Facts and Fictions in Mental Health

Facts and Fictions in Mental Health

Hal Arkowitz

Scott O. Lilienfeld

WILEY Blackwell

This edition first published 2017
© 2017 John Wiley & Sons Inc

Registered Office
John Wiley & Sons, Inc. The Atrium, Southern Gate, Chichester, West Sussex, PO19 8SQ, UK

Editorial Offices
350 Main Street, Malden, MA 02148-5020, USA
9600 Garsington Road, Oxford, OX4 2DQ, UK
The Atrium, Southern Gate, Chichester, West Sussex, PO19 8SQ, UK

For details of our global editorial offices, for customer services, and for information about
how to apply for permission to reuse the copyright material in this book please see our
website at www.wiley.com/wiley-blackwell.

The right of Hal Arkowitz and Scott O. Lilienfeld to be identified as the authors of this work
has been asserted in accordance with the UK Copyright, Designs and Patents Act 1988.

Library of Congress Cataloging-in-Publication data applied for

Hardback ISBN: 9781118311301
Paperback ISBN: 9781118311295

A catalogue record for this book is available from the British Library.

Cover image: Lightspring/Shutterstock
Cover design by Wiley

Set in 10.5/13pt Minion by SPi Global, Pondicherry, India
Printed and bound in Malaysia by Vivar Printing Sdn Bhd

10 9 8 7 6 5 4 3 2 1

To Lollie With Love
Hal Arkowitz

To My Students, From Whom I Continue to Learn So Much
Scott O. Lilienfeld

Contents

Notes on Authors

Hal Arkowitz, Ph.D., is Emeritus Associate Professor at the University of Arizona. He received his bachelor's degree from New York University and his Ph.D. in Psychology (Clinical) from the University of Pennsylvania. His main research interests are in understanding how people change and why they don't. Dr. Arkowitz has published articles and books in the areas of anxiety, depression, psychotherapy, and motivational interviewing. For 10 years, he served as Editor of the *Journal of Psychotherapy Integration*. He also maintains an active clinical practice and has a strong interest in the integration of science and practice in clinical psychology.

Scott Lilienfeld, Ph.D., is Samuel Candler Dobbs Professor of Psychology at Emory University in Atlanta. He received his bachelor's degree from Cornell University in 1982 and his Ph.D. in Psychology (Clinical) from the University of Minnesota in 1990. Dr. Lilienfeld is Associate Editor of the *Journal of Abnormal Psychology*, and past President of the Society for a Science of Clinical Psychology President and the Society for the Scientific Study of Psychopathy. Dr. Lilienfeld has published over 300 manuscripts on personality disorders (especially psychopathy), dissociative disorders, psychiatric classification, pseudoscience in psychology, and evidence-based practices in clinical psychology.

In 1998, Dr. Lilienfeld received the David Shakow Award for Outstanding Early Career Contributions to Clinical Psychology from APA Division 12, and in 2012 he received the James McKeen Cattell Award for Distinguished Career Contributions to Applied Psychological Science from the Association for Psychological Science.

Preface

"Exercise great caution if you decide to change an answer (on a multiple choice test). Experience indicates that many students who change answers change to the wrong answer." This quote is taken from a highly influential book to help people prepare for the Graduate Record Examination, a test that is immensely important in gaining entry to graduate programs. This sounds like good advice except for one thing – it's wrong. Numerous studies have found that test-takers who stick with their first instinct in answering multiple choice items tend to do more poorly than if they had changed their answers more often.

Dr. Phil (Phil McGraw), the popular television "shrink," appears to create significant change in his guests' problems in 10–15 minutes. Yet, there is not one shred of evidence to suggest that this is the case. In fact, scientific evidence suggests that his and other approaches characterized by high confrontation and low empathy tend not only to be ineffective, but may increase resistance to change. His main messages are based on a philosophy of "Just do it!" Consider the following Dr. Phil quote: "A lot of people do have tragic childhoods. But you know what? Get over it." If change were this easy, the number of people with psychological problems would dwindle dramatically.

Both of these examples demonstrate how some of our firmly held beliefs are contradicted by findings from scientific research. In this book, we use the word "myths" to describe these beliefs. Our goal is to present the scientific evidence that bears on these myths.

Often, these beliefs contain a grain of truth, but they become myths when stated in exaggerated and absolute ways. For example, many believe that sex offenders almost always repeat their crimes and can't be helped. Studies have found that only a relatively small number recidivate and those who receive treatment are much less likely to reoffend than those who do not. We have a long way to go to prevent recidivism among sexual offenders because even though it is lower than most people think, it is still too high. The myth does possess a kernel of truth, but as stated, it is contradicted by findings from research.

Some of the other myths we consider in this book are:

- Talking to suicidal persons about their wish to die increases the likelihood of suicide.
- Depression is due to a chemical imbalance in the brain.
- There is an epidemic of autism.
- Divorce always leads to serious problems in children.
- People can have multiple personalities.
- Marijuana is addictive.
- A full moon triggers strange behaviors.
- Herbal treatments have been demonstrated to be effective for anxiety and depression.
- Obesity is caused primarily by a lack of willpower.
- Electroconvulsive therapy is a hazardous procedure that often leaves people incoherent and zombie-like.

We learn myths from a variety of sources, including the media and the views voiced by untrained people. There are several reasons why we are prone to believing them. One of us (Scott Lilienfeld), along with his collaborators, has written extensively on this topic (e.g., in his book *50 Great Myths of Popular Psychology*). This discussion draws from this work.

First, myths make things simple so we don't have to deal with the complexities often present in reality. A good example of this is Dr. Phil's message that all we have to do to change problem behaviors is to "just do it." This message is simple, clear, and wrong. There are many reasons why problem behaviors are so hard to change (see Chapter 43, this volume), as well as factors that need to be present for effective change to occur. It's easier just to accept Dr. Phil's simplified thesis.

Second, the reality that we experience is subjective, and influenced by selective perception and memory. In other words, we tend to perceive and remember what fits best with our preconceived notions. For example, if people perceive others with psychological problems as weak and fearful, they will be favorably inclined toward the belief that all others have to do is muster up the courage and make the needed changes.

The third reason is called "confirmation bias," which is the tendency to selectively attend to and remember information that confirms one's beliefs or hypotheses, and to neglect or distort information that doesn't. If we believe that most people with schizophrenia are violent, we will be more likely to attend to information consistent with previously held views and ignore or forget information inconsistent with them.

Fourth, people confuse correlation and causation. Just because two things are correlated or associated, doesn't mean that one causes the other. An example of this occurred in a state mental hospital where researchers noticed that there was a distinct odor in the ward of people with schizophrenia that was not present in other wards. The researchers formed the apparently reasonable hypothesis that the perspiration of those with schizophrenia may contain some chemicals that contribute to the development of this disorder. As they were conducting the study, a psychiatric aide came by and asked what they were studying. When the researchers told him, he laughed and said something like, "Oh yes, it does smell in there. The shower's been broken for a week now." The association between the body odor and schizophrenia was only correlational. The cause of both was the broken shower. In many instances, a correlation between two variables may be due to a third variable rather than to a causal connection between the two events.

Unfortunately, myths about mental health are widespread. Holding beliefs based on facts instead of fictions can reduce stigma and lead to more appropriate attitudes and behaviors toward people with mental illnesses. Our goal in this book is to supply precisely this corrective information.

Undergraduate and graduate students will find this book helpful in dispelling myths about mental health. This book can be used as a valuable adjunct to the main textbook in undergraduate classes in introductory, abnormal, and clinical psychology. It is also a good fit for graduate courses in clinical psychology, counseling, social work, and psychiatry programs. Laypersons and journalists will also find a great deal of value in this book to further their understanding of mental illness.

Most of these chapters have previously been published in a bimonthly column entitled Facts and Fictions in Mental Health in the magazine *Scientific American Mind* and updated for this book. Three new chapters (on myths concerning suicide, bipolar disorder and creativity, and popular conceptions of psychotherapy) have been added.

We want to thank *Scientific American Mind* for generously granting us permission to publish the chapters in this book. In addition, we wish to express our deep appreciation to our two editors, Mariette DiChristina and Ingrid Wicklegren, for their invaluable feedback and suggestions on earlier drafts of the chapters. Their comments and suggestions significantly improved the liveliness and readability that we strived to achieve.

We also appreciate the help from others at *Scientific American Mind* who did outstanding work finding the illustrations for the chapters and helped in many other ways.

References

Lilienfeld, S. O., Lynn, S. J., Ruscio, J., & Beyerstein, B. L. (2010). *50 great myths of popular psychology*. Chichester, UK: John Wiley & Sons.

McGraw, P. (n.d.) Retrieved from http://www.brainyquote.com/quotes/authors/p/phil_mcgraw_2.html#XHu9

Acknowledgments

This book would not have been possible without the assistance of many exceedingly helpful individuals. We are especially grateful to Mariette DiChristina and Ingrid Wickelgren at *Scientific American* and *Scientific American Mind* for their expert assistance in editing the original articles, Karen Shield at Wiley-Blackwell for her help with permissions, and Andrew Peart and Liz Wingett at Wiley-Blackwell for making the book possible and for their help with assembling the manuscript. Finally, we thank the scores of colleagues who provided us with useful input on the original articles, and to scores of readers who provided thoughtful feedback on them.

Section 1
Anxiety-Related Disorders

Introduction

Most of us know at least one person who has been afflicted with an anxiety-related disorder. In many cases, it's the person staring back at us in the mirror. Approximately 3 out of every 10 people in the United States will suffer from one of these disorders at some point in their lives. Because these problems cause so much distress in so many people, it is imperative that we have a correct understanding of their nature and treatments.

Anxiety disorders are characterized by expectations that distressing or dangerous events may occur in certain situations, even when there is little or no chance they will. These expectations are often associated with pronounced physiological arousal and strong tendencies to avoid the feared situations. Anxiety is also part of the symptom picture of several anxiety-related disorders including posttraumatic stress disorder (PTSD), obsessive-compulsive disorder (OCD), and hoarding disorder.

The fifth edition of the American Psychiatric Association's diagnostic manual (*DSM-5*), published in 2013, lists several anxiety disorders including specific phobias; social phobia; panic disorder; agoraphobia; and generalized anxiety disorder.

Facts and Fictions in Mental Health, First Edition. Hal Arkowitz and Scott O. Lilienfeld.
© 2017 John Wiley & Sons, Inc. Published 2017 by John Wiley & Sons, Inc.

People with specific phobias usually experience anxiety about one particular situation (e.g., driving on freeways), object (e.g., needles), or living creatures (e.g., snakes). Often, phobias are given names derived from Greek. One of our favorites is hexakosioihexekontahexaphobia, which refers to a fear of the number 666, biblically associated with Satan. Try pronouncing that! Social anxiety disorder is an intense and often paralyzing fear of situations involving scrutiny by others, as in having a conversation or giving a speech in public. A diagnosis of panic disorder requires recurrent panic attacks with a fear of having more in the future. The name of this disorder also owes its origins to ancient Greece, in this case the mythical Greek god Pan, whose main diversion was scaring travelers in the forest, preferably at night. Apparently, Pan was good at his job. Panic attacks are terrifying experiences involving an abrupt surge of intense fear accompanied by physical symptoms that include accelerated heart rate, chest pain, shortness of breath, and trembling, as well as mental symptoms like a fear of losing control, going crazy, or dying. People diagnosed with agoraphobia become anxious in and avoid situations perceived as difficult to escape, embarrassing, or in which help would be unavailable in case of panic-like symptoms. Examples are crowded places, movie theaters, or being alone and away from home. Generalized anxiety disorder is characterized by excessive and pervasive worry, usually in several areas such as work, school, finances, and the safety of oneself or loved ones.

Several anxiety-related disorders appear in other sections of the *DSM*. These include PTSD, OCD, and hoarding disorder. In order to receive a diagnosis of PTSD, a person must experience exposure to traumas such as actual or threatened death, serious injury, or sexual violence. Exposure to trauma can be direct, as in the case of a victim of torture, or indirect, as in observing a fatal automobile crash. Common symptoms include trauma-related distressing and intrusive memories, flashbacks, or dreams; distress at exposure to cues relating to the trauma (e.g., media depictions of similar events); sleep disturbances; inability to experience positive emotions; and irritability and anger. Recently, researchers have found that this disorder is even more prevalent than previously thought, with rates of at least 7%.

A diagnosis of OCD requires the presence of either obsessions, which are persistent and intrusive thoughts, urges, or images recalled that cause anxiety, or compulsions, which are maladaptive attempts to reduce that anxiety. In most cases, both obsessions and compulsions are present. A common example of OCD is when a person engages in excessive and frequent hand washing to reduce the anxiety caused by obsessions about dirt and contamination. In some cases, people with this disorder wash their hands so much that they rub off several layers of skin. A particularly good portrayal of a person with OCD was by Jack Nicholson in the 1997 movie *As Good as It Gets*. In contrast, people with hoarding disorder experience excessive anxiety about parting with possessions regardless of their value or utility. They retain them in an attempt to reduce anxiety. Some keep so much that it may be difficult for them to move around comfortably in their living quarters. A 2004 movie entitled *The Aviator* portrayed Howard Hughes, who was one of the wealthiest people in the world, and who developed a severe hoarding disorder.

There are a number of treatments that have been employed to treat anxiety. While the one that has shown the most success involves a number of methods that fall under the rubric of cognitive-behavior therapy, and to some extent psychoanalytically oriented psychotherapy. Others have also been used. They include anti-anxiety medication, herbal remedies, a form of meditation known as mindfulness, and a recently developed treatment known as eye movement desensitization and processing (EMDR). In the latter, the therapist asks clients to think of memories of anxiety-provoking events while tracing the therapist's back-and-forth finger movements with their eyes.

A number of questions have been raised about the nature and treatment of anxiety-related disorders. In this section, we will examine some of them, including:

- Do panic attacks come out of the blue?
- Do most people who experience trauma develop PTSD?
- Is trauma involving physical threat necessary to trigger PTSD?
- In *DSM-5*, is hoarding a symptom of obsessive-compulsive disorder?
- Are there any down sides to using anti-anxiety medications?
- How effective are herbal remedies, mindfulness meditation, and EMDR in the treatment of anxiety-related disorders?

1

Why Do We Panic?

"I was driving home after work," David reported. "Things had been very stressful there lately. I was tense but looking forward to getting home and relaxing. And then, all of a sudden – boom! My heart started racing, and I felt like I couldn't breathe. I was sweating and shaking. My thoughts were racing, and I was afraid that I was going crazy or having a heart attack. I pulled over and called my wife to take me to the emergency room."

David's fears turned out to be unjustified. An emergency room doctor told David, a composite of several therapy patients seen by one of us (Hal Arkowitz), that he was suffering from a panic attack.

The current edition of the *Diagnostic and Statistical Manual* (*DSM-5*) defines a panic attack as "An abrupt surge of intense fear or intense discomfort that reaches a peak within minutes." In addition, 4 out of a list of 13 symptoms must be present. Some of these symptoms are: trembling or shaking; sensation of shortness of breath or smothering chest pain or discomfort; feelings of unreality or detachment; and fears of dying or losing control and "going crazy." Most attacks occur without obvious provocation, making them even more terrifying. Some 8%–10% of the population experience an occasional attack, but only 5% develop panic

Facts and Fictions in Mental Health, First Edition. Hal Arkowitz and Scott O. Lilienfeld.
© 2017 John Wiley & Sons, Inc. Published 2017 by John Wiley & Sons, Inc.

disorder. Contrary to common misconception, these episodes aren't merely rushes of anxiety that most of us experience from time to time. Instead patients who have had a panic attack typically describe it as the most frightening event they have ever undergone.

Research has provided important leads to explain what causes a person's first panic attack – clues that can help ward off an attack in the first place. When stress builds up to a critical level, a very small additional amount of stress can trigger panic. As a result, the person may experience the event as coming out of the blue.

Some people may have a genetic predisposition toward panic, as psychologist Regina A. Shih, then at Johns Hopkins University, and her colleagues described in a review article. The disorder runs in families, and if one identical twin has panic disorder, the chance that the other one also has it is two to three times higher than for fraternal twins, who are genetically less similar. Although these findings do not rule out environmental factors, they do strongly suggest a genetic component.

Panic disorder imposes serious restrictions on patients' quality of life. They may be plagued by a persistent concern about the possibility of more attacks. Agoraphobia involves fear of specific situations in which escape might be difficult or help might not be available in the event of panic-like or other anxiety-related symptoms. The feared situations include using public transportation, being in enclosed places, and being outside of the home alone. In the most severe cases, sufferers may even become housebound.

From Normal Anxiety to Crippling Fear

What are the roots of these incapacitating panic attacks? Psychologist David H. Barlow of Boston University, who has conducted pioneering research on understanding and treating panic disorder and related disorders, and others believe that panic attacks result when our normal "fight-or-flight" response to imminent threats – including increased heart rate and rapid breathing – is triggered by "false alarms," situations in which real danger is absent. (In contrast, the same response in the face of a real danger is a "true alarm.")

When we experience true or false alarms, we tend to associate the biological and psychological reactions they elicit with cues that were present at the time. These associations become "learned alarms" that can evoke further panic attacks.

Both external situations and internal bodily cues of arousal (such as increased breathing rate) can elicit a learned alarm. For example, some people experience panic attacks when they exercise because the physiological arousal leads to bodily sensations similar to those of a panic attack.

Why do some people experience only isolated attacks, whereas others develop full-blown panic disorder? Barlow has synthesized his research and that of others to develop an integrated theory of anxiety disorders, which states that certain predispositions are necessary to develop panic disorder:

- *a generalized biological vulnerability* toward anxiety, leading us to overreact to the events of daily life;
- *a generalized psychological vulnerability* to develop anxiety caused by early childhood learning (such as overprotection from our parents) that the world is a dangerous place and that stress is overwhelming and cannot be controlled;
- *a specific psychological vulnerability* in which we learn in childhood that some situations or objects are dangerous even if they are not.

Panic disorder develops when a person with these vulnerabilities experiences prolonged stress and a panic attack. The first attack activates the psychological vulnerabilities, creating a hypersensitivity to external and internal cues associated with the attack. As a result, even medication containing a mild stimulant can provoke an attack.

Still, there is good news. Two findings in particular can provide reassurance for those with panic disorder. The first is that all panic attacks are triggered by known events, even though the sufferer may be unaware of them. This knowledge can reduce the anxiety associated with the sense of unpredictability. Second, it can be reassuring to learn that a panic attack is a misfiring of the fight-or-flight response in the absence of danger.

Basic research not only has helped us understand panic disorder but also has led to effective treatments. In particular, Barlow and his associates developed panic-control treatment, described in their 2006 book *Mastery of Your Anxiety and Panic*. It involves education about panic disorder and somewhat gradual exposure to the internal and external cues that trigger panic attacks, along with changing the catastrophic interpretations of bodily cues so that they no longer trigger the attacks. This treatment has in most instances surpassed drug therapies for the disorder over the long term.

Further Reading

Barlow, D. H. (2002). *Anxiety and its disorders* (2nd ed.). New York, NY: Guilford Press.

Barlow, D. H., & Craske, M. G. (2006). *Mastery of your anxiety and panic: Workbook (treatments that work)* (4th edn.). Oxford, England: Oxford University Press.

Craske, M. G., & Barlow, D. H. (2014). Panic disorder and agoraphobia. In D. H. Barlow (Ed.), *Clinical handbook of psychological disorders* (5th edn.) (pp. 1–61). New York, NY: Guilford Press.

For a referral to a therapist in your area who uses panic-control treatment or similar treatments, contact the Center for Anxiety and Related Disorders at www.bu.edu/card or the Association for Behavioral and Cognitive Therapies at www.aabt.org.

2

Does Posttraumatic Stress Disorder Require Trauma?

Stress is an inevitable part of our life. Yet whether our daily hassles include the incessant gripes of a nasty boss or another hectoring letter from the Internal Revenue Service, we usually find some way of contending with them. In rare instances, though, terrifying events can overwhelm our coping capacities, leaving us psychologically paralyzed. In such cases, we may be at risk for posttraumatic stress disorder (PTSD).

PTSD is an anxiety disorder marked by flashbacks, nightmares, and other symptoms that impair everyday functioning. The disorder is widespread. At least in the United States, it is thought to affect about 8% of individuals at some point during their lifetime.

Although PTSD is one of the best known of all psychological disorders, it is also one of the most controversial. The intense psychological pain, even agony, experienced by sufferers is undeniably real. Yet the conditions under which PTSD occurs – in particular, the centrality of trauma as a trigger – have come increasingly into question. Mental health professionals have traditionally considered PTSD a typical, at times even ubiquitous, response to trauma. They have also regarded the disorder as distinct from other forms of anxiety spawned by life's slings and arrows. Still, recent data fuel doubts about both assumptions.

Facts and Fictions in Mental Health, First Edition. Hal Arkowitz and Scott O. Lilienfeld.
© 2017 John Wiley & Sons, Inc. Published 2017 by John Wiley & Sons, Inc.

Figure 2.1 Source: Anxiety Spirale by Linoillustration.com

Shell Shock

PTSD did not formally enter psychiatry's diagnostic bible, the *Diagnostic and Statistical Manual of Mental Disorders* (*DSM*), until 1980. Yet accounts of syndromes that mirror PTSD date back to Sumeria and ancient Greece, including a mention in Homer's *Iliad*. In the American Civil War, veterans suffered from "soldier's heart"; in World War I, it was called "shell shock," and in World War II, the term used was "combat fatigue." In the 1970s some soldiers returning from the war in Southeast Asia received informal diagnoses of "post-Vietnam syndrome," which also bore a striking resemblance to the *DSM*'s description of PTSD.

According to *DSM-5*, PTSD occurs in the wake of "trauma" – defined by the manual as an extremely frightening event in which a person experiences or witnesses death, severe injury, or sexual violation. (Less violent experiences such as serious relationship or financial problems do not count.) The most frequent triggers of PTSD thus include wartime combat, rape, murder, car accidents, fires, and natural disasters such as tornadoes, floods, and earthquakes.

PTSD is now officially characterized by four sets of symptoms. These include reliving the event through intrusive memories and dreams; emotional avoidance such as steering clear of reminders of the trauma; negative thoughts and mood, including blaming oneself for the traumatic event and detaching emotionally from others; and hyper-arousal that causes sufferers to startle easily, sleep poorly, and be on alert for potential threats. These problems must last for a month or more for someone to qualify for the PTSD label.

Immune to Trauma?

After the terrorist attacks of September 11, 2001, many mental health experts confidently predicted an epidemic of PTSD, especially in the most severely affected locations: New York City and Washington, DC. The true state of affairs was much more nuanced, however. It is certainly true that many Americans experienced at least a few posttraumatic symptoms following the attacks, but most of the afflicted recovered rapidly. In a 2002 study psychologist Roxane Cohen Silver of the University of California, Irvine, and her colleagues showed that about 12% of Americans suffered significant posttraumatic stress between 9 and 23 days after the attacks. Six months later this number had declined to about 6%, suggesting that time often heals the psychic wounds.

Work by epidemiologist Sandro Galea of the New York Academy of Medicine and his colleagues, also published in 2002, revealed that 5–8 weeks after 9/11, 7.5% of New Yorkers met the diagnostic criteria for PTSD; among those who lived south of Canal Street – that is, close to the World Trade Center – the rates were 20%. Consistent with other data, these findings suggest that physical proximity is often a potent predictor of stress responses. Yet they also indicate that only a minority develops significant posttraumatic pathology in the aftermath of devastating stressors. Indeed, the overall picture following the 9/11 attacks was one of psychological resilience, not breakdown.

More broadly, research that psychologist George A. Bonanno of Columbia University and his colleagues reviewed in 2011 suggests that only about 5%–10% of people typically develop PTSD after experiencing traumatic life events. And although the rates rise when stressors are severe or prolonged, they hardly ever exceed 30%. The rare exceptions may occur with repeated trauma. In another 2011 study psychologist Stevan Hobfoll of Rush Medical College and his colleagues reported that of 763 Palestinians living in areas rife with political violence, more than 70% exhibited moderate PTSD symptoms and about 26% had severe symptoms.

The finding that PTSD is not an inevitable sequela to trauma has spurred investigators to pursue factors that forecast relative immunity to the condition. Across studies, higher income and education, strong social ties and male gender tend to confer heightened resilience, although these predictors are far from perfect. People who usually experience very little anxiety, guilt, anger, alienation, and other unpleasant emotions – that is, who have low "negative emotionality" – are also less likely to suffer from PTSD following trauma. Thus, in ways that researchers do not yet understand, individual characteristics must combine with trauma to produce this illness.

Emotional Triggers

Not only is trauma insufficient to trigger PTSD symptoms, it is also not necessary. Although by definition clinicians cannot diagnose PTSD in the absence of trauma, recent work suggests that the disorder's telltale symptom pattern can emerge from stressors that do not involve bodily peril. In 2008 psychologist Gerald M. Rosen of the University of Washington and one of us (Scott Lilienfeld) reviewed data demonstrating that significant PTSD symptoms *can* follow emotional upheavals resulting from divorce, significant employment difficulties, or loss of a close friendship. In a 2005 study of 454 undergraduates, psychologist Sari Gold of Temple University and her colleagues revealed that students who had experienced nontraumatic stressors, such as serious illness in a loved one, divorce of their parents, relationship problems, or imprisonment of someone close to them, reported even higher rates of PTSD symptoms than did students who had lived through bona fide trauma. Taken together, these findings call into question the long-standing belief that these symptoms are tied only to physical threat.

In light of these and other data, some authors have suggested that the PTSD diagnosis be extended to include anxiety reactions to events that are stressful but not terrifying. Yet such a change could lead to what Harvard University psychologist Richard J. McNally calls "criterion creep" – expanding the boundaries of the diagnosis beyond recognition.

This and other controversies aside, recent results raise the possibility that PTSD is a less distinctive affliction than originally thought and that its symptoms may arise in response to a plethora of intense stressors that are part and parcel of the human condition.

Further Reading

Bonanno, G. A., Westphal, M., & Mancini, A. D. (2011). Resilience to loss and potential trauma. *Annual Review of Clinical Psychology*, *11*, 511–535.
Rosen, G. M., & Lilienfeld, S. O. (2008). Posttraumatic stress disorder: An empirical evaluation of core assumptions. *Clinical Psychology Review*, *28*(5), 837–868.

3

Clutter, Clutter, Everywhere
The Problem of Hoarding

Stuff, stuff, and more stuff. Many of us love to buy and keep things, even when the items are not useful. About 70% of children amass collections of favored objects, such as coins, dolls, or baseball cards; many adults do the same. People often regard possessions as extensions of themselves and become attached to them accordingly.

Yet in rare cases, the habit of gathering and retaining things reaches unhealthy extremes, culminating in hoarding disorder, a condition that is poorly understood. Many laypeople believe that clinical hoarders are too lazy to discard their junk or that they enjoy living with it. Neither of those assumptions appears to be true. Moreover, most experts have long assumed that extreme hoarding is a variant of obsessive-compulsive disorder (OCD), even though most recent research suggests otherwise. Instead, the ailment may stem from an exaggerated version of a basically adaptive tendency to accumulate materials that are important to us.

Distinct Pathology

Nikolai Gogol's 1842 novel, *Dead Souls*, featured a character named Plyushkin, a landowner who saved almost everything he found. Sigmund Freud regarded hoarding as a symptom of what he termed the "anal character," purportedly stemming from overly harsh toilet training. (Few psychologists today share this view.) In the early and mid-1990s, however, hoarding increasingly came to be recognized as a serious clinical problem. Systematic research criteria for pathological hoarding, introduced in 1993 by psychologist Randy O. Frost of Smith College, spread awareness of the malady, as did a parade of television documentaries and reality shows, such as *Hoarders*, *Clean House*, and *Hoarding: Buried Alive*.

Until recently, most mental health professionals regarded pathological hoarding as a subtype of OCD. Hoarding was considered a compulsion – a repeated, ritualized action intended to ward off anxiety, such as checking the stove repeatedly to make sure that it is turned off. According to a 2010 review by psychologist David Mataix-Cols of King's College London, however, 80% or more of people who engage in extreme hoarding do not meet criteria for OCD. For example, many do not experience the obsessions – recurrent or intrusive thoughts, images, or impulses – that are widespread in OCD. Moreover, hoarders tend to be poorer, older, and more prone to mood and anxiety disorders than those with OCD; they are also less likely than OCD sufferers to be aware that they are disordered.

In recognition of these differences, the fifth edition of the American Psychiatric Association's diagnostic manual (*DSM-5*), published in 2013, for the first time included pathological hoarding as a distinct condition. According to this volume, "hoarding disorder" is characterized by extreme and enduring difficulties parting with possessions, even if they have no tangible value. The afflicted have powerful urges to retain items or become very upset about tossing them out. Their home or workplace is filled with so much clutter that the space is unusable – and their problems seriously impair their everyday functioning or cause distress. Before diagnosing hoarding disorder, clinicians must rule out medical conditions that can lead to hoarding. For instance, in a 1998 study psychiatrist Jen-Ping Hwang of the Veterans Administration of Taipei and his colleagues found that 23% of patients with dementia displayed clinically significant hoarding behavior.

Hoarding disorder appears to be present in between 2% and 5% of the population, making it more prevalent than schizophrenia. It afflicts men and women in about equal numbers. People most often hoard books, magazines, newspapers, and clothes; in some cases, they accrue scores of shirts, pants, and dresses that have never been removed from their packaging. More rarely, individuals stockpile animals. In one case in 2010 authorities found more than 150 cats living in a home in Powell, Wyoming. Animal hoarders tend to be more psychologically impaired than other hoarders and live in more squalid conditions, according to a 2011 article by Frost and his colleagues.

Deadly Business

Hoarding can be a serious, even deadly, business. The clutter may reach such proportions that living spaces become essentially uninhabitable, and patients may need to construct narrow tunnels or "goat paths" to get from one location to another. In a 2008 study psychologist David Tolin of the Institute of Living in Hartford, Connecticut, and his co-workers reported that 2% of hoarders had been evicted because of their mess. In a 2009 investigation, psychology student Gregory Lucini and his colleagues at the Worcester Polytechnic Institute Project Center in Melbourne, Australia, revealed that hoarding contributed to 24% of preventable deaths in house fires. In other cases, hoarders have been smothered to death by their clutter; in 2013, a 68-year-old New Jersey woman was found dead underneath piles of rotting garbage, clothing, tote bags and other possessions.

No one knows for sure why hoarders hoard. One clue to the condition, however, is that they often report a powerful emotional attachment to objects; some may imbue them with humanlike qualities, such as feelings, while recognizing that doing so is irrational. In other cases, hoarders insist on maintaining old items, such as clothing, "just in case." Hoarding runs in families; in a 1993 study by Frost and psychology student Rachel C. Gross, now a professor at American University, 85% of pathological hoarders described one or more first-degree relatives (parents, children, siblings) as "pack rats"; this percentage significantly exceeded that of nonhoarders. In a 2009 study of more than 5,000 twin pairs, psychologist Alessandra C. Iervolino of King's College London and her collaborators found that this family pattern is genetically influenced; they estimated the heritability of severe hoarding at 50%.

Hoarding may have evolutionary origins. The behavior is present in a host of species, including honeybees, crows, rodents and monkeys, as psychologist Jennifer G. Andrews-McClymont, now at Morehouse College, and her colleagues pointed out in a 2013 review. This observation raises the possibility that the condition reflects a naturally selected urge to stockpile resources for times of scarcity.

Help for Hoarders

Hoarding disorder is challenging to treat, but some types of cognitive-behavior therapy can reduce its severity, according to a 2007 literature review by Tolin and his colleagues. The treatment focuses on altering irrational beliefs about the value of objects and providing supervised practice with organizing and discarding things. This intervention is not a panacea, however, given that many people with hoarding disorder do not complete their "homework," which typically involves rearranging and tossing out clutter.

The limited treatment options for hoarders partly reflect our relatively poor understanding of this serious ailment. With the formal recognition of hoarding disorder in *DSM-5*, however, research into the causes of pathological hoarding will likely increase and, along with it, the promise of more effective therapies.

Further Reading

Frost, R. O., & Steketee, G. (2010). *Stuff: Compulsive hoarding and the meaning of things*. Boston, MA: Houghton Mifflin Harcourt.
Mataix-Cols, D., Frost, R. O., Pertusa, A., Clark, L. A., Saxena, S., Leckman, J. F. … Wilhelm, S. (2010). Hoarding disorder: A new diagnosis for *DSM-V*? *Depression and Anxiety, 27*(6), 556–572.

4

Eye Movement Desensitization and Reprocessing (EMDR) for Anxiety
Taking a Closer Look

More than 500 brands of psychotherapy exist, with new ones springing up on a nearly monthly basis. Although a handful of these neophyte treatments have been tested in scientific studies, it is anybody's guess whether the others actually work.

Over the past 20 years or so, one of these new kids on the therapy block has stood out from the pack for the remarkable attention it has received from the media, practitioners, and mental health consumers. This treatment carries a mouthful of a label – "eye movement desensitization and reprocessing" – and it has made an impressive splash on the psychotherapy scene. Not surprisingly, most therapists refer to it simply as "EMDR," and we'll do the same here.

Like some other psychotherapies, EMDR was the brainchild of serendipity. One day in 1987 Francine Shapiro, a California psychologist in private practice, went for a walk in the woods. She had been preoccupied with a host of disturbing thoughts. Yet she discovered that her anxiety lifted after moving her eyes back and forth while observing her surroundings. Intrigued, Shapiro tried out variants of this procedure with her clients and found that they, too, felt better. EMDR was born.

Facts and Fictions in Mental Health, First Edition. Hal Arkowitz and Scott O. Lilienfeld.
© 2017 John Wiley & Sons, Inc. Published 2017 by John Wiley & Sons, Inc.

After an initial published study in 1989, EMDR became the focus of dozens of investigations and scores of presentations at professional conferences. Shapiro initially developed EMDR to help clients overcome the anxiety associated with posttraumatic stress disorder (PTSD) and other anxiety disorders, such as phobias. Nevertheless, therapists have since extended this treatment to a host of other conditions, including depression, sexual dysfunction, schizophrenia, eating disorders, and even the psychological stress generated by cancer.

EMDR therapists ask their clients to hold the memories of anxiety-provoking stimuli – for example, the painful memories of a frightening accident – in their minds. While doing so, clients track the therapist's back-and-forth finger movements with their eyes, much like a person in an old Hollywood movie following a hypnotist's swinging pocket watch. EMDR proponents have invoked a dizzying array of explanations for the apparent effectiveness of the lateral eye movements: distraction, relaxation, synchronization of the brain's two hemispheres, and simulation of the eye movements of rapid eye movement (REM) sleep have all emerged as candidates. In conjunction with their therapists, EMDR clients also learn to replace negative thoughts (such as "I'll never get this job") with more positive thoughts (such as "I can get this job if I try hard enough").

Few psychological treatments have been as widely heralded as EMDR. Some EMDR proponents have called it a "miracle cure" and "paradigm shift," and ABC's *20/20* proclaimed it an "exciting breakthrough" in the treatment of anxiety. More than 80,000 clinicians have undergone formal training in EMDR, and the EMDR International Association (EMDRIA), a group of mental health professionals dedicated to promoting the technique, boasts over 4,000 members. The organization estimates that this procedure has been administered to approximately 2 million clients. Moreover, in some American cities, psychotherapists proudly list their certifications in EMDR on their Yellow Page advertisements. But does it work?

The Evidence

The answer is not entirely straightforward. As with all psychotherapies, one can look at the question of whether EMDR "works" in several different ways. Here we will address three important variants of this question:

Does EMDR work better than doing nothing? Yes. Numerous controlled studies show that EMDR produces more improvement than absence of treatment, at least for alleviating the symptoms of civilian PTSD, such as those triggered by rape. The evidence regarding EMDR's efficacy for other anxiety disorders is promising but preliminary. EMDR's effects are most marked on self-reported measures of anxiety; its impact on physiological measures linked to anxiety (such as heart rate) is less clear-cut.

Does EMDR work better than supportive listening? Probably. Although the research evidence on this front is less extensive, most studies indicate that EMDR produces more improvement than control conditions in which therapists merely listen attentively to a client's problems but do not attempt to intervene directly. (Studies generally show, however, that such supportive listening conditions produce positive effects in their own right.) So the therapeutic effects of EMDR probably cannot be attributed entirely to the beneficial consequences of interacting with a warm and empathic therapist. Something more seems to be going on.

Does EMDR work better than standard behavioral and cognitive-behavior therapies? No. Most behavioral and cognitive-behavior therapies for anxiety rely on a core principle of change: exposure. That is, these treatments work by exposing clients repeatedly to anxiety-provoking stimuli, either in their imagination ("imaginal exposure") or in real life ("in vivo exposure"). When exposure to either type is sufficiently prolonged, clients' anxiety dissipates within and across sessions, generating improvement.

When scientists have compared EMDR with imaginal exposure, they have found few or no differences. Nor have they found that EMDR works any more rapidly than imaginal exposure. Most researchers have taken these findings to mean that EMDR's results derive from the exposure, because this treatment requires clients to visualize traumatic imagery repeatedly.

Lastly, researchers have found scant evidence that the eye movements of EMDR are contributing anything to its effectiveness. When investigators have compared EMDR with a "fixed eye movement condition" – one in which clients keep their eyes fixed straight ahead – they have typically found no differences between conditions. So the panoply of hypotheses invoked for EMDR's eye movements appears to be "explanations in search of a phenomenon."

So, now to the bottom line: EMDR ameliorates symptoms of traumatic anxiety better than doing nothing and probably better than talking to a supportive listener. Yet little or no compelling evidence exists that EMDR is superior to exposure-based treatments that behavioral and cognitive-behavior therapists have been administering routinely for decades. Paraphrasing British writer and critic Samuel Johnson, Harvard University psychologist Richard McNally nicely summed up the case for EMDR: "What is effective in EMDR is not new, and what is new is not effective."

Further Reading

Davidson, P. R., & Parker, K. C. H. (2001). Eye movement desensitization and reprocessing (EMDR): A meta-analysis. *Journal of Consulting and Clinical Psychology, 69,* 305–316.

Devilly, G. J. (2002). Eye movement desensitization and reprocessing: A chronology of its development and scientific standing. *Scientific Review of Mental Health Practice, 1,* 113–138.

Shapiro, F. (1995). *Eye movement desensitization and reprocessing: Basic principles, protocols, and procedures.* New York, NY: Guilford Press.

5

The Down Sides of Anti-Anxiety Medication

> Mother needs something today to calm her down
> And though she's not really ill
> There's a little yellow pill
> She goes running for the shelter of a mother's little helper

As these lines of the 1966 Rolling Stones song "Mother's Little Helper" remind us, Valium and other members of the benzodiazepine class of tranquilizing drugs have long been a part of popular culture. But how well do these medications work, and what are their dangers?

At some point in their lives, 25% of Americans will develop an anxiety disorder: panic disorder, generalized anxiety disorder, phobias, obsessive-compulsive disorder, or posttraumatic stress disorder. Many other people will experience significant problems with anxiety and stress that are not severe enough to qualify for a formal diagnosis. It is therefore not surprising that psychiatrists and psychologists have sought effective treatments for anxiety. Psychologists have looked primarily to psychotherapy and psychiatrists primarily to drug therapy.

The main type of psychotherapy that has been shown to be helpful in the treatment of anxiety problems is cognitive-behavior therapy (CBT).

Facts and Fictions in Mental Health, First Edition. Hal Arkowitz and Scott O. Lilienfeld.

Table 5.1   Commonly prescribed benzodiazepines for anxiety

Common brand name	Generic name
Xanax	Alprazolam
Klonopin	Clonazepam
Valium	Diazepam
Ativan	Lorazepam

This therapy involves gradual exposure to feared situations and the implementation of cognitive methods to reduce the catastrophic thinking that is so common in anxiety. This therapy typically yields positive effects in approximately 16 sessions. When the anxiety problem is severe, however, or when other significant psychological problems are present, therapy may take considerably longer.

Two main types of drugs are used to treat anxiety: selective serotonin reuptake inhibitors (SSRIs) and benzodiazepines. SSRIs, which include Prozac, Zoloft, and Lexapro, constitute the most common drug therapy for depression, and they also have proved helpful for anxiety. They typically require 2 to 4 weeks before they start to work and need to be taken daily. In contrast, benzodiazepines work soon after the patient swallows the pill – in most cases leading to relaxed feelings within 10 to 30 minutes. Benzodiazepines can be taken on either a regular or an as-needed basis. Given how they act, it is not surprising that they are among the most commonly prescribed medicines for anxiety (see Table 5.1).

Despite this understandable appeal, numerous concerns and controversies surround the use of benzodiazepines. Further, many people are unaware of many of the potential problems with these drugs.

Side Effects and Withdrawal

In general, benzodiazepines all have the same calming effects, but they differ in the strength of these effects (which also depends on dosage) and how long they stay in the system. Most people who take benzodiazepines experience few side effects if they take them for short periods or on an as-needed basis. Yet because anxiety disorders are usually chronic, benzodiazepine treatment is often prolonged, resulting in an increased risk of side effects.

Side effects that can occur primarily with regular and extended use include physical and psychological dependence, withdrawal symptoms (especially when the medication is discontinued abruptly), reduced alertness, drowsiness, physical fatigue, impaired physical coordination, and memory loss. When benzodiazepines are ingested along with alcohol, the likelihood and strength of these side effects increase greatly, because both are central nervous system depressants. In rare cases, the results can be fatal.

One of the most common withdrawal symptoms is rebound anxiety – return of the anxiety at the same or worse levels than before. Studies have shown that 50% to 75% of people with panic disorder relapse when they stop taking benzodiazepines. Other possible withdrawal symptoms include abdominal pains and cramps, depression, dizziness, lethargy (physical and mental inertness), flu-like symptoms, palpitations, insomnia, and irritability. People who experience withdrawal often return to the medication to avoid these symptoms, which can result in a vicious cycle of dependence.

New Options

Benzodiazepines and newer related medications that aid sleep – for example, Ambien and Lunesta – are also commonly prescribed for people with insomnia, which is often associated with anxiety disorders. Although both sets of medications can cause dependence, this problem is less serious for the newer sleeping medications. A recent study of a new nonbenzodiazepine sleeping medication called Rozerem raises the possibility that it may not have potential for substance abuse or for motor or cognitive impairment, although psychological dependence is still a possibility.

Research studies show that a viable alternative to anxiety or sleeping medications of any kind is CBT, which has proved quite helpful for patients. CBT and the benzodiazepines are about equally effective for anxiety when subjects are compared before and after treatment. After discontinuation of treatment, however, those who relied on a benzodiazepine experience much higher relapse rates. Generally, if patients keep taking the drug, they will relapse at a lower rate, but then they risk the side effects of regular and long-term use. In contrast, no such problems exist with CBT. Moreover, drug therapy is considerably more expensive than CBT because the medications must be taken continuously for their effects to persist. In contrast, the effects of CBT endure fairly well after treatment has ended.

Is combining CBT and antianxiety medication better than using either alone? Studies have found that combined treatments (when the drug is either a benzodiazepine or SSRI) do not do any better than either treatment alone and that subjects administered medication show significantly higher relapse rates when it is discontinued.

So, what's the bad and good news? First, the bad news. Benzodiazepines work only as long as you continue to take them. They can cause psychological and physiological dependence, lead to serious withdrawal symptoms and engender a number of other undesirable consequences.

Now the good news. Used on an as-needed or short-term basis, benzodiazepines can alleviate anxiety problems while minimizing side effects. Used regularly, they are effective in reducing anxiety problems but cause side effects. Tapering off the drug, rather than stopping abruptly, can minimize problems with withdrawal.

Anyone seeking treatment for an anxiety problem would do well to first consider CBT. This treatment is more effective and cheaper than drug therapy and does not cause dependence, withdrawal, or other side effects. A second option to explore before taking benzodiazepenes are SSRIs, which have fewer problems with dependence and withdrawal. As a third option, benzodiazepines may be helpful when their use is closely monitored by a knowledgeable psychiatrist or other medical professional.

Further Reading

Barlow, D. (Ed.). (2001). *Clinical handbook of psychological disorders* (3rd ed.). New York, NY: Guilford Press.

Montgomery, S. A., & Den-Boer, J. A. (Eds.). (2001). *SSRIs in depression and anxiety*. New York, NY: John Wiley & Sons.

Offidani, E., Guidi, J., Tomba, E., & Fava, G. A. (2013). Efficacy and tolerability of benzodiazepines versus antidepressants in anxiety disorders: A systematic review and meta-analysis. *Psychotherapy and Psychosomatics, 82*, 355–362.

6

Is Mindfulness Good Medicine for Anxiety and Depression?

In a typical mindfulness meditation session, participants sit on the floor, eyes closed, backs straight, and legs crossed, their bodies positioned to facilitate their inner experiences. For 10 to 15 minutes, they observe their thoughts as if they were outsiders looking in. They pay particular attention to their breathing, and when their minds wander to other thoughts, they bring their attention back to their breath. As they practice, their minds empty of thoughts, and they become calmer and more peaceful.

Meditation has long been used for spiritual growth. More recently, in psychotherapy, researchers and practitioners have demonstrated interest in a type of Buddhist meditation designed to foster mindfulness, a state of being engaged in the moment without judgment. Mindfulness meditation has shown promise in treating disorders ranging from pain to psoriasis (see "Being in the Now," by Amishi P. Jha, *Scientific American Mind*, March/April 2013). But when it comes to treating diagnosed mental disorders, the evidence that mindfulness helps is decidedly mixed, with the strongest data pointing toward its ability to reduce clinical depression and prevent relapses. In this chapter, we will discuss these findings and some of the controversies regarding applications of mindfulness.

Facts and Fictions in Mental Health, First Edition. Hal Arkowitz and Scott O. Lilienfeld.
© 2017 John Wiley & Sons, Inc. Published 2017 by John Wiley & Sons, Inc.

Openness and Acceptance

People have practiced meditation throughout history. It has evolved into many forms and is found in virtually every major religion. In 2004 psychologist Scott Bishop, then at the University of Toronto, and his associates defined mindfulness as maintaining attention on present experiences and adopting an attitude toward them characterized by curiosity, openness, and acceptance.

Psychotherapy researchers have developed and evaluated variations of mindfulness for therapeutic purposes. For example, mindfulness-based stress reduction acts, as the name suggests, to reduce psychological stress. Mindfulness-based cognitive therapy, on the other hand, integrates mindfulness with methods designed to change the dysfunctional thoughts that may contribute to problematic emotions and behaviors. Both are usually delivered through 8 weekly classes and an all-day workshop.

As a remedy for depression and anxiety, mindfulness meditation may help patients let go of negative thoughts instead of obsessing over them. Training people to experience the present, rather than reviewing the past or contemplating the future, may help keep the mind out of a depressive or anxious loop.

Indeed, some support exists for the efficacy of such training in ameliorating symptoms of depression and possibly anxiety. In a 2010 meta-analysis (quantitative review), psychologist Stefan Hofmann of Boston University and his colleagues examined studies that tested both forms of mindfulness meditation as a remedy for anxiety disorders and depression. They found that the meditation sessions led to significant improvements in both conditions immediately after therapy, as well as approximately three months later. Given the relatively small number of well-designed studies available at that time, however, the authors were appropriately cautious in their conclusions.

Still, a 2013 meta-analysis partly backs up the 2010 assessment. In that review, psychologist Bassam Khoury, then at the University of Montreal, and his colleagues found that both types of mindfulness-based therapies were effective for depression and anxiety disorders, though not more so than cognitive therapy without mindfulness.

Mindfulness has fared less well as a therapy for anxiety disorders in some studies. In another meta-analysis published in 2015, psychologist

Clara Strauss of the University of Sussex in England and her associates found that mindfulness treatments were effective for depression but not for anxiety disorders. The results for anxiety may differ across investigations for various reasons, but one possibility points to differences in patient populations. For instance, some studies include individuals afflicted with anxiety disorders who also have significant health problems such as cancer, whereas others do not. How well mindfulness works may depend somewhat on the source of a patient's anxiety.

Averting Relapse

The clearest mental health benefit for mindfulness may be in reducing relapse rates for a subset of individuals with depression. Preventing relapse is a crucial challenge for therapists because relapse rates for clinical depression are extremely high. Up to 60% of those who have had one depressive episode will have one or more additional episodes; for those who have already relapsed once, 60%–90% will have further episodes; and for those who have experienced three or more depressive episodes, 95% will relapse.

Mindfulness seems to be particularly potent as a preventive in patients who have relapsed three or more times. In a pioneering study of mindfulness-based cognitive therapy for depression recurrence, published in 2000, psychologist John Teasdale, then at the Medical Research Council (MRC) in Cambridge, England, and his colleagues compared individuals receiving treatment as usual, such as visits to family doctors, psychiatrists, and therapists, with those who also received mindfulness-based cognitive therapy. Subjects were followed for more than a year. Among those who had experienced three or more episodes of depression, mindfulness therapy significantly reduced relapse rates compared with the usual treatment. No difference between the groups emerged, however, for people who had experienced two or fewer depressive episodes. These surprising results have been replicated in several studies.

Although no one knows precisely why the benefits of mindfulness would be greater for the sample of three or more, a 2004 replication by Teasdale and psychologist S. Helen Ma, then also at the MRC, provides some leads. The researchers found that in individuals who had experienced two or fewer depressive episodes, adverse life events, such as a death in the family or a relationship breakup, were a common trigger for relapse but that such external occurrences were less often associated with relapse in those who became depressed more than twice. The researchers speculated that by the time a person has had three or more depressive episodes, a significant negative event is not necessary for relapse. Instead a strong association has been formed in the mind between more ordinary negative moods and depressive thoughts. When a person who has recovered from depression experiences a mild negative mood, that mood may activate thoughts such as "Here it comes again," triggering a full-blown depressive episode. In those cases, mindfulness might help break the cycle by enabling individuals to be less affected by fleeting unhappy thoughts so that they do not lead to emotional turmoil.

Through such mechanisms, mindfulness-based cognitive therapy and mindfulness-based stress reduction hold promise as remedies for depression and possibly anxiety. What is more, mindfulness-based cognitive therapy offers clear advantages for preventing relapse in patients who have had more than two episodes of depression. (Its ability to avert relapse for anxiety disorders is unknown.) No one fully understands how, or to what extent, mindfulness-based treatments contribute to recovery in these illnesses. Nevertheless, such treatments constitute an exciting new direction in psychotherapy.

Further Reading

Gu, J., Strauss, C., Bond, R., & Cavanagh, K. (2015). How do mindfulness-based cognitive therapy and mindfulness-based stress reduction improve mental health and wellbeing? A systematic review and meta-analysis of mediation studies. *Clinical Psychology Review, 37*, 1–12.

Hofmann, S. G., Sawyer, A. T., Witt, A. A., & Oh, D. (2010). The effect of mindfulness-based therapy on anxiety and depression: A meta-analytic review. *Journal of Consulting and Clinical Psychology, 78*(2), 169–183.

Teasdale, J. D., Williams, J. M. G., & Kabat-Zinn, J. (2014). *The mindful way workbook: An 8-week program to free yourself from depression and emotional distress.* New York, NY: Guilford Press.

7

Can Herbs Ease Anxiety and Depression?

Herbal therapies are astoundingly popular among the American public. In 2008 statistician Patricia M. Barnes of the National Center for Health Statistics and her colleagues reported that almost 20% of children and adults in the United States had used an herbal medicine during the past year. In 1998 a team led by physician David M. Eisenberg of Harvard Medical School determined that use of herbs for physical and mental problems had risen 380% between 1990 and 1997.

Our enthusiasm for herbal medicine is undoubtedly fueled by the high cost of prescription drugs, the fact that these drugs do not work for everyone, and a burgeoning interest in natural remedies. Moreover, many people erroneously assume that natural substances are inherently safer than synthetic medications.

The use of plants as treatments dates to at least 3000 B.C. Today this practice is part of a broader movement known as complementary and alternative medicine. Many people turn to such treatments – which also include remedies such as acupuncture, aromatherapy, and massage – for psychological problems. In a 2001 study sociologist Ronald C. Kessler of Harvard Medical School and his associates found that more than half of people with panic attacks or severe depression

Facts and Fictions in Mental Health, First Edition. Hal Arkowitz and Scott O. Lilienfeld.
© 2017 John Wiley & Sons, Inc. Published 2017 by John Wiley & Sons, Inc.

used some form of alternative therapy, including herbs, during the previous year, usually without medical supervision.

Nevertheless, most plants have not been studied for their therapeutic value or side effects. Studies of two herbal treatments – kava for anxiety and St. John's wort for depression – indicate that some plant-derived substances might help individuals with psychological problems, but the evidence is so far inconclusive.

Kick Back, Relax

Pacific Islanders have long used an extract of the root of the kava plant (*Piper methysticum*), which grows on those islands, for social, ceremonial, and medicinal purposes, including relaxation and the reduction of anxiety. Introduced in the United States in the 1980s, kava extract is most often served as a drink, which Americans can now sample in any of various kava bars. The Purple Lotus Kava Bar in West Palm Beach, Florida, for example, offers "a popular alternative to the same old nightlife, a place to truly kick back and relax."

For the treatment of anxiety, people generally purchase kava in drug and health food stores. Some experimental results suggest the root has anti-anxiety properties. In a review article published in 2010, physician Max H. Pittler of the German Cochrane Center at the University of Freiburg and physician Edzard Ernst of the Peninsula Medical School in Exeter, England, analyzed 12 well-designed studies comparing kava with a placebo for the treatment of anxiety. They found that kava was more effective than the inert substance for ameliorating general anxiety, but the difference between the two was small. Unfortunately, relatively few studies qualified for inclusion, and the investigations differed in the dosages used, strains of kava, duration of treatment, and severity of the patients' anxiety.

In addition, although the herb is relatively safe, it should not be used with abandon. Its side effects may include stomach complaints, restlessness, headache, and fatigue. Reports of the root causing liver damage led to a 2002 warning from the Food and Drug Administration, along with bans on kava in several countries. Further research has quieted this concern, and the bans have since been lifted. Even so, we cannot rule out the possibility that kava causes liver damage because alternative explanations for a few cases of liver problems remain unexplained by other factors.

Of more concern are interactions between kava and other medications. Kava can intensify sleepiness if taken with sedatives, sleeping pills, antipsychotics, or alcohol, raising the risk of injury during activities such as driving and using heavy machinery. It may also enhance the sedating effects of anticonvulsants and worsen the side effects associated with antipsychotic medication.

Scientists have studied other herbal remedies for anxiety, too. A few studies hint, for example, that lemon balm and valerian may be calming. Still, the evidence supporting their efficacy is even more preliminary than that for kava. And their potential dangers are equally uncertain.

Weeding Out Despair

St. John's wort (*Hypericum perforatum*), a plant historically used to drive out evil spirits, is the most widely studied herbal medicine for depression. In a 2009 review physician Klaus Linde of the Munich Technical University and his colleagues evaluated 29 well-designed studies of St. John's wort, usually taken as a pill for major depression. Overall, the studies suggested that the herb was more effective than a placebo and just as effective as antidepressants such as Prozac yet came with fewer side effects.

Not all of the studies Linde's team analyzed, however, found an advantage for St. John's wort over a placebo. In addition, two large-scale U.S. investigations revealed scant support for the idea that St. John's wort could ease depression. One of these, a 2011 study led by psychiatrist Mark H. Rapaport, then at Cedars-Sinai Hospital in Los Angeles, indicated that the plant was no more effective than a placebo for mild to moderate depression. Thus, this herb may ease some cases of depression, but the evidence is far from overwhelming.

St. John's wort is not without some risks. It can cause stomach upset, skin rashes, fatigue, restlessness, headache, and confusion. More serious is the possibility, though slight, that it can interfere with becoming pregnant, worsen dementia, or trigger psychosis in vulnerable individuals. And as with traditional antidepressants, St. John's wort can trigger a manic episode in people with bipolar disorder. The herb also may interact dangerously with other drugs. If taken with certain antidepressants, it may cause potentially life-threatening increases in the neurotransmitter serotonin. It also can reduce the effectiveness of birth-control pills, heart medications, and HIV treatments, among other drugs.

Approved drugs for anxiety and depression carry risks, too, but in those cases, the FDA is supposed to monitor and publicize them. In contrast, no government agency regulates herbal treatments. In addition, the fact that doctors do not prescribe herbs – and often do not even know their patients are using them – raises the risk of drug interactions. Further, relatively little is known about the purity or long-term effects of herbal remedies or what dose is optimal for a particular ailment.

Despite these concerns, advertisements for herbal remedies often make exaggerated and unsubstantiated claims. One online ad for an anti-anxiety pill called Seredyn containing a combination of largely untested herbs asserts that "over 93% of Seredyn users with occasional anxiety and 85% with chronic anxiety report positive results, and 80–83% of users with panic and anxiety attacks say that Seredyn helps prevent and stop their attacks." Such testimonials are essentially meaningless if not backed by verifiable data.

Nevertheless, more safe and effective herbal treatments for anxiety and depression may still be in our future. Perhaps one day scientists will discover in nature a large medicine cabinet offering new remedies for a broad spectrum of mental disorders.

Further Reading

Sarris, J., McIntyre, E., & Camfield, C. A. (2013). Plant-based medicines for anxiety disorders, part 2: A review of clinical studies with supporting preclinical evidence. *CNS Drugs, 27,* 301–319.

Wallach, H., & Kirsch, I. (2015). Herbal treatments and antidepressant medication: Similar data, divergent conclusions. In S. O. Lilienfeld, S. J. Lohr, & J. Lohr (Eds.), *Science and pseudoscience in clinical psychology* (2nd ed.) (pp. 364–388). New York, NY: Guilford Press.

Section 2
Mood Disorders

Introduction

DSM-5 separates depression-related disorders into two categories: depressive disorders and bipolar disorders (previously known as manic-depressive disorder). The lifetime prevalence of the former is approximately 20% and the latter approximately 1%.

There are several types of depressive disorders including major depression and persistent depressive disorder. Symptoms of major depression include severe sadness and loss of interest or pleasure in everyday activities, feelings of worthlessness, suicidal thinking and attempts, fatigue, and problems with attention and concentration. This type of depression is often self-limiting and interspersed with periods of relatively normal mood, but has a very high rate of recurrence. The related condition of persistent depressive disorder is typically milder but more chronic; it may even be life-long. Many famous people have probably suffered from one or both of these conditions, including actor Brad Pitt, singer Lady Gaga, British Prime Minister Winston Churchill (who referred to depression as his "black dog") and U.S. President Abraham Lincoln.

Facts and Fictions in Mental Health, First Edition. Hal Arkowitz and Scott O. Lilienfeld.
© 2017 John Wiley & Sons, Inc. Published 2017 by John Wiley & Sons, Inc.

People with a bipolar disorder typically cycle between periods of depression and mania or a less severe form known as hypomania. Symptoms may include grandiosity, euphoria, hyperactivity, little need for sleep, and impulsive behaviors such as extreme spending sprees. Many famous people have probably suffered from bipolar disorder, including comedian Robin Williams, actor Jean-Claude Van Damme, artist Vincent van Gogh, and composer Ludwig van Beethoven.

Despite the severity of depressive and bipolar disorders, these famous figures and others with a mood disorder have managed to function well. In contrast, the lives of many other people with these disorders are significantly impaired.

Some of the questions about depressive and bipolar disorders that we critically examine in this section are:

- Is depression caused by bad chemistry?
- Can talking about suicide increase suicidal tendencies?
- Do suicide rates peak during the winter holidays?
- Is depression almost always the primary cause of suicide?
- Is it the case that a person who has made one suicide attempt is unlikely to make another?
- Is electroconvulsive therapy, often called "shock therapy," a brutal procedure that does more harm than good?
- Are people with serious mental illness, such as bipolar disorder, usually more creative than others?
- Does loss of a loved one inevitably lead to serious distress and depression?

8

Bipolar Disorders and Creativity
Psychological Truth or Urban Legend?

The belief that madness and creativity are intimately linked has a lengthy history. Aristotle maintained that genius never emerges without a touch of madness, and the 17th-century British poet John Dryden wrote that "great wits are sure to madness near allied, and thin partitions do their bounds divide." Even today, the perception that severe mental illness and creativity are closely associated is widespread. The view of the tortured artistic genius finds its expression in a host of popular books and films, such as the 2000 movie *Pollock*, a biographical depiction of the talented but troubled American abstract painter Jackson Pollock (jokingly nicknamed "Jack the Dripper" for his unique style of splashing paint on canvass).

As we will discover, research reveals that there is at least a kernel of truth to this popular stereotype. At the same time, the link between mental illness and creativity appears to be largely specific to bipolar disorder (once called manic depression) and closely allied conditions. Even here, this association is more complex than scientists had once assumed.

Facts and Fictions in Mental Health, First Edition. Hal Arkowitz and Scott O. Lilienfeld.
© 2017 John Wiley & Sons, Inc. Published 2017 by John Wiley & Sons, Inc.

On Top of the World

Although early research suggested that persons with schizophrenia are prone to creativity, most of this work has not stood the test of time. More recently, interest has turned to individuals with bipolar disorder, who are prone to manic episodes (mania), often alternating with bouts of severe depression. During mania, people experience dramatic upsurges in energy, positive moods, and self-confidence to the point of self-aggrandizement. They typically require much less sleep than usual, take uncharacteristic risks, are easily distracted, and report racing thoughts. At these times, they often become more talkative and active than usual, frequently making grand and unrealistic plans without any follow-through. Given that manic episodes are usually marked by enormous bursts of energy, exhilaration, and rapid thinking, it is not surprising that some researchers have proposed that it is tied to a heightened likelihood of creative accomplishments.

Tortured Geniuses

Indeed, a 1987 paper published by psychiatrist Nancy Andreasen of the University of Iowa revealed that 80% of a sample of 30 authors recruited from the Iowa Writer's Workshop (compared with only 30% of a control group of nonwriters) had suffered from mood disorders at some point in their lives; the rates of bipolar disorder were especially elevated. Similarly, in a 1989 examination of 47 British authors who had won prestigious awards, psychologist Kay Redfield Jamison of Johns Hopkins University reported that 38% of the sample had a lifetime history of treatment for mood disorders, with bipolar disorder and related conditions being the most frequent.

As Jamison and others have observed, the links to bipolar disorder extend beyond writing to art and music. Among great composers, for example, such figures as Georg Fredric Handel, Hector Berlioz, Peter Iliach Tchaikovsky, and Gustav Mahler have been retrospectively diagnosed by some experts as bipolar sufferers, although such assessments should be interpreted with caution given their basis in indirect historical evidence. One striking example is 19th-century German composer Robert Schumann, who kept detailed diaries and wrote numerous letters that documented his mood changes. Based on these writings, many psychological and psychiatric historians have concluded that Schumann met criteria for bipolar disorder. As Jamison demonstrated, Schumann's productivity soared when he apparently experienced manic or hypomanic (mild manic) episodes; for example, in 1850, when manic, he wrote a remarkable 24 compositions. In contrast, when Schumann was apparently clinically depressed, his productivity plummeted; for example, in 1840, during a profound depression, he did not write a single piece.

Still, as psychologist Judith Schlesinger of the Learning Research Institute of San Bernardino, California, observed in a 2009 paper, the studies of Andreasen and Jamison had serious methodological problems. Diagnoses of bipolar disorder in both investigations were made by Andreasen and Jamison themselves, who may have been biased in their evaluations; moreover, Jamison's study lacked a control group of nonwriters. Subsequent research has largely addressed these criticisms, however. For example, in analyses of a large 2010 general population survey, economist Carol Tremblay of Oregon State University and her colleagues found that bipolar disorder was disproportionately represented among artistic and craft professions, including writing, painting, music teaching, and arranging stage lighting.

A Complex Link

Although the association between bipolar disorder and creativity is reasonably robust, this relationship is qualified by other variables. As psychologists Greg Murray of Swinborne University of Technology (Australia) and Sheri Johnson of the University of California at Berkeley noted in a 2010 review, most work suggests that the link to creativity is stronger for hypomanic than for manic episodes. The former episodes are often seen in a condition called cyclothymic disorder, which is characterized by pronounced mood swings that are less extreme than those of mania or clinical depression. This research raises the intriguing possibility that although a moderate "dose" of mania is helpful for creativity, an extreme dose may hamper creativity, perhaps because it impairs judgment and concentration. As Murray and Johnson pointed out, a further wrinkle is that the association between bipolar disorder and creativity seems to be limited to artistic, literary, and musical, rather than to scientific creativity. Perhaps outstanding scientific accomplishment necessitates an intense mental discipline and persistent focus on a single problem that is largely incompatible with manic tendencies.

A further question is whether mania is correlated with a greater quality of artistic and musical production, or merely a greater quantity. Perhaps people in the midst of manic episodes simply generate more "stuff," both good and bad. A 1994 analysis of Schumann's compositions by psychologist Robert Weisberg of Temple University may shed light on this issue. Weisberg measured the quality of Schumann's works by tabulating the number of times each had been recorded by musicians. Weisberg found that Schumann's manic and hypomanic episodes were associated with heightened compositional quantity, not quality. Nevertheless, as psychologist Bruno Repp of Yale University observed in a 1995 commentary on Weisberg's analysis, popularity does not necessarily reflect quality. Moreover, because Weisberg examined only one composer, the jury on the quality–quantity question is still out.

Manic Mechanisms

Scientists do not why know bipolar tendencies are associated with heightened creativity. Still, researchers have unearthed some tantalizing clues. Even while healthy individuals prone to manic episodes tend to exhibit elevated levels of a personality trait called "openness to experience," which captures intellectual curiosity and willingness to try new things. In between episodes, individuals with bipolar disorder usually have high levels of impulsivity and positive emotions, each of which may propel them toward creative risk-taking during the heightened bursts of energy of hypomania and mania. Moreover, during manic episodes, individuals may be able to perceive connections among seemingly unrelated events, a hallmark of creative thinking. Other scholars have argued that the depression experienced by bipolar individuals plays a role too. In a 1988 review, psychiatrists Hagop Akiskal and Karen Akiskal, then at the University of Tennessee College of Medicine, conjectured that the psychological suffering experienced by depressed individuals provides them with deep emotional insights that can be transformed into artistic products during hypomanic and manic episodes. Nevertheless, systematic research supporting this hypothesis is lacking.

In the coming years, researchers will almost certainly come to better understand the fascinating linkage between bipolar disorder and creativity. When they do, their discoveries are likely to shed light not only on the manifestations of bipolar disorder, but on the enigmatic sources of creative genius.

Further Reading

Murray, G., & Johnson, S. L. (2010). The clinical significance of creativity in bipolar disorder. *Clinical Psychology Review, 30*(6), 721–732.

Schlesinger, J. (2009). Creative mythconceptions: A closer look at the evidence for the "mad genius" hypothesis. *Psychology of Aesthetics, Creativity, and the Arts, 3*(2), 62–72.

9

Grief Without Tears?

Virtually all of us experience the loss of a loved one at some point in our life. So it is surprising that the serious study of grief is not much more than 30 years old. Yet in that time, we have made significant discoveries that have deepened our understanding of this phenomenon – and challenged widely held assumptions.

In this chapter, we confront two common misconceptions about grief. The first is that the bereaved inevitably experience intense symptoms of distress and depression. The second is that unless those who have experienced the death of a loved one "work through" their feelings about the loss, they will surely experience delayed grief reactions, in which strong emotions may be triggered by events unrelated to the loss, even long after it occurred. As we will show, neither belief holds up well to scientific scrutiny.

Bouncing Back

Most people believe that distress and depression almost always follow the death of someone close, according to psychologists Camille B. Wortman of Stony Brook University and Kathrin Boerner of Mount Sinai

Facts and Fictions in Mental Health, First Edition. Hal Arkowitz and Scott O. Lilienfeld.
© 2017 John Wiley & Sons, Inc. Published 2017 by John Wiley & Sons, Inc.

School of Medicine. Symptoms of distress include yearning for the deceased, feeling that life has lost its meaning, having anxiety about the future, and experiencing shock at the loss. Depression involves feeling sad and self-critical, having suicidal thoughts, lacking energy, and undergoing disturbed appetite and sleep.

To examine this belief, several groups of investigators tracked bereaved people, mostly widows and widowers, for up to 5 years. Results revealed that between 26% and 65% had *no* significant symptoms in the initial years after their loss; only 9%–41% did. (The variability results partly from differences in how the symptoms were measured.) And the depression of some may be chronic rather than a reaction to the death.

Psychologist George A. Bonanno of Columbia University and his colleagues examined this possibility and other questions in a prospective study published in 2002. They followed about 1,500 elderly married individuals over several years. During that time 205 subjects lost a spouse, after which the investigators continued to track them for 18 months. Surprisingly, about half of the bereaved spouses experienced no significant depression either before or after the loss. Nor did they display serious distress, although some did feel sad for a short time. Eight percent of the participants were depressed *before* losing their partner – and stayed that way. For about 10% – individuals who had reported being very unhappy in their marriage – the death actually brought relief from preexisting depression.

The spouse's death did precipitate depression in 27%. Of these individuals, a substantial proportion (about 11% of the total) started improving after 6 months and became symptom-free within 18 months. The rest of that subgroup did not get better – but even so, more than 70% of the study's participants neither developed depression nor became more depressed as a result of their spouse's demise. (The small number of remaining subjects fit various other patterns.) These results tell a clear story, at least where an elderly partner is concerned: Most people are resilient and do not become seriously depressed or distressed when someone close to them dies.

Working It Out

In her 1980 book *The Courage to Grieve*, social worker Judy Tatelbaum wrote that after the death of a loved one "we must thoroughly experience all the feelings evoked by our loss," and if we don't "problems and symptoms of unsuccessful grief" will occur. The idea that people need to work through grief originated with Sigmund Freud and is still pervasive. It usually includes expressing feelings about the loss, reviewing memories about the deceased, and finding meaning in the loss. According to this view, those who do not explore their emotions will suffer the consequences later.

Yet grief work may be unnecessary for the large proportion of people who do not become significantly distraught after a loss. And when researchers have tested the common grief-work techniques of writing or talking about the death, some have found small benefits for the procedures, but most have not. In addition, the jury is still out on grief counseling, in which professionals or peers try to facilitate the working-through process. Results from two quantitative reviews of the efficacy of such therapy found no significant gains from it, and a third found just a modest positive effect. One caveat: The benefits might be slightly greater than these studies indicate because most of the subjects were recruited by the researchers, and these individuals may be less in need of counseling than those who seek help.

Finally, two teams of researchers followed bereaved persons, including spouses, adult children, and parents, for up to 5 years after their loss and found little or no evidence of a delayed grief reaction. When such reactions have been found, they occur only in a very small percentage of the bereaved. Thus, the overall risk of reexperiencing a flood of negative emotions appears to be quite minimal.

Given that most people who have experienced the death of a loved one show few signs of distress or depression, many bereaved individuals may need no particular advice or help. The few who experience intense and lasting despair may benefit from interventions, although traditional grief counseling may not be the best choice. Instead people might consider seeking empirically supported psychotherapies for depression (see Chapter 12, this volume).

That said, our conclusions are based largely on studies of Caucasian American widows and widowers. We cannot say for sure that they extend to people of all ages, ethnicities, and genders. In addition, reactions to a loss may depend on a person's relationship to the deceased – be it a parent, sibling, or child – as well as whether the death was sudden, violent, or drawn out. The consequences of these varying perspectives and circumstances have yet to be carefully explored.

Nevertheless, we can confidently say that just as people live their lives in vastly different ways, they cope with the death of others in disparate ways, too. Despite what some pop-psychology gurus tell us, grief is not a one-size-fits-all experience.

Further Reading

Bonanno, G. A. (2009). *The other side of sadness: What the new science of bereavement tells us about life after loss.* New York, NY: Basic Books.

Lotterman, J. H., Bonanno, G. A., & Galatzer-Levy, I. (2014). The heterogeneity of long-term grief reactions. *Journal of Affective Disorders, 167,* 12–19.

Wortman, C. B., & Boerner, K. (2007). Beyond the myths of coping with loss: Prevailing assumptions versus scientific evidence. In H. S. Friedman & R. Cohen Silver (Eds.), *Foundations of health psychology* (pp. 285–324). New York, NY: Oxford University Press.

10

Is Depression Just Bad Chemistry?

A commercial sponsored by Pfizer, the drug company that manufactures the antidepressant Zoloft, asserts, "While the cause [of depression] is unknown, depression may be related to an imbalance of natural chemicals between nerve cells in the brain. Prescription Zoloft works to correct this imbalance." Using advertisements such as this one, pharmaceutical companies have widely promoted the idea that depression results from a chemical imbalance in the brain.

The general idea is that a deficiency of certain neurotransmitters (chemical messengers) at synapses, or tiny gaps, between neurons interferes with the transmission of nerve impulses, causing or contributing to depression. One of these neurotransmitters, serotonin, has attracted the most attention, but many others, including norepinephrine and dopamine, have also been granted supporting roles in the story.

Much of the general public seems to have accepted the chemical imbalance hypothesis uncritically. For example, in a 2007 survey of 262 undergraduates, psychologist Christopher M. France of Cleveland State University and his colleagues found that 84.7% of participants found it "likely" that chemical imbalances cause depression. In reality, however, depression cannot be boiled down to an excess or deficit of any particular

Facts and Fictions in Mental Health, First Edition. Hal Arkowitz and Scott O. Lilienfeld.
© 2017 John Wiley & Sons, Inc. Published 2017 by John Wiley & Sons, Inc.

Figure 10.1   Source: Getty Images

chemical or even a suite of chemicals. "Chemical imbalance is sort of last-century thinking. It's much more complicated than that," neuroscientist Joseph Coyle of Harvard Medical School was quoted as saying in a blog by National Public Radio's Alix Spiegel.

Indeed, it is very likely that depression stems from influences other than neurotransmitter abnormalities. Among the problems correlated with the disease are irregularities in brain structure and function, disturbances in neural circuitry, and various psychological contributions, such as life stressors. Of course, all these influences ultimately operate at the level of physiology, but understanding them requires explanations from other vantage points.

Are Your Chemicals out of Balance?

Perhaps the most frequently cited evidence in support of the chemical imbalance hypothesis is the effectiveness of antidepressants, many of which increase the amounts of serotonin and other neurotransmitters at synapses. Zoloft, Prozac, and similar selective serotonin reuptake inhibitors (SSRIs) result in such an increase and can often relieve depression, at least when it is severe. As a result, many believe that a deficiency in serotonin and other neurotransmitters causes the disorder. But just because a drug reduces symptoms of a disease does not mean that those symptoms were caused by a chemical problem the drug corrects. Aspirin alleviates headaches, but headaches are not caused by a deficiency of aspirin.

Evidence against the hypothesis comes from the efficacy of a newly developed antidepressant, Stablon (Tianeptine), which *decreases* levels of serotonin at synapses. Indeed, in different experiments, activation or blockage of certain serotonin receptors has improved or worsened depression symptoms in an unpredictable manner. A further challenge to the chemical imbalance hypothesis is that many depressed people are not helped by SSRIs. In a 2009 review article psychiatrist Michael Gitlin of the University of California, Los Angeles, reported that one third of those treated with antidepressants do not improve, and a significant proportion of the remainder get somewhat better but remain depressed. If antidepressants correct a chemical imbalance that underlies depression, all or most depressed people should get better after taking them. That they do not suggests that we have only barely begun to understand the disorder at a molecular level. As a result, we must consider other nonchemical leads.

This is Your Brain on Depression

A possible clue lies in brain structures. Imaging studies have revealed that certain brain areas differ in size between depressed and mentally healthy individuals. For example, the amygdala, which responds to the emotional significance of events, tends to be smaller in depressed people than in those without the disorder. Other emotional regulatory centers that appear to be reduced in volume are the hippocampus, an interior brain region involved in emotional memory, the anterior cingulate cortex, which helps to govern impulse control and empathy, and certain sections of the prefrontal cortex, which plays an important role in emotional regulation. Nevertheless, the effects of these shrinkages on depression, if any, remain an open question.

Neuroimaging studies have revealed that the amygdala, hypothalamus, and anterior cingulate cortex are often less active in depressed people. Some parts of the prefrontal cortex also show diminished activity, whereas other regions display the opposite pattern. The subcallosal cingulate gyrus, a region near the anterior cingulate, often shows abnormal activity levels in depressed individuals. These differences may contribute to depression, but if they do, scientists are not sure how.

In 2012 neurosurgeon Andres M. Lozano of the University of Toronto and his associates studied the effects of deep brain stimulation of the subcallosal cingulate gyrus in depressed patients who had not benefited from standard treatments. The intervention led to a significant reduction in symptoms of depression, supporting the possibility that a dysfunction in this brain area may be involved in the illness.

Findings also point to a crucial role for psychosocial factors such as stress, especially when it arises from a loss of someone close to you or a failure to meet a major life goal. When someone is under a good deal of stress, a hormone called cortisol is released into the bloodstream by the adrenal glands. Over the short term, cortisol helps humans cope with dangers by mobilizing energy stores for flight or fight. But chronically high cortisol levels can harm some bodily systems. For example, at least in animals, excess cortisol reduces the volume of the hippocampus, which in turn may contribute to depression. Despite such data, we still do not know if stress alters the human brain in ways that can lead to depression.

Seeing the Elephant

Throughout this chapter, we have described associations between various brain changes and depression. We have not talked about "causes," because no studies have established a cause-and-effect relation between any brain or psychosocial dysfunction and the disorder. In addition, depression almost certainly does not result from just one change in the brain or environmental factor. A focus on one piece of the depression puzzle – be it brain chemistry, neural networks, or stress – is shortsighted.

The tunnel-vision approach is reminiscent of a classic story in which a group of blind men touch an elephant to learn what the animal looks like. Each one feels a different part, such as the trunk or the tusk. The men then compare notes and learn that they are in complete disagreement about the animal's appearance. To understand the causes of depression, we have to see the entire elephant – that is, we must integrate what we know at multiple levels, from molecules to the mind to the world we live in.

Further Reading

France, C. M., Lysaker, P. H., & Robinson, R. P. (2007). The "chemical imbalance" explanation for depression: Origins, lay endorsement, and clinical implications. *Professional Psychology: Research and Practice, 38*(4), 411–420.

Lozano, A. M., Giacobbe, P., Hamani, C., Rizvi, S. J., Kennedy, S. H., Kolivakis, T. T. … Mayberg, H. S. (2012). A multicenter pilot study of subcallosal cingulate area deep brain stimulation for treatment-resistant depression. *Journal of Neurosurgery, 116*(2), 315–322.

Park, J. S., & Ho-Young, A. (2013). Direct-to-consumer (DTC) antidepressant advertising and consumer misperceptions about the chemical imbalance theory of depression: The moderating role of skepticism. *Health Marketing Quarterly, 30,* 362–378.

11

Four Myths About Suicide

On August 11, 2014, famed comedian and actor Robin Williams committed suicide. His death shocked the world, especially because many people were at a loss to understand why someone so funny and talented would take his own life. This tragic event once again brought our attention to the phenomenon of suicide. In 2012 (the most recent year for which data are available), 40,600 suicide deaths were reported in the United States, making suicide the 10th leading cause of death for Americans. Experts agree that the actual number may be two to three times higher because many deaths by suicide are reported as due to other causes, such as single-occupancy motor vehicle accidents.

In many cases, suicide can be prevented, but only if we have accurate information that allows us to correctly recognize suicide risk and respond to it appropriately. In this chapter, we examine four commonly held myths about suicide and present the scientific data bearing on them. We also discuss research on the prevention of suicide.

Myth #1: Talking about suicide can increase suicidal tendencies. In 2014, medical student Tomasso Dazzi of King's College London and his associates, reviewed the research on this topic. None of the studies revealed an association between talking about suicide and suicidal thinking.

Facts and Fictions in Mental Health, First Edition. Hal Arkowitz and Scott O. Lilienfeld.
© 2017 John Wiley & Sons, Inc. Published 2017 by John Wiley & Sons, Inc.

To the contrary, some results suggested that talking about suicide might reduce suicidal tendencies, perhaps because revealing such tendencies to others may increase the likelihood of obtaining help.

Myth #2: Suicides rates peak during the winter holidays. Most media portrayals of Thanksgiving and Christmas describe happy and contented people with their loving families in joyous celebration of the winter holidays. Yet, many people are lonely and sad during the winter holidays, leading to the belief that higher suicide rates occur during this season. Research calls this belief into question.

In 2012, psychiatrist Christos Christodoulou of the University of Athens Medical School and his associates reviewed 113 studies from different countries on the relationship between suicide and seasons of the year. Although the results were somewhat mixed, most studies found that the highest rates of suicide occurred in the spring with the second highest in the summer. Suicide can occur at any time, so we need to be vigilant throughout the year.

Myth #3: Depression is almost always the cause of suicide. This widely held belief could lead people to avoid or minimize suicide risk if the person is not depressed. In 2004, psychiatrist Jose Bertoloto of the World Health Organization and his associates reviewed studies on the relationship between psychiatric diagnosis and suicide. They found that 98% of suicides were associated with some type of diagnosable mental disorder. Mood disorders (depression and bipolar disorder) accounted for 30.2%, followed by substance-use related disorders (17.6%), schizophrenia (14.1%), and personality disorders (13.0%). Most of the remaining two thirds had diagnoses other than depression. To detect suicidal risk, we need to attend not only to people who are depressed, but also to those with other disorders as well as those with no diagnosable disorders.

Myth #4: A person who has made one suicide attempt is unlikely to make another. Psychiatrist Erkki Isometsa of the National Public Health Institute of Finland and his associate Jouko Lonnqvist conducted one of the largest-scale studies on this issue. They gained access to the records of all the 1,397 suicides in Finland that occurred over a 10-year period. They found that a previous history of suicide attempts was a significant predictor of completed suicide for women and to a lesser extent for men. Clearly, any suicide attempt needs to be taken seriously because it is tied to higher risk for completed suicide.

How Well Can Suicidal Tendencies Be Detected?

As of yet, there are no measures sufficiently sensitive to accurately identify suicide-prone individuals. Still, studies and the opinions of experts have helped us identify risk factors for suicide. We present some of the best established of these indicators in Box 11.1. Unfortunately, researchers have not yet come up with an algorithm based on these factors to predict suicide attempts. The items in the table should be taken as a rough guide, as prediction of suicide is at best a crude science. For example, one of us (Hal Arkowitz) worked with a depressed mother with a young infant, going through a difficult divorce and custody battle. She had almost all of the risk factors listed and yet the therapist judged that the risk was low. Why? Because she credibly stated that she would never kill herself as long as she had her baby with her. If, however, her husband had obtained custody, in one instant she would move from relatively low risk to extremely high risk. Therefore, readers should use Box 11.1 with care. If you have any questions about whether a friend or family member is suicidal, try to arrange for an evaluation by a mental health professional. If the person refuses to seek treatment, it's often helpful to get professional advice on how to handle the situation.

Box 11.1   Some Warning Signs of Suicide

History or presence of a serious psychiatric disorder
History of one or more suicide attempts
Presence of recent stressors, such as relationship breakup and job loss
Hopelessness
Extreme agitation
Thinking about suicide
Suicide threats
Suicide planning or preparation
Having the means to commit suicide
Few or no reasons for living
Alcohol or drug abuse
Dissatisfaction or denial of treatment
A history of suicide in the immediate family

Can Suicide Be Prevented?

A large number of drug therapies and psychotherapies have been evaluated for those who are at risk. In a 2014 review of drug treatments for suicidal behaviors, Erin F. Ward-Ciesielski, a University of Washington psychology graduate student, and Marsha Linehan found only weak support for these treatments. However, studies in this area have many weaknesses and firm conclusions must await better-designed studies.

In the same review, the authors found more promising results for some types of psychotherapy. Overall, the results for different approaches have been mixed but tend to favor psychotherapy over usual care and other control conditions. Two types of therapy do boast fairly strong support for their effectiveness – cognitive therapy and dialectical behavior therapy. The former treatment encourages clients to challenge their preexisting assumptions and strive toward more rational thinking; the latter consists of weekly therapy sessions and phone consultations as well as skills training in mindfulness, emotion regulation, distress tolerance, and interpersonal effectiveness. In 2005, psychologist Gregory K. Brown of the University of Pennsylvania and his associates compared a 10-session cognitive therapy treatment aimed at reducing suicidal thinking and suicide with usual care for adults who had recently attempted suicide. They followed their subjects for 18 months and found that approximately 76% of the cognitive therapy group did not reattempt suicide during this period compared with 58% of the usual care group. In addition, four well-designed studies have found consistent results for dialectical behavior therapy in reducing suicidal behavior and suicide attempts compared with control conditions.

These studies provide at least some hope for suicidal people who seek treatment. What about those who do not? This is where friends and family members can play a role by recognizing the danger signs and encouraging these individuals to seek help. To do so, people must be armed with accurate information about suicide rather than relying on myths.

Further Reading

Miller, A. L., Rathus, J. H., & Linehan, M. M. (2006). *Dialectical behavior therapy with suicidal adolescents*. New York, NY: Guilford Press.

Nock, M. K. (Ed.). (2014). *The Oxford handbook of suicide and self-injury*. Oxford, England: Oxford University Press.

12

What Is the Best Treatment for Depression

Drugs, Psychotherapy, or Both?

Imagine a treatment for depression that possesses the following properties:

- It is as effective as antidepressant medications but lacks their side effects.
- Its therapeutic results last longer than those of antidepressant medications after treatment has ended.
- Its benefits generalize to many domains of life.
- It causes changes in the brain in processes associated with depression.
- It usually needs to be administered only once a week.
- It generally costs the same or less than medications.

Sound too good to be true? In fact, such a treatment has been around for decades, although many people do not know about it. It is called psychotherapy.

Why are so many people unaware of these facts? One reason is that pharmaceutical companies have huge advertising budgets to aggressively market antidepressant medications to the public and to the physicians who write prescriptions. In contrast, psychotherapists have little

Facts and Fictions in Mental Health, First Edition. Hal Arkowitz and Scott O. Lilienfeld.
© 2017 John Wiley & Sons, Inc. Published 2017 by John Wiley & Sons, Inc.

or no budget for marketing. In this chapter, we will try to level the playing field by providing a scorecard of how antidepressants compare with psychotherapies.

Antidepressants: Pros and Cons

Although a number of different classes of antidepressants exist, we will focus on the most commonly prescribed class today: SSRIs, or selective serotonin reuptake inhibitors (see Box 12.1).

People who take antidepressants usually do not show improvement for 2 to 4 weeks. For any given individual, some antidepressants work better than others; no one antidepressant has been shown to be more effective than any other at a group level. Many people undergoing treatment for depression try two or three SSRIs (or other antidepressants) before they find one that works and that has tolerable side effects. Studies find that about 50%–70% of those who take SSRIs are responders, showing a 50% or greater reduction in symptoms. For some clients, depression is better but still present, whereas others become symptom-free. Residual symptoms after treatment are problematic because they signal a significant risk factor for a repeat depression.

After therapeutic effects appear, clients are usually told to continue on the drug for at least an additional 6 to 12 months to prevent relapse. If patients have had several previous episodes or if their depression is severe, they may be told to remain on the drug longer to avoid recurrence of depression. Using antidepressants for maintenance in this way reduces the relapse rate as compared with a placebo. Save for Prozac, antidepressant therapy has *not* been shown to be effective for children and adolescents and may not be safe for a small percentage of people younger than 24 years old, as we discuss in Chapter 13 (this volume). In addition, antidepressants can cause fetal damage, so pregnant women are strongly advised not to take them.

In most drug trials, all patients receive the same antidepressant. In the real world, however, psychiatrists often try a different medication if one prescription does not work. A study by A. John Rush of the University of Texas Southwestern Medical Center and his colleagues more closely approximated how SSRIs are used in practice. The researchers presented depressed patients with a four-step set of options to be used if necessary.

Box 12.1   Antidepressants and Common Side Effects

Selective serotonin reuptake inhibitors, or SSRIs, can relieve depression but can have drawbacks.

Trade name	Chemical name
Paxil	paroxetine
Prozac	fluoxetine
Lexapro	escitalopram
Celexa	citalopram
Zoloft	sertraline

Common Side Effects of SSRIs

- Short-term (lasting a few weeks): nausea, diarrhea, nervousness, and insomnia
- Long-term (lasting months or longer): low sexual desire or sexual dysfunction (in 50%–75% of patients) and sedation.

Research-Supported Psychotherapies

Scientists have evaluated only a few types of psychotherapy. The most supporting data exist for cognitive-behavior therapy and interpersonal psychotherapy, which have been shown to be effective in treating depression. Only a few studies have examined the performance of the other three therapies listed below, but their outcomes are encouraging.

Name	Approach
Cognitive-behavior therapy	Teaches and encourages new behaviors to help people change overly negative thinking
Interpersonal psychotherapy	Focuses on the social difficulties and conflicts associated with depression
Short-term psychodynamic therapy	Emphasizes understanding and correction of problematic interpersonal patterns

Name	Approach
Client-centered therapy	Emphasizes the therapeutic potential of the therapist–client relationship
Emotion-focused therapy	Builds on client-centered therapy by adding a focus on increasing awareness of thoughts and feelings and resolving persistent and problematic emotional reactions

All subjects started on the same antidepressant (Celexa). At each of three subsequent steps, those who either did not respond or could not tolerate the side effects got a menu of options, which included changing medication, adding medication, or adding or switching to cognitive-behavior therapy (CBT). This study yielded an overall remission rate of 67%, far superior to that of most studies that show remission rates (excluding improvement rates) closer to 33%.

Some studies of adults have shown that combining psychotherapy and medications is more effective than either treatment alone. Further, several studies with adults have found that drug therapy may be more effective than psychotherapy for severe depressions, although the evidence on this point is mixed.

The Scoop on Psychotherapy

Despite the voluminous research on psychotherapy as a treatment for depression, scientists have evaluated only a few types of psychotherapy. CBT has been the most extensively studied by far. Such therapies teach and encourage new behaviors and help people change excessively negative thinking. Interpersonal psychotherapy (IPT) has the second greatest amount of supporting data. Research on other therapies, such as short-term psychodynamic therapy, client-centered therapy, and emotion-focused therapy, has just begun, but outcomes in these few studies have been positive (see Box 12.1). In the remainder of this chapter, our discussion of psychotherapy refers to those practices that have been supported by research.

The findings regarding the efficacy of CBT are remarkably similar to those of most SSRI studies. Approximately two thirds of patients who undergo 12 to 16 sessions of CBT show improvement or remission. (The reason therapy costs the same or less than medications is largely because people are usually on antidepressants far longer than they are in psychotherapy.) So far most comparisons among different therapies have shown them to be about equally effective. As of this writing, however, no studies of psychotherapy have adopted the multistage approach used by Rush and his colleagues with antidepressants; in practice, psychotherapists often switch strategies if the one they are using is not working. Because psychotherapy studies use only one approach for purposes of experimental control, they may underestimate the efficacy of psychotherapy for depression, although that conjecture awaits formal research.

Numerous studies have demonstrated that after treatment has ended, patients treated with medication alone relapse at *twice* the rate of those treated with CBT alone. Further, dropout rates for antidepressant treatments are two to three times as high as those for CBT, with one large-scale study finding a 72% dropout rate for antidepressants by 90 days of use. Recovered patients who had received antidepressants and continued on them for maintenance showed relapse rates roughly equivalent to those who had completed CBT with no further treatment. These findings suggest that CBT may address some of the underlying causal processes better than medication does or that it may provide patients with coping skills that let them deal better with life events. In contrast, antidepressant treatments may be more palliative, suppressing symptoms for as long as the medications are taken. Even so, approximately half of those who respond to CBT relapse within 2 years, suggesting that we psychologists still have our work cut out for us. CBT researchers are working on ways to further reduce posttreatment relapse. For example, recent studies have found that an eight-session group booster treatment known as mindfulness-based cognitive therapy given to recovered depressed patients during the year after the end of initial treatment reduces relapse for those who have had three or more episodes of depression (see Chapter 6, this volume).

In depressed children and adolescents, only one of the antidepressants (Prozac) has been shown to help, whereas several different types of psychotherapies have proved beneficial. In both cases, however, treatment effects have been only moderate. The results of studies on the combination of drug therapy and psychotherapy for these populations show either no advantage or a slight advantage for the combination over either single treatment.

Although results are somewhat mixed, most of the evidence suggests that combined psychotherapy and drug treatments are more effective for adults but not necessarily for children and adolescents. One well-designed large-scale study in chronically depressed adults compared a non-SSRI antidepressant medication, a modified form of CBT that emphasized changing interpersonal relationship patterns and negative thinking, as well as their combination. Whereas response rates for each of the single treatments were comparable to those usually obtained in depression treatment studies, the response rate for the combination treatment was a dramatic 85%!

Putting it Together

Antidepressant medication and certain forms of psychotherapy are reasonably effective for the treatment of adult depression, but there is considerable room for improvement in initial response rates and relapse rates. Response rates (improvement or remission) for both treatments average at around two thirds. This means that many people are helped but are left with some depressive symptoms, whereas others are not helped at all. The combination of psychotherapy and drug therapy may yield better outcomes for adults but little or no added benefits for children and adolescents. Although psychotherapy leads to half the relapse rate of drug therapy over a 2-year follow-up period, relapse rates for both remain disturbingly high.

Psychotherapy, drug therapy, and a combination of the two are all helpful for adult depression, but effects are weaker in children and adolescents who are depressed. Drug therapy may be better for some people, psychotherapy for others, and the combination for others still. We do not know which people will respond best to any given treatment. Moreover, many other important questions remain unanswered. Would longer psychotherapeutic treatments such as those typically used in clinical practice lead to better initial outcomes than those that result from the short-term psychotherapies that have been researched so far? Would a

Box 12.2   Psychotherapy and the Brain

Drug company marketing suggests that depression is caused by a "chemical imbalance" in the brain. For example, an advertisement by the maker of the selective serotonin reuptake inhibitor (SSRI) Zoloft states: "While the cause is unknown, depression may be related to an imbalance of natural chemicals between nerve cells in the brain. Prescription Zoloft works to correct this imbalance." The imbalance to which the SSRI ads refer is a deficit of the neurotransmitter serotonin at receptor sites in the brain. Such advertising is misleading, however, and does *not* reflect scientific findings. There is no clear scientific evidence that neurotransmitter deficits cause depression or that there is an optimal "balance" of neurotransmitter levels in the brain. Moreover, medications that primarily affect chemical messengers other than serotonin are as effective as SSRIs.

Undoubtedly, antidepressants are helpful in alleviating depression. But there is a form of circular reasoning that goes: If SSRIs are helpful in alleviating depression, and if they do change the "chemical imbalance," then depression must be caused by that imbalance. Inferring causality from the success of a treatment is frequently a flawed endeavor: Aspirin is effective for headaches, but no one would seriously claim that headaches are caused by a deficiency of aspirin.

In addition, biological treatments are not unique in their ability to cause changes in the brain. Using neuroimaging techniques, many studies have shown significant brain changes in patients treated with psychotherapy alone. One study with depressed patients demonstrated that cognitive-behavior therapy led to decreased activity in the frontal regions of the brain, some of which may be related to rumination, a common feature of depression. Some studies have found brain changes identical to those caused by antidepressant medications, whereas others have found different brain changes. These findings support the idea that psychotherapy produces measurable changes in the brain, although these modifications may sometimes differ from those produced by medication.

sequential strategy such as that used by Rush and his associates for drug therapy improve psychotherapy outcomes? What can we do to further reduce or eliminate relapse? Are some treatments better for some types of people and depression than for others?

So, to the bottom line. We have learned that psychotherapy and drug therapy are both fairly effective. We know that psychotherapy prevents relapse better than drug therapy does when treatment is discontinued, that there are few, if any, negative side effects of psychotherapy, and that psychotherapy is a safe and moderately effective treatment for depressed children and adolescents. It also can change the biology associated with depression (see Box 12.2). CBT and IPT (the two best empirically supported therapies for depression) and possibly other psychotherapies with some empirical support should be seriously considered for a depressed person seeking treatment. If the response to psychotherapy is not adequate, other types of psychotherapy may be tried or a drug regimen may be added. Although the combination of psychotherapy and drug therapy may be somewhat more effective than either alone, drug side effects can be problematic.

We hope that the information we have provided will counter some of the mistaken impressions fueled by the marketing strategies of some drug companies and that it will encourage readers to think of psychotherapy as a viable treatment for depression that has several advantages over drug therapy.

Further Reading

Cozolino, L. (2010). *The neuroscience of psychotherapy* (2nd ed.). New York, NY: W. W. Norton.

Cuijpers, P., Berking, M., Andersson, G., Quigley, L., Kleiboer, A., & Dobson, K. S. (2013). A meta-analysis of cognitive-behavioural therapy for adult depression, alone and in comparison with other treatments. *Canadian Journal of Psychology, 58*, 376–385.

Hollon, S. D., DeRubeis, R. J., Fawcett, J., Amsterdam, J. D., Shelton, R. C., Zajecka, J. … Gallop, R. (2014). Effect of cognitive therapy with antidepressant medications vs. antidepressants alone on the rate of recovery in major depressive disorder: A randomized clinical trial. *JAMA Psychiatry, 71*, 1157–1164.

13

Can Antidepressants Cause Suicide?

The question posed in the title of this chapter may strike many readers as odd. How can medications that have proved helpful in reducing depression also *cause* suicide? After all, suicide is a tragic complication of some cases of depression. Yet research and clinical observations over the past 40 years have raised concerns that these drugs produce suicidal thoughts, suicide attempts, and possibly even suicide in a small subset of depressed patients. What are the risks?

In 2006 psychiatrist Tarek A. Hammad and his associates at the U.S. Food and Drug Administration published a meta-analysis (quantitative review) of studies involving a large number of children and adolescents taking antidepressants for depression, anxiety disorders, and attention-deficit hyperactivity disorder (ADHD). Their results demonstrated that subjects on antidepressant medications had twice the risk (4% vs. 2%) of suicidality (suicidal thoughts and attempts) as compared with those on placebos. No completed suicides occurred during any of the studies reviewed. A 2007 meta-analysis by psychologist Jeffrey Bridge of Ohio State University and colleagues at several institutions included additional studies and confirmed these results, although the percentages for suicidality were slightly lower.

Facts and Fictions in Mental Health, First Edition. Hal Arkowitz and Scott O. Lilienfeld.
© 2017 John Wiley & Sons, Inc. Published 2017 by John Wiley & Sons, Inc.

These findings point to the drugs as the cause of the increased suicidality rather than depression.

The FDA Acts

The initial results of Hammad's meta-analysis were available to the FDA well before the article's publication. In the wake of these findings, the FDA placed a "black box warning" on all antidepressants in 2004. This warning applied to the entire class of antidepressants and stated that these drugs can increase the risk of suicidality in children and adolescents who have major depressive disorder or other psychiatric disorders. The black-box warning is the strongest one that the FDA can issue (and is so named because of the black border that usually surrounds the text of the warning). In 2007 the agency extended this warning to include people up to the age of 24, noting that the data did not show this increased risk in adults older than 24.

The risk for suicidality usually occurs within the first days or weeks of starting the medication. According to a 2004 FDA Public Health Advisory, public health officials are concerned that patients showing certain symptoms early in treatment or during a change in medication dosage may be at heightened risk for worsening depression or suicidality. This added risk is more likely if the symptoms are severe, abrupt in onset, and not part of the depressive symptoms for which the patient initially sought treatment. These symptoms include anxiety, agitation, panic attacks, insomnia, irritability, hostility, impulsivity, severe restlessness, hypomania, and mania. Fortunately, only a small percentage of people who show these symptoms are at risk for suicidality. Nevertheless, if these symptoms start to occur, they should be reported to the prescribing physician.

Advice About Antidepressants

Numerous studies in patients of all age ranges have found that antidepressants are helpful in about two thirds of depression cases. For children and adolescents, the data show that Prozac (fluoxetine) is fairly effective but that other antidepressants are not any more effective than a placebo pill. For adults, many different antidepressants have proved helpful. One major problem with antidepressants is the high rate of relapse (approximately 40%) that occurs after they are discontinued. Many researchers have found that the combination of an antidepressant and psychotherapy (especially cognitive-behavior therapy) leads to greater symptom reduction and less suicidality and suicide than either treatment affords alone.

Box 13.1   Fast Facts

Issues of Concern

1. Suicide is a tragic complication of some cases of depression. Antidepressants have proved helpful in reducing depression.
2. Suicide is the third leading cause of death in adolescents (10 to 14 years old). Increased antidepressant use has been associated with a decrease in completed suicides.
3. Some studies, however, have shown that use of antidepressants in children and adolescents might cause a disturbing increase in suicidality (suicidal thoughts and attempts).

At a practical level, the risk of suicidality can often be adequately addressed by careful monitoring of patients, especially early in treatment. Unfortunately, most primary care doctors and psychiatrists do not do this; they usually arrange a follow-up meeting several weeks or more after the drug is prescribed. This may be the result of the doctors' lack of awareness of the risk of suicidality or the limits placed on the number of sessions by some insurance companies. Some even tell patients that such side effects are possible and that they will wear off in a week or two. This warning may discourage patients from calling doctors if the symptoms do occur. Treatment with both antidepressants and psychotherapy carries the built-in safeguard that the psychotherapist can monitor side effects and inform the patient and prescribing physician if any problems do occur.

Although there have been no research findings demonstrating completed suicide resulting from antidepressant usage in children and adolescents, a number of case reports suggest that there might be cause for concern. Case reports, however, are only suggestive and do not constitute hard scientific evidence. In addition, most studies that have found suicidality have been relatively short-term with small samples as compared with those needed to address this question; long-term risks have not yet been carefully evaluated. Most studies of people older than 24 have not reported increased suicidality with antidepressants. Nevertheless, we should be cautious about accepting this conclusion because we do not know the mechanism that explains why antidepressants can trigger suicidality in younger people.

In addition, these data may be subject to serious sources of bias, as we will discuss. To be on the safe side, physicians should also closely monitor adults who are taking antidepressants. If people who are taking antidepressants wish to stop, it is important that they consult their doctor before doing so and that they gradually taper off the drug rather than going "cold turkey." Stopping antidepressants abruptly can trigger an array of distressing symptoms, including dizziness, nausea, headache, fatigue, anxiety, irritability, and sadness, to name just a few.

Conflicts of Interest?

The controversy regarding antidepressants and suicidality has both scientific and economic dimensions. In 2004 sales of commonly prescribed classes of antidepressants (including selective serotonin reuptake inhibitors, or SSRIs) in the United States alone reached $10.9 billion. Clearly, pharmaceutical companies have a large stake in these drugs. David Healy, a psychiatrist and former secretary of the British Association for Psychopharmacology, has argued that some drug makers have often published biased results of studies on these medications and hidden or disguised their risks for more than 40 years. Others have vigorously challenged his conclusions.

Pharmaceutical makers have funded most drug trials to date, creating a potential conflict of interest for investigators and leading to the increased likelihood of an "experimenter expectancy effect." This effect occurs when researchers expect certain results – in this case, that antidepressants are safe and effective – and unintentionally influence the study design or analyses to find these results. Although double-blind procedures (in which neither the patient nor the research staff knows whether the patient is receiving an active medication or a dummy pill) can provide some protection against this bias, often controversy exists with respect to how well these procedures are implemented in medication studies.

It is also relevant that a major study funded by the National Institute of Mental Health found higher suicidality rates than those obtained in studies funded by drug companies. Moreover, many drug companies have provided ghostwriters to write up drug trials for publication, potentially biasing the document by slanting its descriptions toward favorable drug effects. Finally, there have been reported instances (e.g., the scandal regarding the drug Vioxx) in which pharmaceutical companies have hidden negative evidence. Although this type of nondisclosure has not been clearly demonstrated for antidepressants, it remains a disturbing possibility.

In response to these concerns, the International Committee of Medical Journal Editors (ICMJE) has recently required that authors submitting papers must disclose all financial and personal relationships that might bias their work, state whether potential conflicts exist, identify individuals who provided writing assistance, and disclose the funding sources for this assistance. Perhaps most important, the ICMJE requires authors to register all clinical trials they have conducted with a not-for-profit organization, whether or not the studies have been published. In this way, *all* studies will be publicly available at no charge, not just those that have obtained positive results. In addition, the FDA requires drug companies to submit the results of all studies that have been conducted, including efficacy and safety data, in their application for FDA approval.

So, do antidepressants cause suicide? The available data suggest that they probably do not, but potential biases in the research render this conclusion tentative. Nevertheless, some antidepressants do appear to cause at least a slight increase in suicidal thoughts and attempts in children, adolescents, and young adults.

Suicide is the third leading cause of death in adolescents (10 to 14 years of age) in the United States. Many investigators have found that increased antidepressant use is associated with decreased rates of completed suicides. If black-box warnings lead physicians to decrease their administration of antidepressants, the rate of completed suicides may increase. Results of a recent study in the Netherlands suggest that this may be the case: The suicide rate in children and adolescents has increased by more than 40% since 2003, when prescription rates of antidepressants began to *decrease.*

A better alternative to prescribing antidepressants to fewer children and adolescents would be to continue to prescribe them but with close and careful monitoring by the physician. Otherwise, we may be faced with a tragic irony: Efforts to protect children from suicidal thoughts and attempts through lower antidepressant prescription rates may lead to greater harm through increased suicide rates because of inadequately treated depression.

Many questions remain. Will future studies conducted independently of the influences of drug companies show different risks of suicidality and suicide in young people? Will we continue to find a lack of antidepressant-induced suicidality and suicide in adults? What will longer-term studies reveal about the effects of antidepressants on suicide and suicidality? We hope that recent efforts to reduce sources of bias in research will provide us with more accurate answers to these important questions.

Fortunately, there is a safe alternative to antidepressants. Many, but not all, studies have shown that short-term psychotherapies (12 to 16 sessions), with or without medication, are at least as effective as medication for depression and anxiety, maintain patient improvement better in the long run, and carry little or no associated risk of suicide. Yet because psychotherapists do not have advertising budgets remotely approaching those of drug companies, many mental health consumers are unaware of these important findings.

Given the present state of knowledge, we support the use of antidepressants, particularly fluoxetine, as one treatment for depression and anxiety in children, adolescents, and young adults, as long as the treatment is closely monitored. Fluoxetine and many other antidepressants have proved effective in adult populations, and we support their use with those older than 24 as well. The data show, however, that a combination of psychotherapy, particularly cognitive-behavior therapy, and antidepressant medication is the most effective, enduring, and safe treatment.

Further Reading

Gupta, S., Gersing, K. R., Erkani, A., & Tal, B. (2015). Antidepressant regulatory warnings, prescription patterns, suicidality and other aggressive behaviors in major depressive disorder and anxiety disorders. *Psychiatric Quarterly*, *86*, 1–14.

Hammad, T. A., Laughren, T., & Racoosin, J. (2006) Suicidality in pediatric patients treated with antidepressant drugs. *Archives of General Psychiatry*, *63*(3), 332–339.

Healy, D. (2004). *Let them eat Prozac: The unhealthy relationship between the pharmaceutical industry and depression*. New York, NY: New York University Press.

14

The Truth About Shock Therapy

A rabble-rousing patient on a psychiatric ward is brought into a room and strapped to a gurney. He is being punished for his defiance of the head nurse's sadistic authority. As he lies fully awake, the psychiatrist and other staff members place electrodes on both sides of his head and pass a quick jolt of electricity between them. Several orderlies hold the patient down while he grimaces in pain, thrashes uncontrollably, and lapses into a stupor.

This scene from the 1975 Academy Award-winning film *One Flew Over the Cuckoo's Nest*, starring Jack Nicholson as the rebellious patient, has probably shaped the general public's perceptions of electroconvulsive therapy (ECT) far more than any scientific description. As a result, many laypeople regard ECT as a hazardous, even barbaric, procedure. Yet most data suggest that when properly administered, ECT is a relatively safe and often beneficial last-resort treatment for severe depression, among other forms of mental illness.

Facts and Fictions in Mental Health, First Edition. Hal Arkowitz and Scott O. Lilienfeld.
© 2017 John Wiley & Sons, Inc. Published 2017 by John Wiley & Sons, Inc.

Cuckoo Conceptions

One Flew Over the Cuckoo's Nest is far from the only negative portrayal of ECT in popular culture. In a 2001 survey of 24 films featuring the technique, psychiatrists Andrew McDonald of the University of Sydney and Garry Walter of Northern Sydney Central Coast Health of New South Wales reported that the depictions of ECT are usually pejorative and inaccurate. In most cases, ECT is delivered without patients' consent and often as retribution for disobedience. The treatment is typically applied to fully conscious and terrified patients. Following the shocks, patients generally lapse into incoherence or a zombielike state. In six films, patients become markedly worse or die.

Probably as a result of such portrayals, the general public holds negative attitudes toward ECT. In a 2012 survey of 165 students in undergraduate psychology courses, who are presumably more likely than most to be informed about mental illness therapies, psychologists Annette Taylor and Patricia Kowalski of the University of San Diego found that roughly 74% agreed that ECT is physically dangerous. And a 2006 survey of 1,737 Swiss citizens led by psychologist Christoph Lauber, then at the Psychiatric University Hospital in Zurich, revealed that 57% perceived ECT as harmful; only 1.2% supported its use.

Minimal Risk

ECT, colloquially called "shock therapy," was introduced in 1938 by Italian neurologists Ugo Cerletti and Lucio Bini as a treatment for psychosis. (Cerletti apparently got the idea after observing that cows that had been shocked prior to slaughter became sedated.) The treatment is simple: Electrodes are attached to a patient's head, and electric current is passed between them, causing changes in brain chemistry and activity.

In line with the public's perceptions, the intervention often was perilous before the mid-1950s. Back then, patients were awake during ECT. The shocks caused convulsions, and broken bones were a fairly common result of the body thrashing about. After all, when properly administered, ECT induces a seizure; indeed, many researchers argue that a seizure is needed for the procedure to work.

Nowadays in the United States and other Western countries, patients receive ECT in conjunction with a muscle relaxant and a general anesthetic, both given largely to tamp down muscular activity during the seizure and decrease overall discomfort. Hence, although patients still undergo a seizure, they are unconscious during the procedure and do not experience pain or observable convulsions. During ECT, the patient's brain waves, along with other vital signs, are monitored to ensure safety.

These advances have made ECT much safer and less frightening than it once was. In a 1986 survey of 166 patients who had received ECT, psychiatrists C. P. L. Freeman and R. E. Kendell of the University of Edinburgh found that 68% reported that the experience was no more upsetting than a visit to the dentist. For the others, ECT was more unpleasant than dentistry, but it was not painful.

Still, the treatment is not hazard-free. In some countries, physicians deliver ECT much as they did in the pre-1950s era. In a 2010 review psychiatrist Worrawat Chanpattana of Samitivej Srinakarin Hospital in Bangkok and his colleagues found that 56% of patients across 14 Asian countries received ECT with no muscle relaxant or anesthetic. And ECT performed anywhere has some downsides. Patients typically emerge from a session temporarily disoriented. More seriously, most patients experience retrograde amnesia afterward: They no longer remember many events that occurred a few weeks to months before the treatment. The loss is less pronounced when electrodes are placed on one side of the head rather than on both. And recent technologies, including brief-pulse machines that permit the electricity doses to be carefully calibrated, minimize the extent of the amnesia. But some memory problems virtually always accompany the procedure. In addition, some studies hint that ECT can in rare cases lead to lasting cognitive deficits beyond the limited retrograde amnesia, although the data backing this possible outcome are far from definitive.

Mysterious Mechanisms

Given its adverse effects on memory, patients should consider ECT only after other treatments have failed. Yet the bulk of research suggests that ECT can be effective at alleviating the symptoms of several mental illnesses, including severe depression and the manic phase of bipolar disorder. It also seems to ease catatonia, a condition marked by striking movement abnormalities, such as remaining in a fetal position or gesturing repeatedly, that may accompany schizophrenia and bipolar disorder.

The case for the intervention would be even stronger if researchers could determine why it works. According to a 2011 review, psychiatrist Tom Bolwig of Copenhagen University Hospital noted that ECT increases the secretion of certain hormones that are disturbed in depression. Others have suggested that the electricity stimulates neural growth and helps to rebuild brain areas that are protective against depression. A third idea is that the seizures themselves fundamentally reset brain activity in ways that often bring relief, Bolwig concludes.

ECT may also ameliorate illness by altering the sensitivity of receptors for neurotransmitters, such as serotonin (see Chapter 10, this volume). None of these hypotheses, however, has yet to garner convincing research support. As we learn more about this widely misunderstood intervention, we may be able to refine our delivery methods and reduce ECT's negative effects. Even in its current form, however, the treatment is a far cry from the barbaric punishment portrayed in the media. Hence, it is often worth considering as an option for unremitting psychological distress after all else has failed.

Further Reading

Dukakis, K., & Tye, L. (2006). *Shock: The healing power of electroconvulsive therapy.* New York, NY: Avery Publishing Group.

McDonald, A., & Walter, G. (2009). Hollywood and ECT. *International Review of Psychiatry, 21*(3), 200–206.

Section 3
Child and Adolescent Disorders

Introduction

In 2013, the *DSM-5* introduced a new group of diagnoses called neuro-developmental disorders, which usually begin in childhood, often before the youngster enters grade school. These problems usually continue into adolescence and often adulthood. Included in this category are attention-deficit hyperactivity disorder; autism spectrum disorder; motor disorders, which include Tourette's syndrome; and problems in intellectual development, learning, and communication. The problems of young people also appear in many other places throughout the *DSM*. Children and adolescents can be diagnosed with anxiety, mood, and eating disorders, as well as disruptive, impulse control, and conduct disorders. In this section, we will examine myths regarding some of these psychological difficulties.

Most people, especially parents, have heard the term attention-deficit hyperactivity disorder (ADHD). Youngsters who are given this diagnosis are primarily inattentive, primarily hyperactive, or a combination of the two. Symptoms of the primarily inattentive type include distractibility, disorganization, and forgetfulness, whereas symptoms of the primarily

Facts and Fictions in Mental Health, First Edition. Hal Arkowitz and Scott O. Lilienfeld.
© 2017 John Wiley & Sons, Inc. Published 2017 by John Wiley & Sons, Inc.

hyperactive group include overactivity, impulsivity, fidgeting, and an inability to wait. In individuals with ADHD, symptoms from either or both category interfere with school performance as well as relationships with peers and adults.

The main features of autism spectrum disorder, formerly called autism, are serious problems in communication and social interaction along with repetitive patterns of behaviors, interests, and activities. The spectrum stretches from milder forms, which were formerly subsumed under a diagnosis called Asperger's syndrome, to more severe autism. A 1988 movie that introduced many people to this disorder was *Rain Man*, in which Dustin Hoffman portrayed a severely autistic man modeled after an actual individual, Kim Peek (who was nicknamed the "Kimcomputer" in view of his remarkable memory for statistics, such as the batting averages of major league baseball players). Although an eminent psychologist, Bernard Rimland, was a consultant who helped develop this role, the depiction created problems in how the public perceived this disorder. Rimland later said that he created the role of severe autism, someone who would now be diagnosed at the top end of the autism spectrum. By doing so, he unintentionally created a stereotype of people with autism as interpersonally odd, even weird. But autism can be mild as well, and many people at this end of the spectrum function effectively. Dan Akroyd, the brilliantly talented actor, writer, and comedian, was diagnosed with both autism spectrum disorder and Tourette's disorder. One of his symptoms of autism was a preoccupation with ghosts. This provided the inspiration for the movie *Ghostbusters*, which he cowrote and in which he played one of the leading characters (not one of the ghosts). Tourette's disorder is classified as a motor disorder and involves bodily and vocal tics. A tic is a sudden, rapid, repetitive movement or vocalization.

The question of whether children can have bipolar disorder is highly controversial (see the introduction to Section 2 for a description of this diagnosis). Another controversial area involves the effectiveness of methods to teach adolescents about the dangers of drug use and to "just say no" to taking drugs.

In this section, we take a closer look at this issue and others in the area of child and adolescent disorders.

- Is attention-deficit hyperactivity disorder overdiagnosed and overtreated?
- Has the prevalence of autism increased dramatically?

- Do most children with Tourette's syndrome curse?
- Are the problem behaviors of people with Tourette's syndrome voluntary or caused by psychological problems?
- Are people with Tourette's syndrome always incapacitated by their disorder?
- Is bipolar disorder in children either rare or nonexistent?
- Does divorce almost always cause serious and long-lasting problems for children?
- Do "get tough" approaches help juvenile offenders?

15

Are Doctors Diagnosing Too Many Children With ADHD?

A German children's book from 1845 by Heinrich Hoffman featured "Fidgety Philip," a boy who was so restless he would writhe and tilt wildly in his chair at the dinner table. Once, using the tablecloth as an anchor, he dragged all the dishes onto the floor. Yet it was not until 1902 that a British pediatrician, George Frederic Still, described what we now recognize as attention-deficit hyperactivity disorder (ADHD). Since Still's day, the disorder has gone by a host of names, including organic drivenness, hyperkinetic syndrome, attention-deficit disorder – and now ADHD.

Despite this lengthy history, the diagnosis and treatment of ADHD in today's children could hardly be more controversial. On his television show in 2004, Phil McGraw ("Dr. Phil") opined that ADHD is "so over-diagnosed," and a survey in 2005 by psychologists Jill Norvilitis of the University at Buffalo, SUNY, and Ping Fang of Capitol Normal University in Beijing revealed that in the United States, 82% of teachers and 68% of undergraduates agreed that "ADHD is overdiagnosed today." According to many critics, such overdiagnosis raises the specter of medicalizing largely normal behavior and relying too heavily on pills rather than skills – such as teaching children better ways of coping with stress.

Facts and Fictions in Mental Health, First Edition. Hal Arkowitz and Scott O. Lilienfeld.
© 2017 John Wiley & Sons, Inc. Published 2017 by John Wiley & Sons, Inc.

Yet although data point to at least some overdiagnosis, at least in boys, the extent of this problem is unclear. In fact, the evidence, with notable exceptions, appears to be stronger for the undertreatment than overtreatment of ADHD.

Medicalizing Normality

The American Psychiatric Association's diagnostic manual, *DSM-5*, outlines two major sets of indicators for ADHD: inattention (a child is easily distracted) and either hyperactivity (he or she may fidget a lot, for example) or impulsivity (the child may blurt out answers too quickly). A child must display at least six of the nine listed symptoms for at least half a year from both the inattention and hyperactivity/ impulsivity categories. In addition, at least some problems must be present before the age of 12 and produce impairment in at least two different settings, such as school or home. Studies suggest that about 5% of school-age children have ADHD; the disorder is diagnosed in about 3 times as many boys as girls.

Many scholars have alleged that ADHD is massively overdiagnosed, reflecting a "medicalization" of largely normative childhood difficulties, such as jitteriness, boredom, and impatience. Nevertheless, it makes little sense to refer to the overdiagnosis of ADHD unless there is an objective cutoff score for its presence. Data suggest, however, that a bright dividing line does not exist. In a study published in 2011 psychologists David Marcus, now at Washington State University, and Tammy Barry of the University of Southern Mississippi measured ADHD symptoms in a large sample of third graders. Their analyses demonstrated that ADHD differs in degree, not in kind, from normality.

Yet many well-recognized medical conditions, such as hypertension and type 2 diabetes, are also extremes on a continuum that stretches across the population. Hence, the more relevant question is whether doctors are routinely diagnosing kids with ADHD who do not meet the levels of symptoms specified by the *DSM-5*.

Some studies hint that such misdiagnosis does occur, although its magnitude is unclear. In 1993 Albert Cotugno, a practicing psychologist in Massachusetts, reported that only 22% of 92 children referred to an ADHD clinic actually met criteria for ADHD following an evaluation, indicating that many children referred for treatment do not have the disorder as formally defined. Nevertheless, these results are not conclusive, because it is unknown how many of the youth received an official diagnosis, and the sample came from only one clinic.

Clearer, but less dramatic, evidence for overdiagnosis comes from a 2012 study in which psychologist Katrin Bruchmüller of the University of Basel and her colleagues found that when given hypothetical vignettes of children who fell short of the *DSM-IV* diagnosis, about 17% of the 1,000 mental health professionals surveyed mistakenly diagnosed the kids with ADHD. These errors were especially frequent for boys, perhaps because boys more often fit clinicians' stereotypes of ADHD children. (In contrast, some researchers conjecture that ADHD is underdiagnosed in girls, who often have subtler symptoms, such as daydreaming and spaciness.)

Pill Pushers?

Published reports of using stimulants for ADHD date to 1938. But in 1944 chemist Leandro Panizzon, working for Ciba, the predecessor of Novartis, synthesized a stimulant drug that he named in honor of his wife, Marguerite, whose nickname was Rita. Ritalin (methylphenidate) and other stimulants, such as Adderall, Concerta, and Vyvanse, are now standard treatments; Strattera, a nonstimulant, is also widely used. About 80% of children diagnosed with ADHD display improvements in attention and impulse control while on the drugs but not after their effects wear off. Still, stimulants sometimes have side effects, such as insomnia, mild weight loss, and a slight stunting of height. Behavioral treatments, which reward children for remaining seated, maintaining attention, or engaging in other appropriate activities, are also effective in many cases.

Many media sources report that stimulants have been widely prescribed for children without ADHD. As Dutch pharmacologist Willemijn Meijer of PHARMO Institute in Utrecht and his colleagues observed in a 2009 review, stimulant prescriptions for children in the United States rose from 2.8% to 4.4% between 2000 and 2005. Yet most data suggest that ADHD is undertreated, at least if one assumes that children with this diagnosis should receive stimulants. Psychiatrist Peter Jensen, then at Columbia University, noted in a 2000 article that data from the mid-1990s demonstrated that although about 3 million children in the United States met criteria for ADHD, only 2 million received a stimulant prescription from a doctor.

The perception that stimulants are overprescribed and overused probably has a kernel of truth, however. Data collected in 1999 by psychologist Gretchen LeFever, then at Eastern Virginia Medical School, point to geographical pockets of overprescription. In southern Virginia, 8%–10% of children in the second through fifth grades received stimulant treatment compared with the 5% of children in that region who would be expected to meet criteria for ADHD. Moreover, increasing numbers of individuals with few or no attentional problems – such as college students trying to stay awake and alert to study – are using stimulants, according to ongoing studies. Although the long-term harms of such stimulants among students are unclear, they carry a risk of addiction.

A Peek at the Future

The new edition of the diagnostic manual, *DSM-5*, which appeared in 2013, has broadened the diagnosis of ADHD relative to its predecessor (*DSM-IV*) by specifying a lower proportion of total symptoms for the diagnosis and raising the age of onset from 7 to 12 years old. In a commentary in 2012 psychologist Laura Batstra of the University of Groningen in the Netherlands and psychiatrist Allen Frances of Duke University expressed concerns that these modifications will result in erroneous increases in ADHD diagnoses. Whether or not their forecast is correct, this next chapter of ADHD diagnosis will almost surely usher in a new flurry of controversy regarding the classification and treatment of the disorder.

Further Reading

Bruchmüller, K., Margraf, J., & Schneider, S. (2012). Is ADHD diagnosed in accord with diagnostic criteria? Overdiagnosis and influence of client gender on diagnosis. *Journal of Consulting and Clinical Psychology, 80*(1), 128–138.

16

Autism

An Epidemic?

If the figure of "1 in 68" has a familiar ring, perhaps that's because you recently heard it on a television commercial or read it in a magazine. According to widely publicized estimates, 1 in 68 is now the proportion of children who suffer from autism. This proportion is astonishingly high compared with the figure of 1 in 2,500 that autism researchers had accepted for decades. Across a mere 10-year period – 1993 to 2003 – statistics from the U.S. Department of Education revealed a 657% increase in the nationwide rate of autism, now officially termed autism spectrum disorder.

Not surprisingly, these bewildering increases have led many researchers and educators to refer to an autism "epidemic." Representative Dan Burton of Indiana also declared in 2001 that "we have an epidemic on our hands." But what's really going on?

Before we explore this question, a bit of background is in order. Autism is a severe disorder that first appears in infancy. Individuals with autism are characterized by problems in language, social bonding, and imagination. All suffer from serious communication deficits, and some are mute. They do not establish close relationships with others, preferring to remain in their own mental worlds. They engage in highly stereotyped

Facts and Fictions in Mental Health, First Edition. Hal Arkowitz and Scott O. Lilienfeld.
© 2017 John Wiley & Sons, Inc. Published 2017 by John Wiley & Sons, Inc.

and repetitive activities, exhibiting a marked aversion to change. About two thirds of autistic individuals are marked by intellectual deficiency, formerly known as mental retardation. For reasons that are unknown, most are male.

The causes of autism remain enigmatic, although studies of twins suggest that genetic factors play a prominent role. Still, genetic influences alone cannot account for such a rapid and astronomical rise in a disorder's prevalence over a matter of just a few years.

As a consequence, investigators have turned to environmental factors for potential explanations. The causal agents proposed include antibiotics, viruses, allergies, enhanced opportunities for parents with mild autistic traits to meet and mate, and, in one recent study conducted by Cornell University researchers, elevated rates of television viewing in infants. Few of these explanations have been investigated systematically, and all remain speculative.

Problem Shots?

Yet one environmental culprit has received the lion's share of attention: vaccines. At first blush, vaccines would seem to make a plausible candidate for the source of the epidemic. The debilitating symptoms of autism typically become apparent shortly after age 2, not long after infants have received vaccinations for a host of diseases. Indeed, many parents claim that their children developed autism shortly after receiving inoculations, either following a vaccine series for mumps, measles, and rubella (German measles) – the so-called MMR vaccine – or following vaccines containing thimerosal, a preservative containing mercury.

Much of the hype surrounding a vaccine–autism link was fueled by a widely covered investigation of 12 children published in 1998 by British gastroenterologist Andrew Wakefield and his colleagues. The study revealed that symptoms of autism emerged shortly after the children received the MMR vaccine. (Ten of the 13 authors have since published a retraction of the article's conclusions.) Public interest in the vaccine–autism link was further stoked by the provocatively titled book *Evidence of Harm* (St. Martin's Press, 2005), written by investigative journalist David Kirby, which was featured in an extended segment on NBC's *Meet the Press*.

Yet recently published research has not been kind to the much ballyhooed vaccine–autism link. The results of several large American, European, and Japanese studies demonstrate that although the rate of MMR vaccinations has remained constant or declined, the rate of autism diagnoses has soared. In addition, after the Danish government stopped administering thimerosal-bearing vaccines, the rates of autism continued to rise. These studies and others, summarized by the Institute of Medicine, suggest there is little evidence that vaccines cause autism. It is possible that vaccines trigger autism in a tiny subset of children, but if so that subset has yet to be identified.

Changing Criteria

Making matters more confusing, ample reason exists to question the very existence of the autism epidemic. Vaccines may be what scientists call an "explanation in search of a phenomenon." As University of Wisconsin–Madison psychologists Morton Ann Gernsbacher and H. Hill Goldsmith and University of Montreal researcher Michelle Dawson noted in a 2005 review, there is an often-overlooked alternative explanation for the epidemic: changes in diagnostic practices. Over time the criteria for a diagnosis of autism have loosened, resulting in the labeling of substantially more mildly afflicted individuals as autistic.

Indeed, the 1980 version of the American Psychiatric Association's diagnostic manual (*DSM-III*) required individuals to meet six of six criteria for an autism diagnosis. In contrast, the 1994 version (*DSM-IV*), which is currently in use, requires individuals to meet any 8 of 16 criteria. Moreover, whereas *DSM-III* contained only two diagnoses relevant to autism, the *DSM-IV* contained five such diagnoses, including Asperger's syndrome, which most researchers regard as a high-functioning variant of autism. *DSM-5*, released in 2013, combined these diagnoses, including Asperger's syndrome, into a broader category of autism spectrum disorder and tightened the diagnostic requirements for this condition, but its long-term impact on the prevalence of autism remains to be determined.

Legal changes may also be playing a significant role. As Gernsbacher and her colleagues noted, an amended version of the Individuals with Disabilities Education Act (IDEA), passed by Congress in 1991, required school districts to provide precise counts of children with disabilities. IDEA resulted in sharp surges in the reported numbers of children with autism. Nevertheless, these numbers are not based on careful diagnoses of autism or on representative samples of the population. As a consequence, researchers who rely on "administrative-based estimates," which come from government data submitted by schools, will arrive at misleading conclusions about autism's prevalence. They must instead rely on "population-based estimates," which are developed from statistically reliable and representative surveys of autism's occurrence in the general population.

Further contributing to the reported increase may be the "Rain Man Effect," the public's increased familiarity with autism following the 1988 Academy Award-winning film starring Dustin Hoffman and Tom Cruise.

Numbers Analyzed

Two studies buttress assertions that the autism epidemic may be more illusory than real. First, in 2005 psychiatrist Suniti Chakrabarti of the Child Development Center in Stafford, England, and psychiatrist Eric Fombonne of McGill University conducted an investigation that used rigorous population-based estimates to track the prevalence of autism diagnoses from 1992 to 1998 in a sample of more than 10,000 children in the same area of England. They found no support for a change in prevalence, suggesting that when researchers maintain the same criteria for autism, the rates of diagnosis do not change over time.

Second, a 2006 article by University of Wisconsin–Madison psychologist Paul Shattuck cited "diagnostic substitution": As the rates of the autism diagnosis increased from 1994 to 2003, the rates of diagnoses of mental retardation and learning disabilities decreased. This finding raises the possibility that the overall "pool" of children with autism-like features has remained constant but that the specific diagnoses within this pool have swapped places.

It is still too early to exclude the possibility that autism's prevalence is growing, but it is unlikely that it is growing at anywhere near the rate many have suggested. As the late Eastern Michigan University sociologist Marcello Truzzi once said, extraordinary claims require extraordinary evidence. The claim of an enormous epidemic of autism diagnoses is indeed extraordinary. Yet the evidence in support of this claim leaves much to be desired.

Further Reading

Fombonne, E. (2003). The prevalence of autism. *Journal of the American Medical Association, 289*(1), 87–89.

Gernsbacher, M. A., Dawson, M., & Goldsmith, H. H. (2005). Three reasons not to believe in an autism epidemic. *Current Directions in Psychological Science, 14*, 55–58.

Herbert, J. D., Sharp, I. R., & Gaudiano, B. A. (2002). Separating fact from fiction in the etiology and treatment of autism: A scientific review of the evidence. *Scientific Review of Mental Health Practice, 1*(1), 23–43.

Institute of Medicine (US) Immunization Safety Review Committee. (2004). *Immunization safety review: Vaccines and autism.* Washington, DC: National Academies Press.

17

What Do We Know About Tourette's Disorder?

On May 22, 2001, radio talk show personality Laura Schlessinger, better known as Dr. Laura, received a call from a woman who was distressed by her sister's decision to exclude their nephew from an upcoming family wedding. When the caller mentioned that the boy suffered from Tourette's disorder (also sometimes called Tourette syndrome), Dr. Laura berated her for even thinking that it might be appropriate to invite a child who would "scream out vulgarities in the middle of the wedding." As we'll soon explain, Dr. Laura's comments embody just one of several common myths regarding Tourette's.

Tourette's disorder is the eponymous name for the condition first formally described in 1885 by French neurologist Georges Gilles de la Tourette, who dubbed it *maladie des tics* ("sickness of tics"). According to the current edition of the American Psychiatric Association's diagnostic manual, Tourette's disorder is marked by a history of both motor (movement) tics and phonic (sound) tics.

Motor tics include eye twitching, facial grimacing, tongue protrusion, head turning, and shrugging of the shoulders, whereas phonic tics encompass grunting, coughing, throat clearing, yelling inappropriate words, and even barking. Some tics are "complex," meaning they are

Facts and Fictions in Mental Health, First Edition. Hal Arkowitz and Scott O. Lilienfeld.
© 2017 John Wiley & Sons, Inc. Published 2017 by John Wiley & Sons, Inc.

coordinated series of actions. For example, a Tourette's patient might continually pick up and smell objects or repeat what someone else just said (echolalia). Often a tic is preceded by a "premonitory urge" – that is, a powerful desire to emit the tic, which some have likened to the feeling we experience immediately before sneezing. Tourette's patients typically report short-term relief following the tic.

Tourette's generally emerges at about age 6 or 7, with motor tics usually appearing before phonic tics. In rare cases, the disorder disappears by adulthood. Data suggest that it may be present in 1–3 out of 1,000 children; about 3 to 4 times as many males as females are affected.

Myths and Realities

As the Dr. Laura incident demonstrates, Tourette's disorder is the subject of popular misconceptions; we'll examine the four that are most widespread.

Misconception 1: *All Tourette's patients curse.* In a survey of undergraduates by University of San Diego psychologists Annette Taylor and Patricia Kowalski, 65% endorsed this view. In fact, coprolalia, the use of curse words, and copropraxia, the use of obscene gestures, occur in only a minority – probably about 10% to 15% – of Tourette's patients. But because these symptoms are so dramatic, they plant themselves firmly in observers' memories. They also garner the lion's share of media attention, as in a 2002 *Curb Your Enthusiasm* episode featuring a chef with Tourette's disorder, who curses uncontrollably in front of his customers.

Misconception 2: *Tourette's symptoms are voluntary.* Because Tourette's sufferers can often suppress their tics for brief periods, some have concluded mistakenly that patients generate them of their own accord. In fact, they have little or no control over premonitory urges and can inhibit tics only for so long, just as you can only briefly avoid scratching an itch. Although some people believe that tic suppression results in a later "rebound" of tics, research evidence does not support this view.

Misconception 3: *Tourette's disorder is caused by underlying psychological conflict.* As medical historian Howard Kushner, now at the University of California at San Diego, noted, the idea that Tourette's results from deep-seated psychological factors held sway in American psychiatry for much of the 20th century. As recently as the mid-1980s, one of us (Scott Lilienfeld) was told by a psychologist in training that the tics of Tourette's patients represented symbolic discharges of repressed sexual energies. Today we know that the disorder is substantially heritable. A 1985 study by R. Arlen Price, then at Yale University, and his colleagues found that in identical twins (who share virtually all of their genes) with Tourette's, both twins had the disorder 53% of the time, whereas in fraternal twins (who share half their genes on average) with Tourette's, both twins had the disorder only 8% of the time. Still, stress can increase tic frequency, so genes are unlikely to tell the whole story. Brain-imaging studies of Tourette's patients reveal abnormalities in areas related to movement, such as the basal ganglia, a collection of structures buried deep in the cerebral hemispheres.

Misconception 4: *People with Tourette's are incapacitated by their symptoms.* Many individuals with Tourette's function successfully in society. Mort Doran, a Canadian surgeon with Tourette's, manages to

---

Box 17.1   Tourette's Through History

Some writers have argued that several famous historical figures, including Roman emperor Claudius (of *I, Claudius* fame) and author Samuel Johnson, may have had Tourette's disorder. Others have speculated that composer Wolfgang Amadeus Mozart had Tourette's, although the evidence here is more circumstantial, consisting mostly of suggestions that Mozart was prone to profanity and to hyperactivity, a symptom that commonly occurs with Tourette's.

Psychiatrist Arthur K. Shapiro and psychologist Elaine Shapiro of Cornell University conjectured that the troubled girl who formed the basis for the 1971 book and 1973 blockbuster film *The Exorcist* had Tourette's disorder. Some observers, they contend, misinterpreted her head jerking, grunting, and profane language as hallmarks of demonic possession.

suppress his tics while in the operating room; he is also an amateur pilot. The late neurologist Oliver Sacks wrote of a jazz drummer who reported that his Tourette's disorder enhanced his musical performances by imbuing them with energy. Indeed, some have argued that Tourette's can be a blessing rather than a curse, perhaps in part because the condition forces people to learn impulse-control skills that few of us acquire. This claim is intriguing but anecdotal. Former National Basketball Association point guard Chris Jackson, who changed his name to Mahmoud Abdul-Rauf, said that his Tourette's made him focus with laserlike precision on his shooting. He twice led the league in free-throw percentage; during one stretch of play in 1993, he made 81 consecutive free throws.

Hope for Tourette's Sufferers

There is no known cure for Tourette's, but several treatment options exist. Medications such as Haldol (generic name haloperidol) and Orap (generic name pimozide), which block the action of the chemical messenger dopamine, have been found in studies to be effective in reducing the frequency and intensity of tics. Other promising medications are clonidine, which doubles as a blood pressure drug, and botulinum toxin, better known as Botox. Clonidine inhibits the chemical messenger norepinephrine, which some researchers have argued is implicated in Tourette's. Although Botox's mechanisms of action on Tourette's are unknown, it appears to work by blocking body processes that are involved in facial tics or movement.

Preliminary evidence suggests that some behavioral therapies, especially habit reversal, can be helpful for Tourette's disorder; it is not known whether combining these techniques with medication yields an additive benefit. Habit reversal teaches patients to become aware of the premonitory urges preceding tics and to learn and practice muscular actions incompatible with their tics. For example, patients who repeatedly jerk their arm violently toward others might be taught to direct their arm slowly toward their head, culminating in touching their hair gently. This approach and others are not panaceas, but they can help some Tourette's patients to bring their more troubling symptoms under better control.

Further Reading

Chowdhury, U. (2004). *Tics and Tourette syndrome: A handbook for parents and professionals.* London, England: Jessica Kingsley Publishers.

Kushner, H. I. (1999). *A cursing brain? The histories of Tourette syndrome.* Cambridge, MA: Harvard University Press.

Zinner, S. H. (2004). Tourette syndrome—much more than tics: Moving beyond misconceptions to a diagnosis. *Contemporary Pediatrics, 21*(8), 22–36.

18

Do Children
Get Bipolar Disorder?

Imagine an 8-year-old boy whom we will call Eric. He is irritable and talks incessantly. Unable to sit still and concentrate, he does poorly at school. Nevertheless, he claims to be one of the smartest kids in the world and blames his poor academic performance on his "horrible" teachers. There are periods when his mood changes abruptly from euphoria to depression and then swings back again. Eric's symptoms qualify him for a diagnosis of bipolar disorder, which is characterized by episodes of full-blown mania or a less severe form called hypomania. These moods usually alternate with periods of depression (see Box 18.1).

Until about 1980 most mental health professionals believed that bipolar disorder did not occur in children. Although a few still hold this view, the general opinion of the psychiatric community has drastically shifted over the past 30 years, a period in which diagnoses of the disorder in children have skyrocketed. In a study published in 2007 psychiatrist Carmen Moreno, then at Gregorio Marañón University General Hospital in Madrid, and her colleagues found a 40-fold increase between 1994 and 2003 in the number of visits to a psychiatrist in which a patient younger than 19 was given this diagnosis. By 2003, the researchers reported, the number of office visits resulting in a bipolar diagnosis in

Facts and Fictions in Mental Health, First Edition. Hal Arkowitz and Scott O. Lilienfeld.
© 2017 John Wiley & Sons, Inc. Published 2017 by John Wiley & Sons, Inc.

Box 18.1   Diagnosing Bipolar Disorder

Whether you are a child or an adult, you may qualify for a diagnosis of bipolar disorder if you display symptoms of mania, a state characterized by an elevated, expansive, or irritable mood, usually alternating with periods of major depression. In addition to that mood change, a manic episode includes three or more of the following seven characteristics. (At least four of these symptoms must be present if your manic mood is primarily irritable.)

- Inflated self-esteem or grandiosity
- Decreased need for sleep
- Increased talkativeness
- Racing thoughts
- Distractibility
- Agitation or increase in goal-directed activities such as planning to open a new business
- Engaging in pleasurable activities with high potential for negative consequences.

---

these youths had risen from 25 per 100,000 people to 1,003 per 100,000 people, a rate almost as high as that for adults.

Such data have sparked widespread concern that the condition is egregiously overdiagnosed, perhaps contributing to the use of ineffective and even harmful medical treatments. In this chapter, we discuss controversies regarding the overdiagnosis of bipolar disorder in children and recent attempts to remedy this situation.

Tale of Two Manias

In 1980 the American Psychiatric Association came out with a radically revised third edition of its diagnostic bible, the *Diagnostic and Statistical Manual of Mental Disorders* (*DSM-III*). This edition debuted the term "bipolar disorder" as a replacement for the earlier term "manic-depressive disorder." The diagnosis required a full-blown manic episode lasting at least 1 week, usually alternating with periods of major depression that extended for at least 2 weeks. The symptoms had to be severe enough to interfere with social or occupational functioning; for children, the latter refers to how well they perform in school.

In the view of many professionals, some children did – and still do – fit these criteria. In 1994, however, with the publication of the *DSM-IV*, a new category of bipolar disorder appeared. In this volume, the illness is subdivided into bipolar I, essentially equivalent to the *DSM-III* version of this malady, and bipolar II, which has less stringent diagnostic criteria. A patient can be diagnosed with bipolar II if he or she has hypomania, the less severe form of mania, in which the manic episodes can be shorter – 4 days instead of 1 week – and do not impair functioning. The inclusion of this milder form of the disorder enabled many more children (as well as adults) to qualify for a bipolar diagnosis.

It is no coincidence then that the dramatic rise in cases of childhood bipolar disorder began as soon as *DSM-IV* landed on psychiatrists' desks. Many critics have raised concerns that this manual's loosened criteria have misclassified many children as bipolar II who had features too mild to really qualify them for any type of bipolar disorder – or who suffer from entirely different ailments.

Bad Diagnosis, Bad Treatment

Indeed, bipolar II overlaps substantially with other common childhood conditions. For example, attention-deficit hyperactivity disorder (ADHD) and bipolar are both characterized by distractibility, fidgeting, restlessness, high activity levels, and excessive talking. Bipolar disorder also shares similarities with conduct disorder and oppositional defiant disorder, which are associated with repeated disruptive behaviors. Such overlaps can lead to misdiagnosis.

The consequences of misdiagnosis are not trivial. Stimulant drugs such as Ritalin and Adderall, which are commonly used to treat ADHD, are not only ineffective for bipolar disorder but may worsen its symptoms or even trigger manic episodes. Meanwhile these drugs may produce side effects such as weight loss, insomnia, and nervousness. On the other hand, a child with ADHD who is mistakenly diagnosed with bipolar disorder will usually be prescribed one or more of several medications, including lithium, anticonvulsants such as Depakote or Lamictal, or atypical antipsychotics (Abilify, Zyprexa). All these drugs are ineffective for ADHD and can cause side effects such as weight gain and involuntary movements. Rare but more serious problems such as seizures (from lithium) can show up when the dosage is too high.

Mood Shift

To reduce the problems of overlap and overdiagnosis, the authors of the *DSM-5* have added a category called disruptive mood dysregulation disorder (see "Redefining Mental Illness," by Ferris Jabr, *Scientific American Mind*, May/June 2012). Symptoms of this illness include frequent temper outbursts and chronically irritable, angry, or sad moods. This addition provides a diagnostic home for many children who would be excluded from a bipolar diagnosis but who did display some of its symptoms. With more accurate diagnosis, doctors hope, children in the two bipolar categories, as well as the new one, will receive more appropriate and therefore better treatment.

Despite the proliferation of categories, some children (those with symptoms like Eric's, for example) can be rightly diagnosed with bipolar disorder using stringent criteria. And no matter how they are labeled, children who display pathological mood swings experience significant distress and are in dire need of proper care.

Further Reading

Littrell, J., & Lyons, P. (2010). Pediatric bipolar disorder, part I: Is it related to classical bipolar? *Children and Youth Services Review, 32*(7), 945–964.

Parens, E., & Johnston, J. (2010). Controversies concerning the diagnosis and treatment of bipolar disorder in children. *Child and Adolescent Psychiatry and Mental Health, 4.*

Strakowski, S. M., DelBello, M. P., & Adler, C. M. (Eds.). (2015). *Bipolar disorder in youth: Presentation, treatment, and neurobiology.* New York, NY: Oxford University Press.

19

Kid Gloves for Young Offenders?

Mike S. (not his real name) was 13 years old when one of us (Scott Lilienfeld) met him on an inpatient psychiatric ward, where Lilienfeld was a clinical psychology intern. Mike was articulate and charming, and he radiated warmth. Yet this initial impression belied a disturbing truth. For several years Mike had been in serious trouble at school for lying, cheating, and assaulting classmates. He was verbally abusive toward his biological mother, who lived alone with him. Mike tortured and even killed cats and bragged about experiencing no guilt over these actions. He was finally brought to the hospital in the mid-1980s, after he was caught trying to con railroad workers into giving him dynamite, which he intended to use to blow up his school. According to psychiatry's standard guidebook, the *Diagnostic and Statistical Manual of Mental Disorders* (now in its fifth edition), Mike's diagnosis was conduct disorder, a condition marked by a pattern of antisocial and perhaps criminal behavior emerging in childhood or adolescence.

Psychologists have long struggled with how to treat adolescents with conduct disorder, or juvenile delinquency, as the condition is sometimes called when it comes to the attention of the courts. Given that the annual number of juvenile court cases is about 1.2 million, these efforts are of

Facts and Fictions in Mental Health, First Edition. Hal Arkowitz and Scott O. Lilienfeld.
© 2017 John Wiley & Sons, Inc. Published 2017 by John Wiley & Sons, Inc.

great societal importance. One set of approaches involves "getting tough" with delinquents by exposing them to strict discipline and attempting to shock them out of future crime. These efforts are popular, in part because they quench the public's understandable thirst for law and order. Yet scientific studies indicate that these interventions are ineffective and can even backfire. Better ways to turn around troubled teens involve teaching them how to engage in positive behaviors rather than punishing them for negative ones.

You're in the Army Now

One get-tough technique is boot camp, or "shock incarceration," a solution for troubled teens introduced in the 1980s. Modeled after military boot camps, these programs are typically supervised by a drill instructor and last from 3 to 6 months. They emphasize strict rules and swift punishments (such as repeated pushups) for disobedience, along with a regimen of physical work and demanding exercise. According to the National Institute of Justice, 11 states operated such programs in 2009. Indeed, Mike S. was sent to a boot camp program following his discharge from the hospital.

Even so, research has yielded at best mixed support for boot camps. In a 2010 review of 69 controlled studies, criminologists Benjamin Meade and Benjamin Steiner, both then at the University of South Carolina, revealed that such programs produced little or no overall improvement in offender recidivism. For reasons that are unclear, some of them reduced rates of delinquency, but others led to higher rates. Boot camps that incorporated psychological treatments, such as substance abuse counseling or psychotherapy, seemed somewhat more effective than those that did not offer such therapies, although the number of studies was too small to draw firm conclusions.

Another method is "Scared Straight," which became popular following an Academy Award-winning documentary (*Scared Straight!*), which was filmed in a New Jersey state prison in 1978. Typically these programs bring delinquents and other high-risk teens into prisons to interact with adult inmates, who talk bluntly about the harsh realities of life behind bars. Making adolescents keenly aware of prison life is supposed to deter them from criminal careers. Yet the research on these interventions is not encouraging. In a 2003 meta-analysis (quantitative review) of nine controlled studies of Scared Straight programs, criminal justice researcher Anthony Petrosino, now at the research agency WestEd, and his colleagues showed that these treatments backfired, boosting the odds of offending by 60% to 70%.

The verdict for other get-tough interventions, such as juvenile transfer laws, which allow teens who commit especially heinous offenses to be tried as adults, is no more promising. In a 2010 summary, psychologist Richard Redding of Chapman University found higher recidivism rates among transferred adolescent offenders than among nontransferred ones.

Perils of Punishment

Psychologists do not know for sure why get-tough treatments are ineffective and potentially harmful, but the psychological literature holds several clues. First, researchers have long found that punishment-based strategies tend to be less effective than reward-based strategies for lasting behavioral change, in part because they teach people what *not* to do but not *what* to do. Second, studies indicate that highly confrontational therapeutic approaches are rarely effective in the long term. For example, in a 1993 controlled trial psychologist William Miller of the University of New Mexico and his colleagues found that counselors who used confrontational styles with problem drinkers – for example, by taking them to task for minimizing the extent of their drinking problem – had significantly less success in helping their clients overcome their addictions than did counselors who used supportive styles that relied on empathy. Similarly, a 2010 review by criminal justice researcher Paul Klenowski of Clarion University and his collaborators found that delinquency programs that involved confrontational tactics, such as berating children for misbehavior, were less effective than programs that did not use them.

What is more, adolescents with conduct disorder often enter treatment angry and alienated, harboring feelings of resentment toward authority. Get-tough programs may fuel these emotions, boosting teens' propensity to rebel against parents and teachers. Finally, some programs may inadvertently provide adolescents with role models for bad behavior.

For example, some of the at-risk teens exposed to prisoners in Scared Straight programs may perceive them as cool and worth emulating.

These results show that merely imposing harsh discipline on young offenders or frightening them is unlikely to help them refrain from problematic behavior. Instead teens must learn enduring tools – including better social skills, ways to communicate with parents and peers, and anger management techniques – that help them avoid future aggression. Several effective interventions do just that, including cognitive-behavior therapy, a method intended to change maladaptive thinking patterns and behaviors, and multisystemic therapy, in which parents, schools, and communities develop programs to reinforce positive behaviors. Another well-supported method, aimed at improving behavior in at-risk children younger than 8 years, is parent–child interaction therapy. Parents are coached by therapists in real time to respond to a child's behavior in ways that strengthen the parent–child bond and provide incentives for cooperation (see "Behave!" by Ingrid Wickelgren, *Scientific American Mind*, March/April 2014).

The negative data on get-tough programs remind us that we should be wary of our subjective impressions of strategies that simply seem right or that we feel ought to work. Although we lost track of Mike S., we now know that a concerted effort to teach him more adaptive behaviors would have been more likely to put him on a productive path than would any attempt to scare him straight.

Further Reading

McCord, J. (2003) Cures that harm: Unanticipated outcomes of crime prevention programs. *Annals of the American Academy of Political and Social Science* 587(1), 16–30.

Petrosino, A., Turpin-Petrosino, C., & Buehler, J. (2003). Scared Straight and other juvenile awareness programs for preventing juvenile delinquency: A systematic review of the randomized experimental evidence. *Annals of the American Academy of Political and Social Science* 589(1), 41–62.

20

Is Divorce Bad for Children?

Many of the 1.5 million children in the United States whose parents divorce every year feel as if their worlds are falling apart. Divorcing parents are usually very concerned about the welfare of their children during this troublesome process. Some parents are so worried that they remain in unhappy marriages, believing it will protect their offspring from the trauma of divorce.

Yet parents who split have reasons for hope. Researchers have found that only a relatively small percentage of children experience serious problems in the wake of divorce or, later, as adults. In this chapter, we discuss these findings as well as factors that may protect children from the potentially harmful effects of divorce.

Rapid Recovery

Divorce affects most children in the short run, but research suggests that they recover rapidly after the initial blow. In a 2002 study psychologist E. Mavis Hetherington of the University of Virginia and her then

Facts and Fictions in Mental Health, First Edition. Hal Arkowitz and Scott O. Lilienfeld.
© 2017 John Wiley & Sons, Inc. Published 2017 by John Wiley & Sons, Inc.

graduate student Anne Mitchell Elmore found that many children experience short-term negative effects from divorce, especially anxiety, anger, shock, and disbelief. These reactions typically diminish or disappear by the end of the second year. Only a minority of children suffer longer.

Most children of divorce also do well in the longer term. In a quantitative review of the literature in 2001, sociologist Paul R. Amato, then at Pennsylvania State University, examined the possible effects on children several years after a divorce. The studies compared children of married parents with those who experienced divorce at different ages. The investigators followed these kids into later childhood, adolescence, or the teenage years, assessing their academic achievement, emotional and behavior problems, delinquency, self-concept, and social relationships. On average, the studies found only very small differences on all these measures between children of divorced parents and those from intact families, suggesting that the vast majority of children endure divorce well.

Researchers have consistently found that high levels of parental conflict during and after a divorce are associated with poorer adjustment in children. The effects of conflict before the separation, however, may be the reverse in some cases. In a 1985 study Hetherington and her associates reported that some children who are exposed to high levels of marital discord prior to divorce adjust better than children who experience low levels. Apparently when marital conflict is muted, children are often unprepared when told about the upcoming divorce. They are surprised, perhaps even terrified, by the news. In addition, children from high-discord families may experience the divorce as a welcome relief from their parents' fighting.

Taken together, the findings suggest that only a small percentage of young people experience divorce-related problems. Even here the causes of these lingering difficulties remain uncertain. Some troubles may arise from conflict between parents associated with the divorce. The stress of the situation can also cause the quality of parenting to suffer. Divorce frequently contributes to depression, anxiety, or substance abuse in one or both parents and may bring about difficulties in balancing work and child rearing. These problems can impair a parent's ability to offer children stability and love when they are most in need.

Grown-up Concerns

The experience of divorce can also create problems that do not appear until the late teenage years or adulthood. In 2000, in a book entitled *The Unexpected Legacy of Divorce: A 25 Year Landmark Study*, Judith Wallerstein, then at the University of California, Berkeley, and her colleagues present detailed case studies suggesting that most adults who were children of divorce experience serious problems such as depression and relationship issues.

Yet scientific research does not support the view that problems in adulthood are prevalent; it instead demonstrates that most children of divorce become well-adjusted adults. For example, in a 2002 book, *For Better or For Worse: Divorce Reconsidered*, Hetherington and her coauthor, journalist John Kelly, describe a 25-year study in which Hetherington followed children of divorce and children of parents who stayed together. She found that 25% of the adults whose parents had divorced experienced serious social, emotional, or psychological troubles compared with 10% of those whose parents remained together. These findings suggest that only 15% of adult children of divorce experience problems over and above those from stable families. No one knows whether this difference is caused by the divorce itself or by variables, such as poorer parenting, that often accompany a marriage's dissolution.

In a review article in 2003, psychologists Joan B. Kelly of Corte Madera, California, and Robert E. Emery of the University of Virginia concluded that the relationships of adults whose parents' marriages failed do tend to be somewhat more problematic than those of children from stable homes. For instance, people whose parents split when they were young experience more difficulty forming and sustaining intimate relationships as young adults, greater dissatisfaction with their marriages, a higher divorce rate, and poorer relationships with the noncustodial father compared with adults from sustained marriages. On all other measures, differences between the two groups were small.

Bouncing Back

Even though children of divorce generally do well, a number of factors can reduce the problems they might experience. Children fare better if parents can limit conflict associated with the divorce process or minimize the child's exposure to it. Further, children who live in the custody of at least one well-functioning parent do better than those whose primary parent is doing poorly. In the latter situation, the maladjusted parent should seek professional help or consider limiting his or her time with the child. Parents can also support their children during this difficult time by talking to them clearly about the divorce and its implications and answering their questions fully.

Other, more general facets of good parenting can also buffer against divorce-related difficulties in children. Parents should provide warmth and emotional support, and they should closely monitor their children's activities. They should also deliver discipline that is neither overly permissive nor overly strict. Other factors contributing to children's adjustment include postdivorce economic stability and social support from peers and other adults, such as teachers.

In addition, certain characteristics of the child can influence his or her resilience. Children with an easygoing temperament tend to fare better. Coping styles also make a difference. For example, children who are good problem solvers and who seek social support are more resilient than those who rely on distraction and avoidance.

The good news is that although divorce is hard and often extremely painful for children, long-term harm is not inevitable. Most children bounce back and get through this difficult situation with few, if any, battle scars.

Further Reading

Amato, P. R. (2003). Reconciling divergent perspectives: Judith Wallerstein, quantitative family research, and children of divorce. *Family Relations, 52*(4), 332–339.

Ehrenberg, M., Regev, R., & Lazinski, M. (2014). Adjustment to divorce for children. In L. Grossman & S. Walfish (Eds.), *Translating psychological research into practice* (pp. 1–9). New York, NY: Springer.

Hetherington, E. M., & Kelly, J. (2002). *For better or for worse: Divorce reconsidered.* New York, NY: W. W. Norton.

Section 4
Addictions

Introduction

The use of alcohol and drugs is a significant part of our culture. There are even songs dedicated to various substances, legal and illegal. They include "Jack Daniels If You Please" by David Allan Coe, "Illegal Smile" by John Prine, and "Cocaine" by Eric Clapton. There is also a famous spoonerism: "I'd rather have a bottle in front of me than a frontal lobotomy."

In 2005, sociologist Ronald C. Kessler of Harvard University and his associates published the results of a large-scale epidemiological study on the prevalence of mental disorders in the United States. Using *DSM-IV* criteria for what was then called substance-related disorders, the researchers found that approximately 8.5% of the U.S. population had a diagnosable problem with drug or alcohol dependence at some point in their lives, making it one of the most prevalent of all mental disorders. Although use of these substances can bring pleasure in the short run, their continued and compulsive use causes serious interference with important life activities, such as work, relationships, and mental and physical health.

Facts and Fictions in Mental Health, First Edition. Hal Arkowitz and Scott O. Lilienfeld.
© 2017 John Wiley & Sons, Inc. Published 2017 by John Wiley & Sons, Inc.

Prior to the publication of *DSM-5*, the category most closely associated with addictions was substance-related disorders. *DSM-5* broadened the category to include not only substance addiction, but also behavioral addictions. The category has been renamed Substance-Related and Addictive Disorders. At present, the only behavioral addiction included is gambling disorder, but quite possibly more, such as sexual addiction, will eventually be added.

A variety of treatments have been tried for people with substance-related disorders, many of which have met with considerable success. Two of the most widely studied and helpful approaches are cognitive-behavior therapies (CBT) and motivational interviewing (MI). CBT consists of a variety of related treatments that are aimed at changing dysfunctional thoughts and the problem behaviors resulting from them. MI aims primarily to increase motivation for change and is often used in conjunction with CBT and other treatment approaches.

Despite our progress in understanding and treating addictive conditions, significant misperceptions remain to be addressed. In this section, we raise the following questions about some beliefs in this area.

- Do a very large percentage of people who try marijuana become addicted to it?
- Is marijuana a "gateway" drug, leading to the use of more dangerous substances?
- Are only a relatively small percentage of people who try to change problem drinking on their own successful?
- Does excessive exposure to internet pornography cause few or no problems?
- Is Alcoholics Anonymous the most effective treatment for alcoholism?
- How effective are methods used to teach children and adolescents about the dangers of drug use, underscore the pluses of a drug-free way of life, and "just say no" to taking drugs?

21

The Truth About Pot

In the classic 1936 cult film *Reefer Madness*, well-adjusted high school students who try marijuana suddenly sink into a life of addiction, promiscuity, aggression, academic failure, homicide, and mental illness. The movie concludes with the ominous warning that "The dread marijuana may be reaching forth next for your son or daughter … or yours … or YOURS!" Newspaper headlines of the day often reflected a similar sentiment. On February 10, 1938, a headline in the *Beloit* (*Wisc.*) *Daily News* read, "Authorities Warn Against Spread of Marijuana Habit – Insanity, Degeneracy and Violence Follow Use of Weed."

Such a position on pot seems extreme. Yet just as people have since cast aside the notion that marijuana use inevitably culminates in the destruction of the mind, so have they also begun to question the concept that it is benign. In particular, some evidence suggests that marijuana can, in some cases, be addictive and that it may present other health problems as well, particularly in heavy users. That said, most people suffer no ill effects from a single or occasional use of the drug.

Facts and Fictions in Mental Health, First Edition. Hal Arkowitz and Scott O. Lilienfeld.
© 2017 John Wiley & Sons, Inc. Published 2017 by John Wiley & Sons, Inc.

How Many Get Hooked?

Marijuana, which is also known as cannabis, is the most widely used illicit substance in the world, according to a United Nations report from 2002. Recreational use is widespread in the United States, and medical use is on the rise. In a 2007 study, psychologist Louisa Degenhardt of Michigan State University and her colleagues found that 43% of U.S. adults aged 18 or older have tried marijuana at least once. Many adolescents are drawn to the drug as well. In the large, ongoing Monitoring the Future study, researchers at the University of Michigan found that 14% of eighth graders had used marijuana at least once in the previous year with the number increasing to 35% for 12th graders. Marijuana use will undoubtedly grow in the near future because many states have already legalized it for medical use, and some for recreational use as well. Other states are considering legalization as well.

Given the drug's growing popularity, many people have long been concerned about its potential dangers and, in particular, whether it can be addictive. People tend to use "addiction" and "dependence" interchangeably, although drug experts now favor the term "dependence." In the current version of the mental health profession's "bible," the *Diagnostic and Statistical Manual of Mental Disorders*, a diagnosis of cannabis dependence (a type of substance dependence) requires a person to meet at least 2 of 11 criteria (see Box 21.1).

A number of investigators have addressed this issue and found that only a relatively small percentage of those who try marijuana will become addicted. For example, in a large-scale survey published in 1994, epidemiologist James Anthony, then at the National Institute on Drug Abuse, and his colleagues asked more than 8,000 people between the ages of 15 and 64 about their use of marijuana and other drugs. The researchers found that of those who had tried marijuana at least once, about 9% eventually fit a diagnosis of cannabis dependence. The corresponding figure for alcohol was 15%; for cocaine, 17%; for heroin, 23%; and for nicotine, 32%. So although marijuana may be addictive for some, 91% of those who try it do not get hooked. Further, marijuana is less addictive than many other legal and illegal drugs.

Box 21.1   Cannabis Use Disorder

A problematic use of cannabis in the last year leading to significant impairment or distress as manifest by two or more of the following:

- You have a strong desire or craving to use marijuana.
- Your marijuana use leads to failure to fulfill your major role obligations at work, school, or home.
- You continue to use marijuana despite social problems related to its use.
- You frequently use marijuana in physically hazardous situations.
- You need to use more of the drug over time to obtain the same effects – a phenomenon known as tolerance.
- You feel anxious, have problems sleeping, or experience other unpleasant symptoms when you try to stop using marijuana. This reaction is called withdrawal.
- You are using the drug in larger amounts or for longer periods than you intended.
- Your attempts to reduce or control your use of marijuana have failed.
- You spend a lot of time trying to get the drug, using it, or recovering from its effects.
- You give up important activities such as work, social events, or recreation to use marijuana.
- Your use of the drug continues despite the fact that the habit is making a physical or psychological problem worse.

Possible Perils

A hotly debated issue is whether marijuana is a "gateway" drug, leading to the use of more dangerous substances. Many studies have found that most people who used other illicit drugs had, in fact, used marijuana first. Although results such as these are consistent with the gateway hypothesis, they do not prove that using marijuana causes the use of other drugs. Those who are drawn to marijuana may simply be predisposed to drug use in general, regardless of their exposure to pot. In addition, individuals often smoke cigarettes or drink alcohol before they latch on to marijuana. Should we also be asking whether nicotine and alcohol are gateway drugs?

Researchers have also demonstrated that *heavy* marijuana use can lead to increased tolerance and withdrawal symptoms when trying to stop. In addition, heavy use can contribute to respiratory and cardiovascular problems as well as impairments in short-term memory. Marijuana may also trigger certain disorders, such as schizophrenia, in vulnerable persons (see "A Mind in Danger," by Victoria Costello, *Scientific American Mind*, February 2012, p. 30), although researchers continue to debate the evidence on this issue. Finally, because marijuana is still illegal in many states and under federal law, people who possess or sell marijuana may face legal consequences.

On the other hand, marijuana has significant upsides for individuals with certain illnesses. In glaucoma patients, it can reduce the dangerously high eye pressure that can lead to vision loss. In addition, pot can provide relief from chronic pain, reduce nausea and vomiting from cancer chemotherapy, and limit the severe weight loss that results from AIDS and other diseases.

When a person does become addicted, several types of psychotherapy can help him or her kick the habit. One of the more effective types is a form of cognitive-behavior therapy (CBT) tailored to the addictive mind-set. Using CBT, therapists teach patients practical coping skills that lead to a change in behavior. They also try to modify the thoughts that contribute to a person's addiction. Two faster treatments are motivational interviewing and the closely related motivational-enhancement therapy. The goal of these methods is to boost a person's drive to stop or reduce their use of pot.

Unfortunately, relapse rates remain high for all addiction psychotherapies. In a study published in 2003 psychologist Brent A. Moore, now at Yale University, and his colleagues found that 41% of successfully treated marijuana addicts had relapsed within 6 months. Scientists are searching for ways to bring about long-term abstinence more consistently.

The public needs to be aware of the facts about marijuana so that it can dismiss fictions about the drug's effects. Only by knowing when marijuana presents a real threat and when the risk is minimal can people properly weigh its dangers and benefits in specific situations. Both our health and sound social policy depend on it.

Further Reading

Anthony, J. C., Warner, L. A., & Kessler, R. C. (1994). Comparative epidemiology of dependence on tobacco, alcohol, controlled substances, and inhalants: Basic findings from the National Comorbidity Survey. *Experimental and Clinical Psychopharmacology, 2*(3), 244–268.

Hill, K. (2015). Medical marijuana for treatment of chronic pain and other medical and psychiatric problems: A clinical review. *Journal of the American Medical Association, 313*, 2474–2483.

Roffman, R. J., & Stephens, R. S. (2006). *Cannabis dependence: Its nature, consequences, and treatment*. Cambridge, England: Cambridge University Press.

22

Does Alcoholics Anonymous Work?

Alcoholics Anonymous (AA) counts 2 million members who participate in some 115,000 groups worldwide, about half of them in the United States. How well does it work? Anthropologist William Madsen, then at the University of California, Santa Barbara, claimed in a 1974 book that it has a "nearly miraculous" success rate, whereas others are far more skeptical. After reviewing the literature, we found that AA may help some people overcome alcoholism, especially if they also get some professional assistance, but the evidence is far from overwhelming, in part because of the nature of the program.

Alcoholics Anonymous got its start at a meeting in 1935 in Akron, Ohio, between a businessman named Bill Wilson and a physician, Bob Smith. "Bill W" and "Dr. Bob," as they are now known, were alcoholics. Wilson had attained sobriety largely through his affiliation with a Christian movement. Smith stopped drinking after he met Wilson, whose success inspired him. Determined to help other problem drinkers, the men soon published what has become known as "The Big Book," which spelled out their philosophy, principles, and methods, including the now famous 12-step method (see Box 22.1).

Facts and Fictions in Mental Health, First Edition. Hal Arkowitz and Scott O. Lilienfeld.
© 2017 John Wiley & Sons, Inc. Published 2017 by John Wiley & Sons, Inc.

Box 22.1   Twelve Steps to Sobriety?

In Alcoholics Anonymous, members try to abstain from alcohol by working through the 12 steps listed below. Secular alternatives include Self-Management and Recovery Training (www.smartrecovery.org/) and Secular Organizations for Sobriety (www.cfiwest.org/sos/index.htm).

1. Admit our powerlessness over alcohol.
2. Believe that a Power greater than ourselves can restore us to sanity.
3. Decide to turn our will and lives over to God as we understand Him.
4. Conduct a moral inventory of ourselves.
5. Admit our wrongs to God, ourselves, and another person.
6. Are ready to have God remove all defects of character.
7. Ask Him to remove our shortcomings.
8. List all persons we have harmed, and be willing to make amends to them.
9. Make such amends wherever possible.
10. Continue to take personal inventory and admit any wrongs we find.
11. Pray and meditate to attain knowledge of God's will for us and for the power to carry it out.
12. Awaken spiritually to practice the 12 steps in all of our affairs, and carry this message to other alcoholics.

Source: Adapted from the AA Website: http://aa.org/en_pdfs/smf-121_en.pdf

---

Alcoholics Anonymous was the book's official title and also became the name of the organization that grew from it.

In AA, members meet in groups to help one another achieve and maintain abstinence from alcohol. The meetings, which are free and open to anyone serious about stopping drinking, may include reading from the Big Book, sharing stories, celebrating members' sobriety, as well as discussing the 12 steps and themes related to problem drinking. Participants are encouraged to "work" the 12-step program, fully integrating each step into their lives before proceeding to the next. AA targets more than problem drinking; members are supposed to correct *all* defects of character and adopt a new way of life. They are to accomplish these difficult goals without professional help. No therapists, psychologists, or physicians can attend AA meetings unless they, too, have drinking problems.

A for Abstinence?

Most studies evaluating the efficacy of AA are not definitive; for the most part, they associate the duration of participation with success in quitting drinking but do not show that the program caused that outcome. Some of the problems stem from the nature of AA – for example, the fact that what occurs during AA meetings can vary considerably. Further, about 40% of AA members drop out during the first year (although some may return), raising the possibility that the people who remain may be the ones who are most motivated to improve.

Nevertheless, the results of one well-designed investigation called Project Match, published in 1997, suggest that AA can facilitate the transition to sobriety for many alcoholics. In this study, a group of prominent alcoholism researchers randomly assigned more than 900 problem drinkers to receive one of three treatments over 12 weeks. One was an AA-based treatment called 12-step facilitation therapy that includes contact with a professional who helps patients work the first few of the 12 steps and encourages them to attend AA meetings. The other treatments were cognitive-behavior therapy, which teaches skills for coping better with situations that commonly trigger relapse, and motivational enhancement therapy, which is designed to boost motivation to cease problem drinking.

The AA-based approach seemed to work and compared favorably with the other therapies. In all three groups, participants were abstinent on roughly 20% of days, on average, before treatment began, and the fraction of alcohol-free days rose to about 80% a year after treatment ended. What is more, 19% of these subjects were teetotalers during the entire 12-month follow-up. Because the study lacked a group of people who received no treatment, however, it does not reveal whether any of the methods are superior to leaving people to try to stop drinking on their own.

Other research suggests that AA is quite a bit better than receiving no help. In 2006 psychologist Rudolf H. Moos of the Department of Veterans Affairs and Stanford University and Bernice S. Moos published results from a 16-year study of problem drinkers who had tried to quit on their own or who had sought help from AA, professional therapists or, in some cases, both. Of those who attended at least 27 weeks of AA meetings during the first year, 67% were abstinent at the 16-year follow-up, compared with 34% of those who did not participate in AA. Of the subjects who got therapy for the same time period, 56% were abstinent versus 39% of those who did not see a therapist – an indication that seeing a professional is also beneficial.

These findings might not apply to all problem drinkers or AA programs, however. Because this study was "naturalistic" – that is, an investigation of people who chose their path on their own (rather than as part of the study) – the researchers could not control the precise makeup of the meetings or treatments. Furthermore, the abstinence rates reported might apply only to those with less severe alcohol problems, because the scientists chose people who sought help for the first time, excluding others who had done so in the past. Various studies have found that a combination of professional treatment and AA yields better outcomes than either approach alone.

Constructive Combination

Taken as a whole, the data suggest that AA may be helpful, especially in conjunction with professional treatment, for many people who are addicted to alcohol. We do not know, however, whether AA might occasionally be harmful. When a group is highly confrontational, for example, alcoholics may become resistant to change (see Chapter 40, this volume). Nevertheless, in light of the evidence supporting the program, the wide availability of meetings and the lack of expense, AA is worth considering for many problem drinkers.

Further Reading

Dodes, L., & Dodes, Z. (2015). *The sober truth: Debunking the bad science behind 12-step programs and the rehabilitation industry.* Boston, MA: Beacon Press.

Kaskutas, L. A. (2009). Alcoholics Anonymous effectiveness: Faith meets science. *Journal of Addictive Diseases, 28*(2), 147–157.

Moos, R. H., & Moos, B. S. (2006). Participation in treatment and Alcoholics Anonymous: A 16-year follow-up of initially untreated individuals. *Journal of Clinical Psychology, 62*(6), 735–750.

Project Match Research Group. (1997). Matching alcoholism treatments to client heterogeneity: Project MATCH posttreatment drinking outcomes. *Journal of Studies on Alcohol, 58,* 7–29.

Bill Wilson and Bob Smith, the founders of Alcoholics Anonymous, wrote "The Big Book."

23

Self-Help for Addictions

To cease smoking is the easiest thing I ever did. I ought to know because I've done it a thousand times.

Mark Twain

Samuel Clemens (Twain was his nom de plume) humorously mocked his inability to end his nicotine-fueled habit. But he might have gone for Quitting Round 1,001 had he had the benefit of recent research.

In 1982 Stanley Schachter, an eminent social psychologist then at Columbia University, unleashed a storm of controversy in the addictions field by publishing an article showing that most former smokers and overweight people he interviewed had changed successfully without treatment. He also cited a study that reported even higher rates of recovery among heroin users without treatment.

A particularly controversial finding was that the success rates of his so-called self-changers were actually *greater* than those of patients who underwent professional treatment. Schachter discussed two possible explanations. First, treatment seekers may be more severely addicted than self-changers. Second, studies typically examine only one change

Facts and Fictions in Mental Health, First Edition. Hal Arkowitz and Scott O. Lilienfeld.
© 2017 John Wiley & Sons, Inc. Published 2017 by John Wiley & Sons, Inc.

endeavor, whereas his interviews covered a lifetime of efforts. Perhaps it takes many tries before a person gets it right, he suggested.

Schachter's findings were met with intense skepticism, even outright disbelief, particularly by those who believed in a disease model of addiction. In this view, addictions are diseases caused by physiological and psychological factors that are triggered by using the substance (drugs or alcohol); once the disease is triggered, the addict cannot control his or her substance use, and complete abstinence is the only way to manage the disease. Proponents of this model did not believe that so many people could change their addictions at all, let alone without treatment. Other criticisms came from researchers who questioned the scientific value of Schachter's work because it was based on a small and selective sample and relied on self-reports of past behavior, which often are not accurate pictures of what really happened. Nevertheless, his findings served as a catalyst, encouraging many researchers to study self-change in addictive behaviors. Let us examine what the research tells us about how widespread successful self-change is for problem drinking and drug addiction.

Rates of Success

In 2007, psychologist Reginald Smart of the Center for Addiction and Mental Health in Toronto reviewed the findings on the prevalence of self-change efforts among problem drinkers. We draw the following conclusions from his review and from our reading of the literature:

- Most of those who change their problem drinking do so without treatment of any kind, including self-help groups.
- A significant percentage of self-changers maintain their recovery with follow-up periods of more than 8 years, some studies show.
- Many problem drinkers can maintain a pattern of nonproblematic drinking.
- Those who do seek treatment have more severe alcohol and related problems than those who do not.

Although fewer studies of self-change in drug addiction exist, the results generally mirror those for problem drinking. In summary: Self-change in drug addiction is a much more common choice for solving the problem than treatment is; a substantial percentage of self-changers are successful (but usually after many attempts); a significant percentage of those who were formerly addicted continue to use drugs occasionally without returning to addiction-level use, and they maintain these changes fairly well over time; and those who seek treatment usually have more severe problems than those who do not.

The experiences of Vietnam veterans are especially instructive. Sociologist Lee N. Robins, then at the Washington University School of Medicine in St. Louis, and her associates published a widely cited series of studies beginning in 1974 on drug use and recovery in these veterans. While overseas, about 20% of the soldiers became addicted to narcotics. After discharge to the United States, however, only 12% of those who had been addicted in Vietnam were found to be in that state at any time during the 3-year follow-up. Fewer than 5% had overcome their addiction through therapy. Additional findings from Robins's studies suggested that abstinence is not necessary for recovery. Although nearly half the men who were addicted in Vietnam tried narcotics again after their return, only 6% became readdicted.

The results of Robins's studies suggest the power of self-change in drug addiction, but they also have been the target of many criticisms. For example, most men who became addicted in Vietnam had not had that problem before their tour of duty, suggesting that they may be unrepresentative of the general population of drug addicts. Moreover, their drug use may have been triggered by the stress of serving in Vietnam, making it easier for them to stop when they returned home. This last criticism is weakened, however, by the finding that most men who continued using some narcotics after discharge did not become addicted and by the fact that the return home was also very difficult because of the popular sentiment against that war in the United States.

Next Steps

We need more and better research on the potential for self-change to conquer problem drinking and other addictions. Studies suffer from differences in the definitions of important terms such as "addiction," "treatment," and "recovery." The use of reports of past behavior and relatively short follow-up periods are problematic as well. We also do not know of any studies on self-change with prescription drug addiction. Finally, we need to know if recovery from drug addiction leads to substitution with another addiction. At least one study revealed that many former drug addicts became problem drinkers. Because of these caveats and others, the percentages we have reported should be taken only as rough estimates.

Although we have reviewed some encouraging initial results from the literature, it is our impression that many addictions professionals do not view self-change as very effective. Their conclusion may be largely correct for those problem drinkers and drug addicts to whom they are typically exposed – treatment seekers.

Generalizations from those who seek treatment to the population of problem drinkers and drug addicts as a whole may be incorrect for two reasons, however. First, those who seek treatment have more severe problems than those who do not; second, they may overrepresent those who have failed repeatedly in their attempts at self-change.

We may learn a great deal from people who successfully change addictive behaviors on their own. Whatever they are doing, they are doing something right. In addition to the work with problem drinkers and drug addicts, we are beginning to make headway in the study of self-change in other problem areas, such as smoking, obesity, and problem gambling. Greater knowledge about self-change and how it comes about might be used to help people who are not in treatment find ways of shedding their addictions as well as to enhance the effectiveness of our treatment programs.

Further Reading

Klingemann, H., & Sobell, L. C. (2007). *Promoting self-change from addictive behaviors: Practical implications for policy, prevention, and treatment.* New York, NY: Springer.

Klingemann, H., Sobell, M., & Sobell, L. (2010). Continuities and changes in self-change research. *Addictions, 105*, 1510–1518.

Robins, L. N. (1993). Vietnam veterans' rapid recovery from heroin addiction: A fluke or normal expectation? *Addiction, 88*(8), 1041–1054.

24

How Destructive Is Internet Porn?

Is it possible to have sex with a computer? Well, not exactly, but people can use their computers to engage in a variety of online sexual activities, including hooking up with partners (both virtually and in the flesh) and finding fodder for kinky obsessions.

Online porn is accessible, affordable, and often anonymous, and viewing it has become a popular pastime. A survey of college students in 2008 by psychologist Chiara Sabina of Penn State Harrisburg and her colleagues found that more than 90% of the men and 60% of the women had watched Internet pornography before age 18. In a separate study the rate of use was less than half as frequent among those between the ages of 40 and 49, suggesting that Internet porn consumption may decline with age – although that statistic could reflect generational differences in computer use. Studies have revealed a gender difference in online sexual activities: Men are more likely to watch pornography, whereas women are more apt to participate in sexual chat rooms, suggesting that they prefer sexual stimulation in the context of interaction.

Most people who watch porn seem to be occasional dabblers, but a small percentage of users indulge excessively in online sexual content. In 1998 Alvin Cooper, then at the Marital and Sexuality Center in San

Facts and Fictions in Mental Health, First Edition. Hal Arkowitz and Scott O. Lilienfeld.
© 2017 John Wiley & Sons, Inc. Published 2017 by John Wiley & Sons, Inc.

Jose, California, and his associates conducted an online study of more than 9,000 people who used the Internet for sexual purposes. Slightly fewer than half the respondents – most of them men who were married or in a committed relationship – indulged for an hour or less a week. Forty-five percent reported engaging in online sexual activity between 1 and 10 hours a week. Eight percent used the Internet for such purposes for 11 or more hours weekly, and a small but distinctive 0.5% reported more than 70 hours a week.

Emerging evidence suggests that such heavy use may be associated with harmful effects on the psyche and on relationships. Some experts even contend that Internet porn can be addictive, but the use of the term in this context is controversial.

The Price of Consumption

Although occasional use of pornography sites and other online sexual activities does not appear to be associated with serious problems – at least according to reports from users – even relatively light use may have a negative effect on one's partner or spouse. What is more, heavy consumption of porn, including the Internet variety, may contribute to relationship strains and sexually aggressive attitudes and behaviors toward women.

Numerous studies have found associations between the amount of exposure to pornography and sexually belligerent attitudes such as endorsing coercive sex and sexually aggressive behaviors – say, forcibly holding a woman down. These associations are strongest for men who watch violent pornography and for those who already tend to be sexually aggressive.

Other findings have tied frequent porn use to attitudes such as assigning blame to victims of sexual assault, justifying the actions of sexual perpetrators, and discounting the violence of rape. Enthusiasm for porn often accompanies callousness toward women, dissatisfaction with a partner's sexual performance and appearance, and doubts about the value of marriage. Such attitudes are clearly detrimental to relationships with women and could conceivably be linked to crimes against them.

But should we conclude that watching pornography causes these misogynistic beliefs and actions, as many social commentators assume?

Most of the studies merely show a statistical association between pornography use and such traits. They do not reveal whether watching pornography begets them. For example, although heavy porn use may indeed cause callousness toward women, an existing callousness toward women may instead lead to pornography use. Alternatively, a third factor, such as personal problems of the user, may lead to both pornography use and callousness toward women.

Researchers have also asked the female partners of men who are heavy consumers of pornography how they feel about their partner's habits. Psychologist Ana Bridges of the University of Arkansas and her colleagues found that although most of the women received low overall scores on a measure of distress about their partner's porn use, most of them also endorsed some statements indicative of anguish. For example, 42% agreed that their partner's porn consumption made them feel insecure, 39% that the partner's porn use had a negative effect on their relationship, and 32% that it adversely affected their lovemaking, hinting that the habit may have downsides.

Addicted to Porn?

Even if porn proves detrimental to its users and, in some cases, their partners, it may or may not be addictive. Scientists debate whether addiction is an appropriate term for behaviors such as excessive gambling, shopping, Internet use, sexual activity, and viewing of Internet pornography. Those in favor of recognizing so-called behavioral addictions argue that some immoderate actions share core characteristics with alcohol and drug addiction. These include extreme indulgence and continued use despite a negative effect on the user.

Skeptics counter, however, that although people may partake excessively in certain activities and sometimes suffer detrimental life consequences, they rarely develop tolerance or obvious withdrawal symptoms – two hallmarks of addiction. Some critics further maintain that the label of "addict" adds unnecessary stigma to the problem. Others contend that this description lets people "off the hook" for socially problematic behaviors that are at least partly under their control.

Although researchers have just begun to explore the possible downsides of pornography use in general and Internet pornography in particular, the results of many studies of exposure to pornography suggest that excessive viewing of such material could sometimes be harmful. As a result, psychotherapists need to be alert to such behavior in their clients, especially when it impinges on their romantic relationships. A better understanding of how watching Internet pornography affects the men and women drawn to it may ultimately lead to meaningful treatments for those with a pornography habit that has hurt them and their loved ones.

Further Reading

Döring, N. M. (2009). The Internet's impact on sexuality: A critical review of 15 years of research. *Computers in Human Behavior, 25*(5), 1089–1101.

Malamuth, N. M., Addison, T., & Koss, M. (2000). Pornography and sexual aggression: Are there reliable effects and can we understand them? *Annual Review of Sex Research, 11*, 26–91.

Weir, K. (2014). Is pornography addictive? *Monitor on Psychology, 45*, 46.

Young, K. S. (2008). Internet sex addiction: Risk factors, stages of development, and treatment. *American Behavioral Scientist, 52*(1), 21–37.

25

Just Say No?

"Just say no." In 1982 First Lady Nancy Reagan uttered those three words in response to a schoolgirl who wanted to know what she should say if someone offered her drugs. The first lady's suggestion soon became the clarion call for the adolescent drug prevention movement in the 1980s and beyond. Since then, schools around the country have instituted programs designed to discourage alcohol and drug use among youth – most of them targeting older elementary schoolchildren and a few addressing adolescents.

There is good reason for concern about youth substance abuse. A large U.S. survey conducted in 2012 by psychologist Lloyd D. Johnston and his colleagues at the University of Michigan revealed that fully 24% of 12th graders had engaged in binge drinking (defined as five or more drinks on one occasion) in the past 2 weeks. Moreover, 42% had consumed at least some alcohol in the past month, as had 11% of eighth graders and 28% of high school sophomores. In addition, 1% of 12th graders had tried methamphetamine, and almost 3% had used cocaine in the past year.

In an attempt to reduce these figures, substance abuse prevention programs often educate pupils regarding the perils of drug use, teach

Facts and Fictions in Mental Health, First Edition. Hal Arkowitz and Scott O. Lilienfeld.
© 2017 John Wiley & Sons, Inc. Published 2017 by John Wiley & Sons, Inc.

students social skills to resist peer pressure to experiment, and help young people feel that saying no is socially acceptable. All the approaches seem sensible on the surface, so policy makers, teachers, and parents typically assume they work. Yet it turns out that approaches involving social interaction work better than the ones emphasizing education. That finding may explain why the most popular prevention program has been found to be ineffective – and may even heighten the use of some substances among teens.

Rehearsing Refusal

The most widely publicized teen substance abuse prevention program is Drug Abuse Resistance Education, better known by the acronym D.A.R.E. Created in 1983 by the Los Angeles Police Department, D.A.R.E. asks uniformed police officers to go into schools to warn students about the dangers of drug use and underscore the pluses of a drug-free way of life. In most cases, the officers do so once a week, typically for 45 to 60 minutes, for several months. D.A.R.E. is immensely popular; according to the program Web site, it has been put in place in 75% of U.S. school districts and 52 countries. D.A.R.E. bumper stickers, D.A.R.E. T-shirts, and police cars emblazoned with the word D.A.R.E. are familiar fixtures in many U.S. communities.

Despite this fanfare, data indicate that the program does little or nothing to combat substance use in youth. A meta-analysis (mathematical review) in 2009 of 20 controlled studies by statisticians Wei Pan, then at the University of Cincinnati, and Haiyan Bai of the University of Central Florida, revealed that teens enrolled in the program were just as likely to use drugs as were those who received no intervention.

A few clues to D.A.R.E's deficiencies come from psychologist Pim Cuijpers of the Netherlands Institute of Mental Health and Addiction in Utrecht. In a review of 30 studies published in 2002, she attempted to pinpoint the common elements of successful programs. Cuijpers reported that the most effective ones involve substantial amounts of interaction between instructors and students. They teach students the social skills they need to refuse drugs and give them opportunities to practice these skills with other students – for example, by asking students to play roles on both sides of a conversation about drugs, while instructors coach them about what to say and do. In addition, programs that work take into account the importance of behavioral norms: They emphasize to students that substance use is not especially common and thereby attempt to counteract the misconception that abstaining from drugs makes a person an oddball.

In a 2011 review of various substance abuse prevention programs, epidemiologist Melissa Stigler of the University of Texas School of Public Health and her colleagues buttressed these conclusions. They further observed that programs that unfold during many sessions – ideally, over several years – garner especially strong results, probably because they provide students with lessons that are reinforced over time, as children mature and encounter different environments.

D.A.R.E. lacks some of these key elements. It typically lasts only months rather than years. Moreover, it affords students few opportunities to practice how to refuse offers of drugs. Indeed, Cuijpers noted that purely educational programs that involve minimal or no direct social interaction with other students are usually ineffective. Merely telling participants to "just say no" to drugs is unlikely to produce lasting effects because many may lack the needed interpersonal skills. Programs led exclusively by adults, with little or no involvement of students as peer leaders – another common feature of D.A.R.E. – seem relatively unsuccessful, again probably because students get little practice saying no to other kids.

Good Intentions that Backfire

Worse, D.A.R.E. programs might occasionally backfire when it comes to the use of milder substances, such as alcohol and cigarettes. In a 2002 review psychologist Chudley Werch, now president of PreventionPLUSWellness in Jacksonville, Florida, and health educator Deborah Owen of the University of North Florida reported a slight tendency for teens who went through D.A.R.E. to be more likely to drink and smoke than adolescents not exposed to the program. Small negative effects for D.A.R.E.-like programs on drinking and smoking were also reported in a 2009 study by public health professor Zili Sloboda of the University of Akron and her colleagues. The reasons for these potential boomerang effects are unclear. Yet by emphasizing the hazards of severe drug abuse, D.A.R.E. may inadvertently convey the impression that alcohol and tobacco are innocuous by comparison.

These scientific findings stand in stark contrast to the belief, held by scores of schoolteachers and parents, that D.A.R.E. works. One reason for this discrepancy, clinical psychologist Donald R. Lynam, now at Purdue University, and his colleagues wrote in a 1999 article, is that teachers and parents may overestimate the prevalence of substance use among children. As a consequence, they may assume a decline in use when students of D.A.R.E. abstain from alcohol and drugs. But that conclusion is erroneous if children who did not receive drug prevention education display levels of drug use that are just as low, if not lower. In addition, as Lynam and his colleagues observe, D.A.R.E. makes intuitive sense: It seems plausible that most children exposed to authority figures who warn that drug use is dangerous would hesitate to disobey those admonitions.

The good news is that some proponents of D.A.R.E. are now heeding the negative research findings and incorporating potentially effective elements, such as role playing with peers, into the intervention. Research on these revised programs should soon tell us whether they will make a dent in the considerable problem of substance abuse among vulnerable youth.

Further Reading

Lynam, D. R., Milich, R., Zimmerman, R., Novak, S. P., Logan, T. K., Martin, C. ... Clayton, R. (1999). Project DARE: No effects at 10-year follow-up. *Journal of Consulting and Clinical Psychology, 67*(4), 590–593.

Tripodi, S. J., Bender, K., Litschge, C., & Vaughn, M. G. (2010). Interventions for reducing adolescent alcohol abuse: A meta-analytic review. *Archives of Pediatric and Adolescent Medicine, 164*(1), 85–91.

Section 5
Externalizing Problems

Introduction

Externalizing problems are those whose primary symptoms involve outer-directed, impulsive, and sometimes aggressive behaviors. This broad category of conditions includes antisocial personality disorder, conduct disorder, pedophilia, and intermittent explosive disorder. There is no formal category of externalizing disorders in the *DSM-5*, but it is commonly used in the psychopathology literature, especially for child and adolescent disorders.

The behaviors considered in this section can cause serious physical and legal problems for the perpetrators and serious physical and psychological harm to those at the receiving end. Inaccurate beliefs in these areas can cause problems for developing effective treatments and for social and legal policies that may be helpful to individuals with these conditions and their victims.

Facts and Fictions in Mental Health, First Edition. Hal Arkowitz and Scott O. Lilienfeld.
© 2017 John Wiley & Sons, Inc. Published 2017 by John Wiley & Sons, Inc.

In this section, we raise questions about several beliefs relating to some externalizing problems. These myths include:

- Do almost all sex offenders reoffend?
- Do the majority of road-ragers have anger problems in other areas?
- Are men almost always more aggressive than women?

26

Road Rage

What Is It and What Can We Do About It?

Consider the following recent sobering reports:

- A motorist shot and killed the driver of another car "because he was driving too slowly."
- A large crowd was blocking the parking lot exit of a nightclub. A driver who was growing impatient with waiting for an opening drove his car straight into the crowd, seriously injuring seven people.
- When Jack Nicholson got cut off, the actor waited until both he and the other driver were stopped at a red light, then got out of his car, and hit the windshield and roof of the other car with his golf club. He returned to his car and drove away.

Of course, *you* wouldn't do such things. Or would you?

You might, because road rage is remarkably common. In one survey, 34% reported perpetrating road rage while 41% reported being victims. These statistics actually may be underestimates. For one thing, many respondents may not want to admit to road rage because it is socially undesirable. Also, more people report being the target rather than the initiator of road rage, supporting the idea that initiators may not be fessing up.

Facts and Fictions in Mental Health, First Edition. Hal Arkowitz and Scott O. Lilienfeld.
© 2017 John Wiley & Sons, Inc. Published 2017 by John Wiley & Sons, Inc.

Psychologist Elisabeth Wells-Parker of Mississippi State University and her associates have suggested that the term "road rage" implies specific incidents of anger and aggression directed intentionally at another driver, vehicle, or object. When the behavior erupts, the presence of firearms can worsen the situation. As physician Matthew Miller of the Harvard School of Public Health and his colleagues have pointed out, 11% of a randomly selected sample of 790 drivers reported that they always or sometimes carried a gun (usually loaded) in their vehicle.

Who are these People?

Anybody can be susceptible. Road ragers are men and women, young and old, rich and poor, mentally disturbed and healthy, people with and without generalized anger problems, and members of various ethnicities. Some become angry almost every time they drive, whereas others do so infrequently. Although aggressive retaliation, such as assault or murder, characterizes the extreme end of these behaviors, most crabby drivers engage in milder displays, such as verbal insults, obscene gestures, honking their horn, cutting off other drivers, and chasing other cars.

Still, research does point to some similarities among those who are susceptible to belligerent acts when behind the wheel. People with aggressive tendencies across a variety of situations, including home and work, have an increased likelihood of road rage. Younger drivers are more prone than older drivers are. Men have historically displayed a greater predilection, although women recently have been catching up. Many road ragers are otherwise model citizens who are successful in work and in relationships and well respected in their communities.

Why do some people get angry and even violent in response to the irritating behavior of other drivers, whereas others do not? Psychologist Jerry Deffenbacher of Colorado State University has proposed that some people have a trait for, or predisposition toward, this type of behavior that is triggered by the poor driving of other motorists. Many of his studies have found that those who display lower levels of the trait are far less likely to respond with road rage, even when exposed to the same triggers.

Other researchers have tried to uncover the nature of this trait, and their studies have found that those prone to road rage may show one or more of a variety of characteristics: general aggression (not limited to driving), high levels of stress, antisocial tendencies, or low impulse control and frustration tolerance. Researchers have also demonstrated that road ragers are sensitive to supposed attacks on their self-esteem. For example, in the clinical practice of one of us (Hal Arkowitz), people with road rage problems perceived the irksome behaviors of other drivers as a sign of disrespect and a personal insult rather than attributing those behaviors to the other drivers' carelessness or recklessness. Arkowitz found it useful to help clients learn that "it is not about you." Certain psychological problems have also been found to relate to the road rage trait, including antisocial and borderline personality disorders as well as alcohol and substance abuse.

It is apparent that road ragers represent a very mixed bag of people. They may have only one of the attributes described above or several characteristics, or they may have other features we have yet to discover. Regardless of the initiating factors, however, road ragers seem to respond to various types of therapies.

Prevention and Treatment

Although prevention is the best option, studies have shown that treatment can be effective as well. Deffenbacher conducted two experiments in which subjects received either training in relaxation only or training in relaxation along with other therapies intended to change subjects' dysfunctional thoughts about driving. In general, subjects did better with either of the two treatments than with no treatment. These studies were well designed, but we need to be cautious about generalizing the results to the wider population because all subjects were college students and thus do not represent the full range of road ragers.

Recently psychologist Tara E. Galovski of the University of Missouri–St. Louis and her colleagues evaluated a group treatment for road rage aimed at adults who were either self-referred or court-referred. Treatment consisted of four weekly 2-hour sessions that included education about road rage and anger, recognition of being an angry driver, relaxation techniques, coping skills, and training in different ways to think about anger-eliciting driving situations. Those who received treatment did far better than those who did not and curbed their aggressive behavior by more than 60% on average.

In addition to combating the problem with treatments for individuals, policy leaders could make changes that might reduce road rage in society at large. Sociologist Mark Asbridge of Dalhousie University in Halifax and his associates have made interesting recommendations. One of these is new or increased penalties for road rage. Laws already cover extreme forms, such as assault and dangerously aggressive driving. Asbridge and his coworkers suggest the possible value of broader adoption of an Australian national law that stipulates that drivers must not drive so as to "menace" other persons by threat of personal injury or property damage. Other ideas include mass-media education about road rage and how to avoid it, societal changes such as reducing traffic congestion and promoting public transportation, court programs for convicted road ragers, and redesign of cars to prevent excessive headlight flashing and horn blowing; some cars have already been designed to prevent tailgating.

We conclude with a brief anecdote. Hal Arkowitz used to drive to work on a road that prominently displayed a billboard advertising a funeral home. It showed a picture of the funeral home, along with five simple, but powerful, words: "Drive carefully, we can wait." We hope that greater awareness of road rage and its treatments will help keep them waiting for a long time to come.

Further Reading

Galovski, T., & Deffenbacher, J. (2014). Road rage. In L. Grossman & S. Walfish (Eds.), *Translating psychological research into practice* (pp. 469–475). New York, NY: Springer.

Larson, J., & Rodriguez, C. (1999). *Road rage to road-wise*. New York, NY: Tom Doherty Associates.

27

Once a Sex Offender, Always a Sex Offender

Maybe Not

Sex crimes evince such strong feelings of revulsion and repugnance that it is perhaps not surprising that people misunderstand their nature. The public, whose opinions are reinforced by portrayals in the media and in popular culture, believes that sex offenders will almost always repeat their predatory acts in the future and that all treatments for perpetrators are ineffective. The truth is not so cut and dried – and gives us cause for hope in certain cases.

Before we discuss these beliefs, a few basics are in order. The two most common types of sex offenses are rape and child molestation, but others exist (see Box 27.1). In most cases, the victim, usually female, knows the perpetrator, generally male. By some estimates, one third or more of all sex offenders are under the age of 18, with some even as young as 5 years. Most begin to offend sexually in adolescence. Now what does the research tell us about common beliefs?

Facts and Fictions in Mental Health, First Edition. Hal Arkowitz and Scott O. Lilienfeld.
© 2017 John Wiley & Sons, Inc. Published 2017 by John Wiley & Sons, Inc.

Box 27.1   Categories of Offenses

Many categories of sex offenses exist; precise legal descriptions of types of sex offenses can vary from state to state. Not all uncommon sexual behaviors are illegal. For example, no laws bar transvestism, which usually involves a heterosexual man who dresses in women's clothing.

Sex Offense	General Description
Rape	Sexual intercourse with a minor or unwilling adult
Child molestation	Sexual behaviors between an adult and juvenile who are not blood relatives
Incest	Sexual behaviors between an adult and juvenile who are blood relatives
Exhibitionism	Exposing one's genitals to an unwilling stranger
Voyeurism	Watching unsuspecting others who either are in a state of undress or are having sexual relations
Frotteurism	Sexually oriented touching of an unsuspecting person

Repeat Offenders

First, the notion that recidivism (repeat offending) is inevitable needs a second look. Sex crimes researcher Jill Levenson of Lynn University in Florida and her colleagues found that the average member of the general public believes that 75% of sex offenders will reoffend. This perception is consistent with media portrayals in such television programs as *Law and Order: Special Victims Unit*, in which sex offenders are almost always portrayed as chronic repeaters.

The evidence suggests otherwise. Sex crimes researchers R. Karl Hanson and Kelly E. Morton-Bourgon of Public Safety Canada conducted a large-scale meta-analysis (quantitative review) of recidivism rates among adult sex offenders. They found a rate of 14% over a period averaging 5–6 years. Recidivism rates increased over time, reaching 24% by 15 years. The figures are clearly out of alignment with the public's more dire expectations.

Also contrary to media depictions, most offenders do not "specialize" in one type of sex crime. Most are "generalists" who engage in a variety of sex and nonsexual crimes as well. Hanson and Morton-Bourgon found that sex offenders had a total recidivism rate (for both sex crimes and non-sexual violent crimes) of approximately 36% over a period of 5–6 years. Nevertheless, perpetrators of different types of sex crimes exhibit varying rates of repeat offending. The 15-year recidivism rate is 13% for incest perpetrators, 24% for rapists, and 35% for child molesters of boy victims.

When providing clarifications about the lower than generally acknowledged rates of recidivism, we must be careful not to oversimplify. Recidivism research is as difficult as it is important. For instance, although average rates tell us what percentage reoffends one or more times, we also need to be aware that a subset reoffends at a frighteningly high rate. In addition, there are reasons to think that published findings underestimate the true rates. Most research necessarily omits those offenders who were not detected and arrested or whose victims did not report the crime. Further, many sex offenders plea-bargain down to a nonsexual offense.

Still, there are other reasons to believe that recidivism rates may not be that different from what researchers have found. Frequent offenders are more likely than other offenders to be caught. Many safeguards probably help to keep the recidivism rate in check. Sex offenders released on probation are closely monitored, and those who are considered to be at high risk for recidivism are required to register with authorities. These registries are distributed to law-enforcement personnel. Finally, states are legally required to publicly identify higher-risk sex offenders. The Department of Justice coordinates a Web site (www.fbi.gov/hq/cid/cac/registry.htm) that enables anyone to search for the identity and location of known offenders.

Taking the research and its limitations into account, it is still likely that the public's belief that very high recidivism rates are well documented is incorrect, although this verdict may change in the future.

Treatment Realities

If recidivism is not as common as people generally believe, how do their impressions of treatment's failure or success hold up? Levenson and her colleagues also found that a whopping 50% of the public believes that treatment for sex offenders is ineffective and will not prevent them from relapsing. Yet some studies have shown that treatment can significantly reduce recidivism for both sex and nonsexual crimes. Hanson and his colleagues conducted a meta-analysis on treatment and found that 17% of untreated subjects reoffended, whereas 10% of treated subjects did so. When recidivism rates for sexual and nonsexual violent crimes were combined, 51% of untreated and 32% of treated subjects reoffended.

The advantage for treatment over nontreatment does not appear to be that large; because meta-analyses group studies together, they may mask the fact that some of them found fairly large effects of treatment and others found smaller or no effects. Results of this meta-analysis also suggest that we might be making progress. More recent studies show significantly larger treatment benefits than do the older studies.

Most approaches employ a number of treatments. The majority include two components: cognitive-behavior therapy, which aims to change sexually deviant thoughts, behaviors, and arousal patterns, and relapse prevention, which aims to teach sex offenders how to anticipate and cope with problems (such as feelings of anger or loneliness) that can lead to reoffending.

Although the development of treatments for sex offenders is still in its infancy, studies show that therapy can make a difference. Sex offenders are not all fated to repeat their horrible crimes, and we – through the actions of the general public, policy leaders, and legislators – can encourage hope by supporting further research on such therapies.

Further Reading

Barbaree, H. E., & Marshall, W. L. (2005). *The juvenile sex offender* (2nd ed.). New York, NY: Guilford Press.

Becker, J. V., Johnson, B. R., & Perkins, A. (2014). Paraphilic disorders. In R. Hales, S. C. Yudofsky, & L. W. Roberts (Eds.), *The American Psychiatric Publishing textbook of psychiatry* (6th ed.) (pp. 895–925). Arlington, VA: American Psychiatric Association Publishing.

Hanson, R. K., & Morton-Bourgon, K. E. (2005). The characteristics of persistent sexual offenders: A meta-analysis of recidivism studies. *Journal of Consulting and Clinical Psychology, 73*(6), 1154–1163.

28

Are Men the More Belligerent Sex?

The notion that men have shorter fuses than women has acquired the status of a psychological shibboleth. More than 30 years ago Stanford University psychologists Eleanor Maccoby and Carol Jacklin concluded in an influential book that sex differences were minimal in most psychological traits but considerable when it comes to aggression. This opinion has endured ever since.

Were Maccoby and Jacklin right? Recent research bears out the broad brushstrokes of their claim but reveals that women can be equally, if less dangerously, belligerent.

Mad Men

In 1995 the late psychologist David Lykken of the University of Minnesota wrote that if we could magically place all boys and men between the ages of 12 and 28 in a cryogenic freeze, we would slash the rate of violent crime by two thirds. The data bear out Lykken's thought experiment. In the United States, the rate of violent crime for girls and women aged 10 and older is 1 in 56; the corresponding figure among their male

Facts and Fictions in Mental Health, First Edition. Hal Arkowitz and Scott O. Lilienfeld.
© 2017 John Wiley & Sons, Inc. Published 2017 by John Wiley & Sons, Inc.

counterparts is 1 in 9. Men commit close to 90% of the murders in the United States and more murders than women in all the countries researchers have examined, according to a 1999 report by psychologist Anne Campbell of Durham University in England.

Indeed, investigators have consistently found that short of criminal activity, men exhibit more frequent and more extreme levels of physical aggression with one exception: In domestic disputes, as we will see, the tables are often turned. In a 2004 mathematical synthesis of 196 studies (known as a meta-analysis), psychologist John Archer of the University of Central Lancashire in England found that men are more physically aggressive (by various measures) than women across all ages, with the difference peaking between the ages of 20 and 30. This sex difference extended to all 10 countries Archer examined, which included the United States, Finland, Spain, India, Japan, and New Zealand. Interestingly, researchers have found men to be more physically aggressive in their mental lives as well. Compared with women, men harbor more frequent and enduring homicidal fantasies, more often think about enacting revenge against their enemies, and report more physically aggressive dreams.

Figure 28.1   Source: Getty Images

Evening the Score

Still, studies show that women are at least as prone to feeling anger as men and that they fight plenty. Instead of expressing their angry emotions with their fists, women tend to use what in 1995 the late psychologist Nicki Crick, then at the University of Illinois, termed "relational aggression," a less overt form characterized by social manipulation, especially of same-sex peers. Popularized by such books as *Odd Girl Out: The Hidden Culture of Aggression in Girls*, by Rachel Simmons (Harcourt, 2002), relational aggression includes spreading rumors, gossiping, glaring, eye rolling, giving others the "silent treatment," sending nasty notes or text messages behind rivals' backs, excluding others from social gatherings, poking fun at the appearance of competitors, and assorted other stealth attacks. The so-called gentler sex may opt for such tactics because they are socialized to not show hostility openly and also because their relative lack of physical strength makes violence seem a less promising strategy.

Girls do not have an exclusive claim to relational aggression, however. A 2008 meta-analysis by psychologist Noel Card of the University of Arizona and his colleagues suggests that it is equally common in girls and boys across both childhood and adolescence. Other research suggests this absence of sex differences persists into adulthood.

More surprisingly, women are also just as likely as men to express hostility – in this case physically – in the context of a romantic relationship. The popular stereotype of a domestic abuser is a man who habitually hurts his female partner. Yet research by Archer and sociologist Murray Straus of the University of New Hampshire calls this scenario into question. Surprisingly, their analyses demonstrate that men and women exhibit roughly equal rates of violence within relationships; some studies hint that women's rates of physical aggression are slightly higher. This apparent equality is not solely a result of women fighting back, because it holds even for altercations that women start. Still, domestic abuse within intimate relationships poses a greater threat to women than to men. Women suffer close to two thirds of the injuries, largely because men are stronger on average than women. In addition, women and men differ in the severity of their actions; women are more likely to scratch or slap their partners, and men more commonly punch or choke their partners.

Biology to Blame?

Until recently, most psychologists thought differences in the degree to which men and women exhibit physical aggression stemmed largely from societal reinforcement of traditional gender roles. Social factors undoubtedly account for a part of the differences. But in a study published in 2007 psychologist Raymond Baillargeon of the University of Montreal and his colleagues reveal that as early as the age of 17 months, 5% of boys but only 1% of girls engage in frequent physical aggression, such as kicking and biting. What is more, this gap does not widen between 17 and 29 months, as might be expected if environmental influences such as socialization by parents were to blame. These findings suggest that biological factors – such as the effects of testosterone on brain function – contribute to sex differences in violent behavior.

Bolstering this hypothesis is the fact that males are the more belligerent sex in virtually all mammalian species that biologists have studied. Even the one marked exception to this trend – the spotted ("laughing") hyena – may prove the rule. The female hyena, which is more physically aggressive than her male counterpart, has higher testosterone levels than the male does.

Further Reading

Archer, J. (2004). Sex differences in aggression in real-world settings: A meta-analytic review. *Review of General Psychology, 8*, 291–322.

Bennett, S., Farrington, D. P., & Huesmann, L. R. (2005). Explaining gender differences in crime and violence: The importance of social cognitive skills. *Aggression and Violent Behavior, 10*, 263–288.

Crick, N. R., & Grotpeter, J. K. (1995). Relational aggression, gender, and social-psychological adjustment. *Child Development, 66*(3), 710–722.

Section 6
Personality Disorders

Introduction

DSM-5 defines a personality disorders as "an enduring pattern of inner experience and behavior that deviates markedly from the expectations of the individual's culture, is pervasive and inflexible, has an onset in adolescence or early adulthood, is stable over time, and leads to distress or impairment." Researchers have found that approximately 10% of the population suffers from one or more of these disorders.

The manner in which personality disorders are diagnosed shows little change from *DSM-IV-R* to *DSM-5*. This was surprising to many because this group of diagnoses was known to be seriously flawed. Among the many problems are low reliabilities, considerable overlap in criteria, and the use of a categorical rather than a dimensional system.

The latter has been one of the main criticisms of the *DSM-5* view of personality disorders. In the categorical view, you either meet criteria or you don't. But there is consensus in the field that personality disorders are more accurately captured by a dimensional system. This means that the personality traits that make up these disorders are on a continuum ranging from normal levels to more extreme pathological levels.

Facts and Fictions in Mental Health, First Edition. Hal Arkowitz and Scott O. Lilienfeld.

For example, we've all been suspicious and distrustful of others at times, only to later find out that these feelings were unfounded. This may happen to us occasionally and the feelings associated with these thoughts are usually relatively mild. People with paranoid personality disorder take the suspiciousness and distrust to the extreme. *DSM-5* describes paranoid personality disorder as a "pervasive distrust and suspiciousness of others such that their motives are interpreted as malevolent."

The dimensional version reflects the reality that personality characteristics are on a continuum. But we often need to know if a person fits the diagnosis of one of the personality disorder categories or not. A dimensional system does not tell us how to determine the cut-off points between normal and pathological levels of a trait. In practice, insurance companies often ask therapists for a diagnosis without which they won't cover the patient's treatment. For this practical reason, a categorical system is a practical necessity.

Included in the current *DSM* is a section entitled Alternative DSM-5 Model for Personality Disorders. This is a system proposed for consideration for the next *DSM*. It is a hybrid system giving both categorical and dimensional diagnostic information. It is also likely that the categories of personality disorders will change based on research findings rather than on the armchair speculations that led to the current types of personality disorders.

In this section, we will examine misunderstandings of several of the current personality diagnoses: narcissistic and borderline personality disorders as well as a category that is not in *DSM* despite the fact that many think it should be – psychopathy.

While psychopathy is not included in the *DSM* as a personality disorder, it has all of the characteristics that define this grouping. Instead, *DSM* lists antisocial personality disorder, which has some overlap with psychopathy. Antisocial personality disorders focuses on a pervasive pattern of behaviors that show disregard for and violation of the rights of others. The construct of psychopathy includes deviant behaviors but emotional (e.g., lack of remorse or empathy) and interpersonal (manipulativeness) styles as well. In this section, we will also question the validity of several widespread beliefs about psychopaths. The questions we address here are:

- Can a small dose of narcissism be useful? People with narcissistic personality disorder are often viewed negatively as selfish bullies.

In Chapter 29, we ask the question of whether there can be any positive sides to narcissism.

- Are those diagnosed with borderline personality disorders hopeless, destined to a life of emotional misery, and unable to achieve any success in everyday life? Can people with this disorder be successfully treated?
- Are all psychopaths violent and psychotic?
- Is psychopathy untreatable?

29

A Dose of Narcissism can be Useful

Narcissism has long gotten a bad rap. Its unseemly reputation dates back at least to ancient Greek mythology, in which the handsome hunter Narcissus (who undoubtedly would be gloating over his present-day fame) discovered his own reflection in a pool of water and fell in love with it. Narcissus was so transfixed by his image that he died staring at it. In 1914 Sigmund Freud likened narcissism to a sexual perversion in which romantic attraction is directed exclusively to the self. Contemporary views are hardly more flattering. Enter the words "narcissists are" into Google, and the four most popular words completing the phrase are "stupid," "evil," "bullies," and "selfish."

In 2008 psychologist Jean M. Twenge of San Diego State University and her colleagues found that narcissism scores have been climbing among American college students in the United States for the past few decades. Although the data are controversial, these scholars argue that we are living in an increasingly narcissistic culture.

Some of the opprobrium heaped on narcissists is surely deserved. Yet research paints a more nuanced picture. Although narcissists can be difficult and at times insufferable, they can also make effective leaders and performers. Moreover, because virtually all of us share

Facts and Fictions in Mental Health, First Edition. Hal Arkowitz and Scott O. Lilienfeld.
© 2017 John Wiley & Sons, Inc. Published 2017 by John Wiley & Sons, Inc.

at least a few narcissistic traits, we may be able to learn something about ourselves from understanding them.

Calling all Narcissists

Psychologists conceptualize narcissism as extreme self-centeredness. Of course, we can all be a bit self-focused at times, but for narcissists the self is an overriding concern. In the laboratory, psychologists often measure narcissism using the Narcissistic Personality Inventory. On this questionnaire, individuals pick one statement from pairs such as "I prefer to blend in with the crowd; I like to be the center of attention" and "I am no better or worse than most people; I think I am a special person." Their score reflects how narcissistic they are.

Some items on the test reflect a truth dating back to the Greeks: Narcissists are obsessed with their looks. In 2008 Washington University psychologist Simine Vazire and her colleagues found that such individuals tend to wear expensive clothing and spend a lot of time preening. Data also confirm that narcissistic people like to talk about themselves. In 1988 psychologists Robert Raskin of the University of California, Berkeley, and Robert Shaw of Yale University found that in taped monologues, narcissistic undergraduates were significantly more likely than other students to use the word "I" and less likely to use the word "we."

In extreme forms, narcissism can become pathological. In the latest edition of psychiatry's bible, the *Diagnostic and Statistical Manual of Mental Disorders*, narcissistic personality disorder (NPD) is marked by an excessive sense of self-importance, unrealistic fantasies of success, and intense envy of others' accomplishments. People with NPD are also convinced they deserve special treatment. For example, they may be enraged that they need to wait on line at a restaurant behind other, "lesser" people.

Increasing evidence suggests that the NPD diagnosis is actually a mix of two flavors. Grandiose narcissism is the flamboyant, boastful form that probably characterizes both malignant leaders such as Benito Mussolini and Saddam Hussein and highly venerated figures such as General George S. Patton. The lesser-known "vulnerable" variety of self-devotion afflicts more reserved, fragile individuals who may resemble the self-effacing and thin-skinned characters portrayed by Woody Allen in his films.

No one really knows what causes the intense concern with the self that narcissists display. In one theory, they are compensating for low self-esteem by becoming egotistic. Yet this intriguing conjecture has weak scientific support, and another theory suggests that only vulnerable narcissists lack a sense of self-worth.

The Mirror has Two Faces

Narcissists routinely wreak havoc in everyday life. In a study published in 2004 psychologist W. Keith Campbell of the University of Georgia and his colleagues showed that narcissism is linked to overconfident but rash decision making, such as making unwise bets, and earlier work by Campbell's team tied narcissism to infidelity. Narcissists are also prone to aggression, especially following insults, as a 1998 study revealed. Brad J. Bushman, now at Ohio State University, and Roy F. Baumeister, now at Florida State University, reported that narcissistic college students were more likely than others to retaliate with a loud blast of noise against another "subject" (a confederate of the experimenters) who had derogated an essay they had written. The negative feedback, the authors reasoned, was a threat to their egos.

Even greater damage can stem from the clinical disorder. In 2002 psychologist Paul Nestor of the University of Massachusetts Boston found that individuals with marked features of NPD are at risk for violence and for antisocial personality disorder, a condition that is tied to crime and other irresponsible acts. Self-destructive behaviors may also result from the despair highly narcissistic people feel when others stop noticing them. In a 2009 study a team led by psychologist Aaron L. Pincus of Pennsylvania State University associated features of pathological narcissism with suicide attempts. Vulnerable narcissists may be in particular danger of hurting themselves. Data from 2011 suggest that vulnerable, but not grandiose, narcissism is linked to suicidal thinking, self-harm, and emotional distress.

Yet narcissism may be a double-edged sword. A 2009 investigation led by psychologist Amy B. Brunell of Ohio State University at Newark found that narcissistic individuals readily emerged as leaders in group discussions, and among students enrolled in a graduate business program, narcissists were likely to rise to top positions. These outcomes agreed with an earlier study in which psychologist Ronald J. Deluga of Bryant University asked presidential experts to rate U.S. chief executives on a scale of narcissism. Presidents judged to be more narcissistic were rated by an independent group of historians as particularly effective, charismatic, and creative. Narcissism in a leader may sometimes turn off potential followers, however. Psychologist Timothy A. Judge of the University of Florida and his collaborators found that narcissistic students in management programs tend to perceive themselves as better leaders, but others judged them as worse.

Narcissists' advantages extend beyond leadership, however. In a study published in 2011, psychologist Peter D. Harms of the University of Nebraska–Lincoln and his colleagues showed that narcissistic individuals excelled in simulated job interviews, in part because they were skilled at self-promotion. These findings may dovetail with 2006 results from researchers at the University of Southern California who found that celebrities' narcissism scores exceeded those of the general population.

There is no known effective remedy for narcissism in any of its forms. Yet recognizing that these highly self-centered people probably differ from us in degree rather than kind may give us more empathy for them. If a narcissist is mistreating you, here is a strategy for handling the situation: Find a way to be assertive while assuaging his or her sensitive ego.

Although the extreme self-promotion of grandiose narcissists can be dangerous, such self-focus in moderate doses may be advantageous when it comes to professional success and leadership. In this respect, we may have a thing or two to learn from those who see themselves at the center of the universe.

Further Reading

Campbell, W. K., & Miller, J. D. (Eds.) (2011). *The handbook of narcissism and narcissistic personality disorder: Theoretical approaches, empirical findings, and treatments.* Hoboken, NJ: John Wiley & Sons.

30

The Truth About Borderline Personality

In June of 2011 renowned clinical psychologist Marsha M. Linehan of the University of Washington made a striking admission. Known for her pioneering work on borderline personality disorder (BPD), a severe and intractable psychiatric condition, 68-year-old Linehan announced that as an adolescent, she had been hospitalized for BPD. Suicidal and self-destructive, the teenage Linehan had slashed her limbs repeatedly with knives and other sharp objects and banged her head violently against the hospital walls. The hospital's discharge summary in 1963 described her as "one of the most disturbed patients in the hospital." Yet despite a second hospitalization, Linehan eventually improved and earned a Ph.D. from Chicago's Loyola University in 1971.

Many psychologists and psychiatrists were taken aback by Linehan's courageous admission, which received high-profile coverage in the *New York Times*. Part of their surprise almost surely stemmed from an uncomfortable truth: People with BPD are often regarded as hopeless individuals, destined to a life of emotional misery. They are also frequently viewed as so disturbed that they cannot possibly achieve success in everyday life. As a consequence, highly accomplished individuals such as Linehan do not fit the stereotypical mold of a former BPD sufferer.

Facts and Fictions in Mental Health, First Edition. Hal Arkowitz and Scott O. Lilienfeld.
© 2017 John Wiley & Sons, Inc. Published 2017 by John Wiley & Sons, Inc.

But as Linehan's case suggests, much of the intense pessimism and stigma surrounding this disorder are unjustified. Indeed, few psychological disorders are more mischaracterized or misunderstood.

Fuzzy Borders

New York psychoanalyst Adolf Stern coined the term "borderline" in 1938, believing this condition to lie on the murky "border" between neurosis and psychosis. The term was a misnomer because BPD bears little relation to most psychotic disorders. The name may have perpetuated a widespread misimpression that the disorder applies to people on the edge of psychosis, who have at best a tenuous grasp of reality. Not surprisingly, the popular conception of BPD, shaped by such films as the 1987 movie *Fatal Attraction* (featuring actress Glenn Close as a woman with the condition), is that of individuals who often act in bizarre and violent ways.

An error committed by some clinicians is presuming that patients who do not respond well to treatment or who are resistant to therapists' suggestions are frequently "borderlines." Some mental health workers even seem to habitually attach the label "borderline" to virtually any client who is extremely difficult to deal with. As Harvard University psychiatrist George Valliant observed in a 1992 article, the BPD diagnosis often reflects clinicians' frustrated responses to challenging patients.

In reality, BPD is meant to apply to a specific subgroup of individuals who are emotionally and interpersonally unstable. Indeed, Linehan has argued that a better name for the condition is "emotion dysregulation disorder." Much of the everyday life of individuals with BPD is an emotional roller coaster. Their moods often careen wildly from normal to sad or hostile at the slightest provocation. As Linehan pointed out in a 2009 interview with *Time* magazine, "Borderline individuals are the psychological equivalent of third-degree-burn patients. They simply have, so to speak, no emotional skin." Their perceptions of other people are inconsistent, and they often vacillate between worshipping their romantic partners one day and detesting them the next. Their identity is similarly unstable; patients may lack a clear sense of who they are. And their impulse control is poor; they are prone to explosive displays of anger toward others – and themselves. (For more on the symptoms, causes, and treatment of BPD, see "When Passion Is the Enemy," by Molly Knight Raskin, *Scientific American Mind*, July/August 2010.)

Further fueling the stigma attached to BPD is the assumption that nearly all individuals who engage in self-cutting, such as wrist slashing, are so-called borderlines. In fact, in a 2006 study of 89 hospitalized adolescents who engaged in cutting and related forms of nonsuicidal self-injury, Harvard psychologist Matthew Nock and his colleagues found that 48% did not meet criteria for BPD. The lion's share of these individuals exhibited other personality disorders, such as avoidant personality disorder, which is associated with a pronounced fear of rejection.

Once Borderline Always Borderline?

Two allied myths about BPD are that patients virtually never improve over time and are essentially untreatable. Yet a number of studies indicate that many patients with BPD shed their diagnoses after several years. In a 2006 investigation, for example, psychologists C. Emily Durbin and Daniel N. Klein, both then at Stony Brook University, found that although 16% of 142 psychiatrically disturbed adults initially met criteria for BPD, only 7% did after a decade. Moreover, the average levels of BPD symptoms in the sample declined significantly over time. Work by psychologist Timothy J. Trull and his colleagues at the University of Missouri–Columbia similarly suggests that many young adults who display some features of BPD do not exhibit these features after only a 2-year period, indicating that early signs of BPD often abate.

BPD is not easy to treat. Yet Linehan has shown that an intervention she calls "dialectical behavior therapy" (DBT) is modestly helpful to many sufferers of the condition. DBT encourages clients to accept their painful emotions while acknowledging that they are unhealthy and need help. It teaches patients specific coping skills, such as mindfulness (observing their own thoughts and feelings nonjudgmentally), tolerating distress, and mastering negative emotions. Controlled studies, reviewed by Duke University psychologist Thomas R. Lynch and his colleagues in 2007, indicate that DBT somewhat reduces the suicidal and self-destructive behaviors of patients. Lynch and his collaborators also found that DBT may lessen feelings of hopelessness and other symptoms of depression. Still, DBT is not a panacea, and no clear evidence exists that

DBT can stabilize patients' identity or relationships. Preliminary but promising data suggest that certain medications, including such mood stabilizers as Valproate, can alleviate the interpersonal and emotional volatility that characterize BPD, according to a 2010 review by psychiatrist Klaus Lieb of University Medical Center in Mainz, Germany, and his colleagues.

A Continuing Challenge

Not all BPD patients improve on their own or with treatment, and even those who do typically continue to battle the demons of emotional and interpersonal volatility. Nevertheless, the extreme negative views of this condition are undeserved, as is the mislabeling of a wide swath of the psychiatric population as borderline. It is also undeniable that many clinicians must become more judicious in their use of the BPD label and avoid attaching it to virtually any patient who is oppositional or unresponsive to treatment.

Fortunately, there is room for cautious optimism. As psychiatrist Len Sperry of Barry University noted in a 2003 review, BPD is the most researched of all personality disorders, a fact that remains true today. The fruits of that work promise to yield an improved understanding of BPD, which may reduce the stigma surrounding this widely misunderstood diagnosis. If so, perhaps the day will soon come when successful people who once struggled with BPD, such as Marsha Linehan, are no longer perceived as exceptions that prove the rule.

Further Reading

Crowell, S. E., Beauchaine, T. P., & Linehan, M. M. (2009). A biosocial developmental model of borderline personality: Elaborating and extending Linehan's theory. *Psychological Bulletin, 135*(3), 495–510.

Friedel, R. O. (2004). *Borderline personality disorder demystified: An essential guide for understanding and living with BPD.* Boston, MA: Da Capo Press.

31

What "Psychopath" Means

"Violent psychopath" (89,700). "Psychopathic serial killer" (38,700).
"Psychopathic murderer" (34,500). "Deranged psychopath" (31,300).

We have all heard these phrases before, and the number of Google hits
following them in parentheses attests to their currency in popular
culture. Yet as we will soon discover, each phrase embodies a widespread
misconception regarding psychopathic personality, often called psychopathy (pronounced "sigh-COP-athee") or sociopathy. Indeed, few disorders are as misunderstood as is psychopathic personality. In this chapter,
we will do our best to set the record straight and dispel popular myths
about this condition.

Charming but Callous

First described systematically by Medical College of Georgia psychiatrist
Hervey M. Cleckley in 1941, psychopathy consists of a specific set of
personality traits and behaviors. Superficially charming, psychopaths
tend to make a good first impression on others and often strike observers
as remarkably normal. Yet they are self-centered, dishonest, and

Facts and Fictions in Mental Health, First Edition. Hal Arkowitz and Scott O. Lilienfeld.
© 2017 John Wiley & Sons, Inc. Published 2017 by John Wiley & Sons, Inc.

undependable, and at times they engage in irresponsible behavior for no apparent reason other than the sheer fun of it. Largely devoid of guilt, empathy, and love, they have casual and callous interpersonal and romantic relationships. Psychopaths routinely offer excuses for their reckless and often outrageous actions, placing blame on others instead. They rarely learn from their mistakes or benefit from negative feedback, and they have difficulty inhibiting their impulses.

Not surprisingly, psychopaths are overrepresented in prisons; studies indicate that about 25% of inmates meet diagnostic criteria for psychopathy. Nevertheless, research also suggests that a sizable number of psychopaths may be walking among us in everyday life. Some investigators have even speculated that "successful psychopaths" – those who attain prominent positions in society – may be overrepresented in certain occupations, such as politics, business, and entertainment. Yet the scientific evidence for this intriguing conjecture is preliminary.

Most psychopaths are male, although the reasons for this sex difference are unknown. Psychopathy seems to be present in both Western and non-Western cultures, including those that have had minimal exposure to media portrayals of the condition. In a 1976 study anthropologist Jane M. Murphy, then at Harvard University, found that an isolated group of Yupik-speaking Inuits near the Bering Strait had a term (*kunlangeta*) they used to describe "a man who ... repeatedly lies and cheats and steals things and ... takes sexual advantage of many women – someone who does not pay attention to reprimands and who is always being brought to the elders for punishment." When Murphy asked an Inuit what the group would typically do with a *kunlangeta*, he replied, "Somebody would have pushed him off the ice when nobody else was looking."

The best-established measure of psychopathy, the Psychopathy Checklist-Revised (PCL-R), developed by University of British Columbia psychologist Robert D. Hare, requires a standardized interview with subjects and an examination of their file records, such as their criminal and educational histories. Analyses of the PCL-R reveal that it comprises at least three overlapping, but separable, constellations of traits: interpersonal deficits (such as grandiosity, arrogance, and deceitfulness), affective deficits (lack of guilt and empathy, for instance), and impulsive and criminal behaviors (including sexual promiscuity and stealing).

Three Myths

Despite substantial research over the past several decades, popular misperceptions surrounding psychopathy persist. Here we will consider three of them.

1. **All psychopaths are violent.** Research by psychologists such as Randall T. Salekin, now at the University of Alabama, indicates that psychopathy is a risk factor for future physical and sexual violence. Moreover, at least some serial killers – for example, Ted Bundy, John Wayne Gacy, and Dennis Rader, the infamous "BTK" (Bind, Torture, Kill) murderer – have manifested numerous psychopathic traits, including superficial charm and a profound absence of guilt and empathy.

   Nevertheless, most psychopaths are not violent, and most violent people are not psychopaths. In the days following the horrific Virginia Tech shootings of April 16, 2007, many newspaper commentators described the killer, Seung-Hui Cho, as "psychopathic." Yet Cho exhibited few traits of psychopathy: Those who knew him described him as markedly shy, withdrawn, and peculiar.

   Regrettably, the current (fifth) edition of the American Psychiatric Association's *Diagnostic and Statistical Manual of Mental Disorders* (*DSM-5*), published in 2013, only reinforces the confusion between psychopathy and violence. It describes a condition termed antisocial personality disorder (ASPD), which is characterized by a longstanding history of criminal and often physically aggressive behavior, referring to it as synonymous with psychopathy. Yet research demonstrates that measures of psychopathy and ASPD overlap only moderately.

2. **All psychopaths are psychotic.** In contrast to people with psychotic disorders, such as schizophrenia, who often lose contact with reality, psychopaths are almost always rational. They are well aware that their ill-advised or illegal actions are wrong in the eyes of society but shrug off these concerns with startling nonchalance.

   Some notorious serial killers referred to by the media as psychopathic, such as Charles Manson and David Berkowitz, have displayed pronounced features of psychosis rather than psychopathy. For example, Manson claimed to be the reincarnation of Jesus Christ, and Berkowitz believed he was receiving commands from his neighbor Sam Carr's dog (hence his adopted nickname "Son of Sam"). In contrast, psychopaths are rarely psychotic.

3. **Psychopathy is untreatable.** In the popular HBO series *The Sopranos*, the therapist (Dr. Melfi) terminated psychotherapy with Tony Soprano because her friend and fellow psychologist persuaded her that Tony, whom Dr. Melfi concluded was a classic psychopath, was untreatable. Aside from the fact that Tony exhibited several behaviors that are decidedly nonpsychopathic (such as his loyalty to his family and emotional attachment to a group of ducks that had made his swimming pool their home), Dr. Melfi's pessimism may have been unwarranted. Although psychopaths are often unmotivated to seek treatment, research by psychologist Jennifer Skeem of the University of California at Berkeley and her colleagues suggests that psychopaths may benefit as much as nonpsychopaths from psychological treatment. Even if the core personality traits of psychopaths are exceedingly difficult to change, their criminal behaviors may prove more amenable to treatment.

Psychopathy reminds us that media depictions of mental illness often contain as much fiction as fact. Moreover, widespread misunderstandings of such ailments can produce unfortunate consequences – as Tony Soprano discovered shortly before the television screen went blank.

Further Reading

Edens, J. F. (2006). Unresolved controversies concerning psychopathy: Implications for clinical and forensic decision making. *Professional Psychology: Research and Practice, 37*(1), 59–65.

Hare, R. D. (1999). *Without conscience: The disturbing world of the psychopaths among us.* New York, NY: Guilford Press.

Lykken, D. T. (1995). *The antisocial personalities.* Mahwah, NJ: Lawrence Erlbaum Associates.

Patrick, C. J. (Ed.). (2016). *Handbook of psychopathy* (2nd ed.). New York, NY: Guilford Press.

Section 7

Shattered Selves

Schizophrenia and Dissociative Identity Disorder

Introduction

One of us (Hal Arkowitz) once saw a man for psychotherapy who met diagnostic criteria for schizophrenia. He was not yet on much-needed medication to control his symptoms, so many of them were apparent. As is often the case among individuals with schizophrenia, it was difficult to follow his conversation, as he would jump from one unrelated topic to another. He seemed unrestrained by the need for logical connections in his thinking and speaking. His emotions were often incongruent with the content of what he said. For example, at times he became sad when discussing a happy event in his life. His mind was clearly impaired.

Two of the chapters in this section address myths regarding schizophrenia. The first addresses the association between schizophrenia and violence. In the past 15–20 years, the media have reported on mass murders and other violent acts. The violent acts that receive the most media attention are often those committed by the severely mentally ill. This media coverage has probably contributed to the fact that the majority of people in the United States believe that those diagnosed with schizophrenia, in particular, are likely to engage in violence. Are they correct?

Facts and Fictions in Mental Health, First Edition. Hal Arkowitz and Scott O. Lilienfeld.
© 2017 John Wiley & Sons, Inc. Published 2017 by John Wiley & Sons, Inc.

The second chapter examines whether people with schizophrenia can be helped by treatment. Many mental health professionals, as well as members of the general public, believe that treatments do little to help those with this disorder. How correct is this view?

The third chapter examines beliefs about dissociative identity disorder (previously known as multiple personality disorder).

People diagnosed with dissociative identity disorder seem to exhibit many different personalities and may suddenly shift from one to another. A famous movie entitled *The Three Faces of Eve*, based on real-life events, depicted a woman with three personalities. Later, many more personalities emerged. In this section, we also raise questions about dissociative identity disorder.

- Are those diagnosed with schizophrenia likely to engage in violent behaviors?
- Can treatment reduce or eliminate the symptoms of schizophrenia?
- Can people have many distinct personalities?
- Is dissociative identity disorder the same as, or very similar to, schizophrenia?
- Are people with dissociative identity disorder faking?

32

Can People Have Multiple Personalities?

In the showtime series *United States of Tara,* which aired from 2009 to 2011, actress Toni Collette plays Tara Gregson, a Kansas mother who has dissociative identity disorder (DID), known formerly as multiple personality disorder. As with others with DID, Tara vacillates unpredictably between various personalities, often referred to as alters, over which she does not have control. One of these alters is a flirtatious and flamboyant teenager, another is a traditional 1950s housewife, and a third is a boisterous Vietnam War veteran.

Many films, such as *The Three Faces of Eve* (1957) and *Me, Myself, and Irene* (2000), similarly portray individuals as possessing more than one personality. Some of them even confuse DID with schizophrenia (see Chapter 33, this volume). Even the fifth edition of the American Psychiatric Association's diagnostic manual, published in 2013, specifies the core feature of the disorder as the presence of "two or more distinct identities or personality states." Yet despite the pervasive popular – and professional – portrayal of this disorder, research casts doubt on the idea that anyone truly harbors more than one personality.

Facts and Fictions in Mental Health, First Edition. Hal Arkowitz and Scott O. Lilienfeld.
© 2017 John Wiley & Sons, Inc. Published 2017 by John Wiley & Sons, Inc.

Figure 32.1   Source: *Exit Myself* by Linoillustration.com

Dramatic Differences

Plenty of evidence supports the idea that DID is not merely a matter of faking and that most people with the condition are convinced that they possess one or more alters. Although a few DID patients have only one alter – the so-called split personality – most report having several. In a survey conducted in 1989 by psychiatrist Colin Ross, then at Charter Hospital of Dallas, and his colleagues, the average number of alters was 16. Interestingly, that is the same number of alters purportedly possessed by Shirley Ardell Mason, the woman known as Sybil in the 1973 bestselling book and two made-for-television movies that popularized the diagnosis of multiple personality disorder. (Later evidence emerged suggesting that Sybil's primary therapist encouraged her to display multiple personalities, creating a huge sensation.) In rare cases, the number of alters may reach into the hundreds or even thousands.

Differences among alters can be nothing short of astonishing. Alters within the same patient may be of different ages, genders, races, and even species, including lobsters, ducks, and gorillas. There have even been reported alters of unicorns, Mr. Spock of *Star Trek*, God, the bride of Satan, and Madonna. Moreover, some practitioners claim that alters can be identified by objective characteristics, including distinct handwriting, voice patterns, eyeglass prescriptions, and allergies. Proponents of the idea of multiple personalities have also performed controlled studies of biological differences among alters, revealing that they may differ in respiration rate, brain-wave patterns, and skin conductance, the last being an accepted measure of arousal.

The question of whether people can harbor more than one character has important legal and therapeutic implications. If they can, and if patients are often unaware of their alters' actions, a legal defense of "not guilty by virtue of DID" may be justifiable. Other scholars have argued that each alter is entitled to separate legal representation. As professor of law Ralph Slovenko of Wayne State University noted in a 1999 article, some judges have even required each alter to be sworn in separately prior to testifying.

In treating these patients, many therapists try to get them to integrate their discrete personalities into a coherent whole. In doing so, they may help patients contact "undiscovered" alters and forge lines of communication among alters. For example, Ross has advocated naming alters and holding "inner board meetings" in which they can converse, share opinions, and provide information about missing alters. Psychiatrist Frank Putnam of Cincinnati Children's Hospital has argued for the use of DID "bulletin boards" on which alters can post messages for one another in notebooks or other convenient venues.

Putting the Pieces Together

Despite such practices, persuasive evidence for discrete coexisting personalities in individuals is lacking. The reported distinctions among alters are mostly anecdotal, unconfirmed, and difficult to interpret. For instance, the handwriting and voices of people *without* DID may also vary over brief periods, especially after a mood change. And disparities in physiological reactions, such as brain waves or skin conductance, could be similarly attributable to differences in mood or thoughts over time, according to University of Arizona psychologists John J. B. Allen and Hallam L. Movius. Individuals with DID almost surely experience dramatic psychological changes across situations, so it would be surprising if their physiology did not change as well.

If alters are truly distinct personalities, they should have memories that are inaccessible to other alters. Yet Allen and psychologist William G. Iacono of the University of Minnesota reported in a 2001 review that although most direct memory tests – such as asking patients to recall a list of words in one alter state that they had previously encountered in a different alter state – reveal a lack of transfer of memories across alters, subtler tests usually reveal that memories formed by one alter are in fact accessible to others. In these less direct tests, which tend to be more sensitive and less prone to intentional manipulation of responses, subjects may be asked, for example, to complete a word such as "kin_" after an alter was presented with a related word, say, "queen." Most subsequent studies bear out this conclusion, suggesting that alters are not distinct entities.

If alters are not discrete personalities, what are they? One hint: Individuals who develop DID often meet the diagnostic criteria for borderline personality disorder, bipolar disorder, and other conditions marked by instability. Indeed, a review in 1999 by one of us (Scott Lilienfeld) and his colleagues found that between 35% and 71% of patients with DID also have borderline personality disorder. Understandably, then, many individuals prone to DID are bewildered by their unstable moods, self-destructive behavior, impulsivity, and erratic relationships and are seeking an explanation for these disturbances. If psychotherapists or others ask suggestive questions such as "Is it possible that a part of you you're not aware of is making you do and feel these things?" patients may become convinced that their mind houses multiple identities.

Data show that many therapists who treat DID patients use hypnosis, which may fuel these people's difficulties in distinguishing fantasy from reality. Thus, DID may reflect an effort by individuals to make sense of extremely puzzling behaviors and feelings, a hypothesis proffered by the late psychologist Nicholas Spanos of Carleton University.

If so, techniques for making alters talk to one another may backfire, encouraging patients to falsely believe that the varied thoughts and feelings reside separately in their minds, often rendering them more difficult to integrate. For example, a patient could become convinced that one of her alters is responsible for her intense anger toward her husband, causing her to disregard her true feelings.

A better approach would be to help patients understand that their painful psychological experiences are created not by different personalities but by different aspects of one troubled personality. That way, those suffering could begin to come to grips with these experiences and recognize that their thoughts and feelings are genuinely their own.

Further Reading

Allen, J. J. B., & Iacono, W. G. (2001). Assessing the validity of amnesia in dissociative identity disorder: A dilemma for the DSM and the courts. *Psychology, Public Policy, and Law, 7*(2), 311–344.

Lilienfeld, S. O., & Lynn, S. J. (2014). Dissociative identity disorder: A contemporary scientific perspective. In S. O. Lilienfeld, S. J. Lynn, & J. M. Lohr (Eds.), *Science and pseudoscience in clinical psychology* (2nd ed.) (pp. 113–152). New York, NY: Guilford Press.

Merckelbach, H., Devilly, G. J., & Rassin, E. (2002). Alters in dissociative identity disorder: Metaphors or genuine entities? *Clinical Psychology Review, 22,* 481–497.

33

How Violent are People with Mental Illness?

A 22-year-old college dropout, Jared Lee Loughner, shot Arizona congresswoman Gabrielle Giffords through the head near a Tucson supermarket, causing significant damage to Giffords's brain. In the same shooting spree, Loughner killed or wounded 18 others, including a federal judge and a 9-year-old girl.

Information from Loughner's postings on YouTube and elsewhere online suggests that he is severely mentally ill. Individuals with serious mental illnesses have perpetrated other shootings, including the massacre in 2007 at Virginia Tech in which a college senior, Seung-Hui Cho, killed 32 people and wounded 17. These events and the accompanying media coverage have probably fed the public's perception that most profoundly mentally ill people are violent. Surveys show that 60%–80% of the public believe that those diagnosed with schizophrenia, in particular, are likely to commit violent acts.

Although studies have pointed to a slight increase in the risk of violent behaviors among those afflicted with major psychiatric ailments, a closer examination of the research suggests that these disorders are not strong predictors of aggressive behavior. In reality, severely mentally ill people account for only 3%–5% of violent crimes in the general population.

Facts and Fictions in Mental Health, First Edition. Hal Arkowitz and Scott O. Lilienfeld.
© 2017 John Wiley & Sons, Inc. Published 2017 by John Wiley & Sons, Inc.

The data indicate that other behaviors are likely to be better harbingers of physical aggression – an insight that may help us prevent outbursts of rage in the future.

A Tenuous Tie

Not all psychological and emotional disorders portend violence, even in society's eyes. In this chapter, we refer only to severe mental illness – meaning schizophrenia, bipolar disorder, or psychotic depression. Symptoms of schizophrenia include marked disturbances in thoughts, emotions, and behaviors; delusions (fixed false beliefs); hallucinations (perceiving things that are not physically present); disorganization; and withdrawal from social activities. Bipolar disorder is usually characterized by swings between depression and mania, which involves euphoria and grandiosity, a boost in energy and less need for sleep. Psychotic depression includes acute depressive symptoms, along with delusions or hallucinations, or both.

Most researchers investigating the question of aggression in the mentally ill have found a small but telling association between violence and significant psychological disturbance. In a 2009 meta-analysis, or quantitative review, of 204 studies exploring this connection, psychologist Kevin S. Douglas of Simon Fraser University and his associates found a slightly greater likelihood of aggressive behaviors among those with severe mental illnesses.

Yet this connection is much weaker than the public seems to believe it is and does not necessarily mean that these serious disorders cause violence. The causation could be in the reverse direction: Engaging in chronic aggression (stemming from some other source) may create stress that triggers the illness in those predisposed to it. Alternatively, a third factor could spawn both a psychiatric condition and violence.

Rather than thinking of people with severe mental illness as generally dangerous, scientists are now pinpointing those other factors that might augur violent behavior more reliably. One strong candidate is drug abuse. Revealing results from the MacArthur Violence Risk Assessment Study in 1998, sociologist Henry J. Steadman of Policy Research Associates and his colleagues reported that almost a third of severely mentally ill patients with substance abuse problems engaged in one or more violent acts in the year after they left the hospital. For discharged patients who did not abuse drugs, the corresponding figure was only 18%. (That figure suggests that less than one fifth of severely mentally ill individuals without other issues are dangerously aggressive.)

In its meta-analysis, Douglas's team also flagged drug abuse as one of several factors that contributed to the connection between mental illness and violence. In addition, it found the link was even stronger for patients who suffered from delusions, hallucinations, or disorganized thinking. Thus, a mentally ill person is more at risk of committing an act of aggression when that individual is also abusing a drug and shows particular symptoms.

Substance abuse greatly boosts the chances of violent behavior in healthy subjects, too, suggesting that drug use may be a much better predictor of violence than mental illness. What is more, proper treatment of mental illness can effectively eliminate the small risk of violent behavior posed by a grave disorder. In the MacArthur study, Steadman's team found no difference in the prevalence of violence between the severely mentally ill who were on their medications and mentally healthy people, whereas unmedicated patients lashed out at significantly higher rates. Of course, sick individuals who stop taking their medications could represent more difficult cases. Nevertheless, these results suggest that improving adherence to treatment may lessen the chances that severely ill people will behave violently.

Victims, Not Perpetrators

The stereotype of the crazed individual killing multiple strangers in public simply does not hold up to scrutiny. Although some noteworthy tragedies fit this description, these instances are quite rare. In fact, given how few mentally ill people become violent, a person with a severe psychological disorder is more likely to be a victim than a perpetrator of violence.

Mentally ill people are victims in their own right. A severe psychiatric condition is a terrible burden, even without being treated with suspicion by the community. A widespread belief that the afflicted are violent contributes to the stigma of mental illness and, as such, may interfere with their seeking and obtaining appropriate assistance. Debunking this misconception will likely lead to progress in helping troubled individuals and, by making treatment more broadly accessible, greatly reduce the threat that a small number of these individuals may pose to society.

Further Reading

Douglas, K. S., Guy, L. S., & Hart, S. D. (2009). Psychosis as a risk factor for violence to others: A meta-analysis. *Psychological Bulletin, 135*(5), 679–706.

Flynn, S., Rodway, C., Appleby, L., & Shaw, J. (2014). Serious violence by people with mental illness: National clinical survey. *Journal of Interpersonal Violence, 29,* 1438–1458.

Steadman, H. J., Mulvey, E. P., Monahan, J., Robbins, P. C., Appelbaum, P. S., Grisso, T. ... Silver, E. (1998). Violence by people discharged from acute psychiatric inpatient facilities and by others in the same neighborhoods. *Archives of General Psychiatry, 55*(5), 393–401.

34

Can People with Schizophrenia be Helped?

About 15 years ago psychologist Ronald Levant, then at Nova Southeastern University, was telling some of his colleagues at a conference about patients with schizophrenia whom he had seen recover. One of them asked rhetorically, "Recovery from schizophrenia? Have you lost your mind, too?"

Until recently, virtually all experts agreed that schizophrenia is always, or almost always, marked by a steady downhill progression. But is this bleak forecast warranted? Certainly schizophrenia is a severe condition. Its victims, who make up about 1% of the population, experience a loss of contact with reality that puts them at a heightened risk of suicide, unemployment, relationship problems, physical ailments, and even early death. Those who abuse substances are also at risk for committing violent acts against others. Contrary to popular belief, people with schizophrenia do not have multiple personalities, nor are they all essentially alike – or victims of poor parenting (see Box 34.1).

Nevertheless, research has shown that with proper treatment, many people with schizophrenia can experience significant, albeit rarely

Facts and Fictions in Mental Health, First Edition. Hal Arkowitz and Scott O. Lilienfeld.
© 2017 John Wiley & Sons, Inc. Published 2017 by John Wiley & Sons, Inc.

Box 34.1   Schizophrenia Fictions

Although most people have heard of schizophrenia, many misunderstand the disorder. Here we dispel three widespread misconceptions about this troubling mental illness.

1. **Myth #1: People with schizophrenia have multiple personalities.** **Fact:** This belief reflects a confusion between schizophrenia and dissociative identity disorder – once called multiple-personality disorder – a controversial diagnosis that is supposedly marked by the coexistence of multiple personalities or personality states within individuals. People with schizophrenia possess only one personality, but that personality has been shattered, with severe impairments in thinking, emotion, and motivation.

2. **Myth #2: All people with schizophrenia are essentially alike.** **Fact:** People with schizophrenia experience a bewildering variety of symptoms. Some suffer primarily from "positive" symptoms, such as delusions, which are fixed false beliefs – the idea, say, that government agents are following them – and hallucinations, such as hearing voices. In contrast, others mainly have "negative" symptoms, such as social withdrawal and diminished emotional and verbal expression. Still another set of patients experiences cognitive deficits – problems with paying attention, remembering, and planning. Many patients' deficits span all three categories.

3. **Myth #3: Schizophrenia is caused by family attitudes and behaviors.** **Fact:** In 1948 German psychoanalyst Frieda Fromm-Reichmann introduced the notion of the schizophrenia-inducing mother – one who was hostile and hypercritical – an idea that persisted for decades. Yet research has consistently failed to directly link parenting to the onset of schizophrenia, although numerous investigations suggest that intense familial criticism may hasten its relapse.

complete, recovery from their illness. Many can, for example, live relatively normal lives outside a hospital, holding down a job and socializing periodically with family and friends. As psychiatrist Thomas McGlashan of Yale University concluded in a prescient 1988 publication, "The certainty of negative prognosis in schizophrenia is a myth."

From Desperation to Hope

Around 1900 the great German psychiatrist Emil Kraepelin wrote that schizophrenia, then called dementia praecox (meaning "early dementia"), was characterized by an inexorable downward slide. In 1912 another doctor, A. Warren Stearns, wrote of the "apparent hopelessness of the disease." Some treatments of the day, which included vasectomy and inducement of intense fever using infected blood, reflected this sense of desperation. An attitude of gloom pervaded the field of schizophrenia research for decades, with many scholars insisting that improvement was exceedingly rare, if not unheard of.

Yet experts have lately come to understand that the prognosis for patients with schizophrenia is not uniformly dire. Careful studies tracking patients over time – most of whom receive at least some treatment – suggest that about 20%–30% of people recover substantially over years or decades. Although mild symptoms such as social withdrawal or confused thinking may persist, these individuals can hold down jobs and function independently without being institutionalized.

In one study published in 2005 psychologist Martin Harrow of the University of Illinois College of Medicine and his colleagues followed patients over 15 years and found that about 40% experienced at least periods of considerable recovery, as measured by the absence of significant symptoms as well as the capacity to work, engage in social activities, and live outside a hospital for a year or more. Although most patients do not go into long remissions and may even decline over time, some 20%–30% of this majority experience only moderate symptoms that interfere with – but do not devastate – their ability to perform in the workplace or maintain friendships.

Improved Treatments

Contributing to this less fatalistic view of schizophrenia are the effective treatments that have become available over the past 2 decades. Such atypical antipsychotic medications as Clozaril (clozapine), Risperdal (risperidone), and Zyprexa (olanzapine), most of which were introduced in the 1990s, appear to ameliorate schizophrenia symptoms by affecting the function of neurotransmitters such as dopamine and serotonin, which relay chemical messages between neurons.

In addition, certain psychological interventions developed over the past few decades can often attenuate symptoms such as delusions and hallucinations. For example, cognitive-behavior therapy aims to remedy the paranoid ideas or other maladaptive thinking associated with the disorder by helping patients challenge these beliefs. Family therapies focus on educating family members about the disorder and on reducing the criticism and hostility they direct toward patients. Though not panaceas by any means, these and several other remedies have helped many patients with schizophrenia to delay relapse and, in some cases, operate more effectively in everyday life.

Who is most likely to improve? Researchers have linked a number of factors to better outcomes in patients. These include functioning successfully in their lives before the disease emerged; experiencing severe symptoms suddenly, all at once, rather than little by little; being older when the disease appeared; being female; having a higher IQ; and lacking a family history of the disorder. All these traits and features, however, allow at best modest forecasts of schizophrenia's prognosis.

Clearly, we have made considerable progress in our understanding of schizophrenia's course and are more optimistic than we have ever been about the future of those afflicted. Nevertheless, we need even more effective remedies if our aim is to bring patients back to the productive, happy lives they enjoyed before their illness struck – and shattered their sense of self.

Further Reading

Harding, C. M., & Zahniser, J. H. (1994). Empirical correction of seven myths about schizophrenia with implications for treatment. *Acta Psychiatric Scandinavia*, *90*(Suppl. 384), 140–146.

Walker, E., Kestler, L., Bollini, A., & Hochman, K. H. (2004). Schizophrenia: Etiology and course. *Annual Review of Psychology*, *55*, 401–430.

Section 8

Popular Myths About the Brain and Behavior

Introduction

In 1990, President George H. W. Bush issued a presidential proclamation declaring the 1990s "The Decade of the Brain." The purpose was to make the public more aware of the benefits that can be derived from brain research. Since then, we have continued to make dramatic advances in our understanding of how the brain works. Despite this remarkable progress, some questionable beliefs about the brain continue to be widely accepted by the general public and are discussed in this section. These include: We use only about 10% of our brain's capacity; some people are predominantly right brained (intuitive and creative) and others left brained (logical and rational); increasing our alpha waves causes a deeper sense of consciousness and relaxation.

Hypnosis has remained a fascinating topic for researchers and nonresearchers alike. Here, too, increased knowledge has been accompanied by questionable beliefs. Perhaps the most widespread of these beliefs is that hypnosis is a "trance" or distinct state of consciousness. Many people believe this state is associated with dramatically increased suggestibility during which the hypnotist can induce people to engage in behaviors

Facts and Fictions in Mental Health, First Edition. Hal Arkowitz and Scott O. Lilienfeld.
© 2017 John Wiley & Sons, Inc. Published 2017 by John Wiley & Sons, Inc.

not typical or even possible in the "waking state." There are even claims that hypnosis can generate dramatic psychological and medical cures.

As they get older, most people experience a decline in memory. They often believe that this decline is inevitable and irreversible. Questions have been raised about this belief and whether there are empirically supported methods to help the aging memory.

In this section, we address the following questions:

- Do we use only a very small percentage of our brain's capacity?
- Are some people predominantly right brained (intuitive and creative) and others left brained (logical and rational)?
- Does increasing our alpha brain waves cause a deeper sense of consciousness and relaxation?
- Is what is called a "trance state" in hypnosis a distinct state of consciousness?
- In hypnosis, can people be made to engage in behaviors that they never would engage in in the nonhypnotic state?
- Is the memory loss that accompanies aging an irreversible decline?
- Are there no ways to improve memory in the elderly?

35

Uncovering "Brainscams"

Most of us take our brain for granted. As poet Robert Frost wrote, "The brain is a wonderful organ. It starts working the moment you get up in the morning and does not stop until you get into the office." Weighing in at a mere 3 pounds and possessing the consistency of a lump of Jell-O, our brain looks surprisingly unimpressive in the flesh. Yet it is capable of soaring intellectual feats.

Although our brain underpins virtually every aspect of our thinking, personality, and identity, it is the focus of a host of misconceptions. Without question, the world's expert on "neuromythology" – the study of myths regarding brain structure and function – was Simon Fraser University psychology professor Barry L. Beyerstein, who died in 2007 at the age of 60. Barry coined the term "brainscams" in a 1990 article to draw attention to popular efforts to capitalize on the public's misunderstanding of the brain.

Barry was a friend of one of us (Scott Lilienfeld) and a contributor to both *Scientific American* and *Scientific American Mind*. We think it would be apropos to honor Barry's memory and contribution to neuro-mythology by dedicating this chapter to him and by examining three widespread brainscams that he helped to expose.

Facts and Fictions in Mental Health, First Edition. Hal Arkowitz and Scott O. Lilienfeld.
© 2017 John Wiley & Sons, Inc. Published 2017 by John Wiley & Sons, Inc.

We Use Only 10 Percent of Our Brain's Capacity

This misconception, about which Barry wrote on multiple occasions (including for an Ask the Experts column in the June 2004 issue of *Scientific American*), is among the most deeply entrenched in all of popular psychology. Its seductive appeal is understandable, as we would love to believe that our brain harbors an enormous reservoir of untapped potential. The 10% myth has contributed to a plethora of self-help books and self-improvement gadgets, including commercially available devices that supposedly enable us to harness our unrealized capacities.

Yet the scientific evidence against this myth is overwhelming. Functional brain-imaging studies have consistently failed to turn up any region of the brain that is perpetually inactive. Moreover, research on brain-damaged individuals reveals that a lesion to almost any brain area will produce at least some psychological deficits.

As Barry had noted, the 10% myth probably stemmed in part from a misinterpretation of the writings of William James, one of the founders of American psychology. In his musings around the turn of the 20th century, James wrote that most of us actualize only a small portion of our intellectual potential, an assertion that may well possess some merit. But several popular authors – including Lowell Thomas, who penned the foreword to Dale Carnegie's 1936 best-seller, *How to Win Friends and Influence People* – took liberties with James's writings by proposing that we use only about 10% of our brain. Further contributing to this notion's cachet were early studies suggesting that a substantial majority of the cerebral cortex is "silent." Yet because of advances in the measurement of brain activity, we now know that these areas are far from silent; they make up what neuroscientists term the brain's "association cortex," which plays a vital function in connecting perceptions, thoughts, and emotions across diverse brain areas.

Some People Are Left-Brained; Others Are Right-Brained

Supposedly, left-brained people are analytical, logical, and verbal, whereas right-brained people are creative, holistic, and spatial. Scores of popular books have seized on this purported dichotomy. In his 1972 bestseller, *The Psychology of Consciousness*, Stanford University psychologist Robert Ornstein argued that Western society places too great an emphasis on rational, left-brain thinking and not enough on intuitive, right-brain thinking. In 1979 artist and psychologist Betty Edwards's still popular book, *Drawing on the Right Side of the Brain*, similarly touted the benefits of more creative, right-brained forms of artistic expression.

Yet as Barry and University of Auckland psychologist Michael Corballis noted, the left-brained-versus-right-brained dichotomy is grossly oversimplified. For one thing, this distinction implies that people who are verbally gifted are not likely to be artistically talented, but research suggests otherwise. Moreover, neuroscience studies suggest that the brain's two hemispheres work in a highly coordinated fashion.

Like many brain myths, this one contains a kernel of truth. For several decades, beginning in the 1960s, neuroscientist Roger Sperry of the California Institute of Technology, psychologist Michael S. Gazzaniga of the University of California, Santa Barbara, and their colleagues studied patients who underwent surgery to sever the corpus callosum (the large band of neural fibers connecting the two hemispheres) in an effort to halt intractable epilepsy. The research showed that the left and right hemispheres are indeed different. In most of us, the left hemisphere is specialized for most aspects of language, whereas the right hemisphere is specialized for most visuospatial skills. Yet even these differences are only relative; for example, the right hemisphere tends to play a larger role than the left does in interpreting the vocal tone of spoken language. Moreover, because practically all of us have an intact corpus callosum, our hemispheres are continually interacting.

We Can Achieve a Deeper Sense of Consciousness and Relaxation by Boosting Our Alpha Waves

Purveyors of "alpha consciousness" have encouraged people to undergo brain-wave biofeedback – in some cases using commercially available devices – to increase their production of alpha waves, brain waves that occur at a frequency of about 8–13 cycles per second. Yet research shows alpha-wave output is largely or entirely unrelated to long-term personality traits and short-term states of contentment.

As Barry observed, the myth of alpha consciousness reflects a confusion between "correlation" and "causation." It is true that people tend to display a heightened proportion of alpha waves while meditating or relaxing deeply. But this fact does not mean that an increased production of alpha waves *causes* heightened relaxation. Moreover, research shows that elevated levels of alpha waves are found in some children with attention-deficit hyperactivity disorder, who are anything but relaxed.

These three myths barely scratch the surface of the sprawling field of neuromythology, but they give us a flavor of Barry's valuable role in combating the public's misconceptions about brain function. Fortunately, as readers of *Scientific American Mind* know, the facts about brain function are often far more interesting and surprising than the fictions. By helping laypersons better distinguish brain myths from brain realities, Barry Beyerstein was a pioneer in the ongoing effort to increase the public's scientific literacy. We miss him.

Further Reading

Beyerstein, B. L. (1990). Brainscams: Neuromythologies of the New Age. *International Journal of Mental Health, 19*(3), 27–36.

Della Salla, S. (Ed.). (1999). *Mind myths: Exploring popular assumptions about the mind and brain.* New York, NY: John Wiley & Sons.

Della Salla, S. (Ed.). (2007). *Tall tales about the mind and brain: Separating fact from fiction.* Oxford: Oxford University Press.

Druckman, D., & J. Swets (Eds.). (1988). *Enhancing human performance: Issues, theories, and techniques.* Washington, DC: National Academies Press.

36

Is Hypnosis a Distinct Form
of Consciousness?

The hypnotist, dangling a swinging pocket watch before the subject's eyes, slowly intones: "You're getting sleepy ... You're getting sleepy ..." The subject's head abruptly slumps downward, in a deep, sleeplike trance, oblivious to everything but the hypnotist's soft voice. Powerless to resist the hypnotist's influence, the subject obeys every command, including an instruction to act out an upsetting childhood scene. On "awakening" from the trance half an hour later, there is no memory of what happened.

In fact, this familiar description, captured in countless movies, embodies a host of misconceptions. Few, if any, modern hypnotists use the celebrated swinging watch introduced by Scottish eye surgeon James Braid in the mid-19th century. Although most hypnotists attempt to calm subjects during the "induction," such relaxation is not necessary; people have even been hypnotized while pedaling vigorously on a stationary bicycle. Electroencephalographic (EEG) studies confirm that during hypnosis subjects are not in a sleeplike state but are awake – though sometimes a bit drowsy. Moreover, they can freely resist the hypnotist's suggestions and are far from mindless automatons. Finally, research by the late psychologist Nicholas Spanos of Carleton University in Ontario

Facts and Fictions in Mental Health, First Edition. Hal Arkowitz and Scott O. Lilienfeld.
© 2017 John Wiley & Sons, Inc. Published 2017 by John Wiley & Sons, Inc.

shows that a failure to remember what transpired during the hypnosis session, or so-called posthypnotic amnesia, is not an intrinsic element of hypnosis and typically occurs only when subjects are told to expect it to occur.

The Consciousness Question

The iconic scene we described above also raises a deeper question: Is hypnosis a distinct state of consciousness? Most people seem to think so; in a recent unpublished survey, psychologist Joseph Green of Ohio State University at Lima and his colleagues found that 77% of college students agreed that hypnosis is a distinctly altered state of consciousness. This issue is of more than academic importance. If hypnosis differs in kind rather than in degree from ordinary consciousness, it could imply that hypnotized people can take actions that are impossible to perform in the waking state. It could also lend credibility to claims that hypnosis is a unique means of reducing pain or of effecting dramatic psychological and medical cures.

Despite the ubiquitous Hollywood depiction of hypnosis as a trance, investigators have had an extremely difficult time pinpointing any specific "markers" – indicators – of hypnosis that distinguish it from other states. The legendary American psychiatrist Milton Erickson claimed that hypnosis is marked by several unique features, including posthypnotic amnesia and "literalism" – a tendency to take questions literally, such as responding "Yes" to the question "Can you tell me what time it is?" We have already seen that posthypnotic amnesia is not an inherent accompaniment of hypnosis, so Erickson was wrong on that score. Moreover, research by Green, Binghamton University psychologist Steven Jay Lynn, and their colleagues shows that most highly hypnotizable subjects do not display literalism while hypnotized; moreover, participants asked to simulate hypnosis demonstrate even higher rates of literalism than highly hypnotizable subjects do.

Other experts, such as the late University of Pennsylvania psychiatrist Martin Orne, have argued that only hypnotized participants experience "trance logic" – the ability to entertain two mutually inconsistent ideas at the same time. For example, a hypnotist might suggest to a subject that he is deaf and then ask him, "Can you hear me now?" He may respond,

"No," thereby manifesting trance logic. Nevertheless, research by the late Theodore X. Barber, then at the Medfield Foundation, and his colleagues showed that participants asked to simulate hypnosis displayed trance logic just as often as hypnotized people did, suggesting that trance logic is largely a function of people's expectations rather than an intrinsic component of the hypnotic state itself.

Brain Changes

Still other investigators have sought to uncover distinct physiological markers of hypnosis. Under hypnosis, EEGs, especially those of highly suggestible participants, sometimes display a shift toward heightened activity in the theta band (four to seven cycles per second). In addition, hypnotized participants frequently exhibit increased activity in their brain's anterior cingulate cortex (ACC).

Yet neither finding is surprising. Theta activity is typically associated with states of quiet concentration, which frequently accompany hypnosis. The ACC is linked to the perception of contradictions, which many hypnotized participants experience as they imagine things – such as childhood experiences in the present – that seem to conflict with reality. Further, psychologists have reported similar brain changes among awake subjects. For example, the ACC becomes activated during the famous Stroop task, which requires subjects to name the colors of ink (such as "green") in which competing color words (such as "blue") are printed. Thus, these brain changes are not unique to hypnosis.

Fueling the perception of hypnosis as a distinct trancelike state is the widespread assumption that it leads to marked increases in suggestibility, even complete compliance to the therapist's suggestions. Nowhere is this zombielike stereotype portrayed more vividly than in stage hypnosis shows, in which people are seemingly induced to bark like dogs, sing karaoke, and engage in other comical behaviors in full view of hundreds of amused audience members.

Yet research shows that hypnosis exerts only a minor impact on suggestibility. On standardized scales of hypnotic suggestibility, which ask participants to comply with a dozen suggestions (that one's arm is raising on its own power, for example), the increase in suggestibility following a hypnotic induction is typically on the order of 10% or less.

Moreover, research demonstrates that a formal hypnotic induction is not needed to produce many of the seemingly spectacular effects of hypnosis, such as reduction of extreme pain or various physical feats, popular in stage hypnosis acts, such as suspending a participant horizontally between the backs of two chairs. One can generate most, if not all, of these effects merely by providing highly suggestible people with sufficient incentives to perform them. Stage hypnotists are well aware of this little secret. Before beginning their shtick, they prescreen audience members for high suggestibility by providing those people with a string of suggestions. They then handpick their participants from among the minority who comply.

We agree with Lynn and psychologist Irving Kirsch of the University of Hull in England, who wrote in 1995 that "having failed to find reliable markers of trance after 50 years of careful research, most researchers have concluded that this hypothesis [that hypnosis is a unique state of consciousness] has outlived its usefulness." Increasingly, evidence is suggesting that the effects of hypnosis result largely from people's expectations about what hypnosis entails rather than from the hypnotic state itself. Still, it is always possible that future studies could overturn or at least qualify this conclusion. In particular, research on potential physiological markers of hypnosis may elucidate how hypnosis differs from other states of consciousness. Although hypnosis poses fascinating mysteries that will keep scientists busy for decades, it seems clear that it has far more in common with everyday wakefulness than with the watch-induced trance of Hollywood crime thrillers.

Further Reading

Jamieson, G. A. (2007). *Hypnosis and conscious states: The cognitive neuroscience perspective*. Oxford: Oxford University Press.

Kirsch, I., & Lynn, S. J. (1995). Altered state of hypnosis: Changes in the theoretical landscape. *American Psychologist*, *50*(10), 846–858.

Nash, M. R., & Benham, G. (2005). The truth and the hype of hypnosis. *Scientific American Mind*, *16*(2), 46–53.

37

Memory in Old Age
Not a Lost Cause

When Mick Jagger first sang "What a drag it is getting old," he was 23 years old. Now in his 70s, he is still a veritable Jumpin' Jack Flash on stage. Jagger seems to have found the secret to staying physically fit in his advancing years, but getting old can be a drag on the psyche. Many older adults fear memory loss and worry they are headed down the road to dementia, such as Alzheimer's disease. Every time they forget their keys, leave a door unlocked or fail to remember a name, they are reminded of this nagging concern. In most cases, however, such annoying incidents are part of normal age-related memory loss, not a sign of impending dementia.

Although lots of older adults think such a decline is inevitable, there is good news for many of them. Researchers have developed an array of helpful methods and activities that exercise our minds and bodies that can help keep the older mind in relatively good condition. In this chapter, we examine the most promising ways to shore up memory in the normal aging brain.

Facts and Fictions in Mental Health, First Edition. Hal Arkowitz and Scott O. Lilienfeld.
© 2017 John Wiley & Sons, Inc. Published 2017 by John Wiley & Sons, Inc.

Memory Divided

Memory is not a single entity. The term encompasses several types of remembering, not all of which decline with age. For instance, older people still retain their vocabulary, along with general knowledge about the world (semantic memory). They can also perform certain routine tasks, such as making an omelet or typing on a computer (procedural memory), about as well as they could when they were younger. People do become worse, however, at recalling recent events in their lives (episodic memory) or where they first learned a piece of information (source memory), managing the temporary storage of short-term information (working memory), and remembering to do things in the future (prospective memory).

Prospective memory, in particular, is an important target for memory strategies because forgetting upcoming tasks or appointments can cause considerable frustration or embarrassment. In 2002 psychologist Narinder Kapur of Southampton General Hospital in England and his colleagues reviewed studies on the effectiveness of various common techniques to bolster prospective memory. They found that external aids such as making lists or programming reminders into a cellphone could be helpful in reducing memory problems such as failing to pay bills or attend meetings.

Another successful strategy involves associating information to be recalled with an image, sentence, phrase, or word. The more personally relevant the association is, the more likely it is to be remembered, an approach known as self-referential processing. For example, if we need to return a book to the library, we might imagine ourselves doing just that. Made-up acronyms also can be a big help. In this strategy, a person forms a new word from the initial letters of what he or she wants to remember. To remember to buy a birthday gift for his wife, for example, a man might construct the acronym "BIG" for "Birthday Gift."

In 2008 psychologists Betty L. Glisky of the University of Arizona and Martha L. Glisky of the Evergreen Hospital Medical Center described other useful methods for improving memory that involve visual or semantic elaboration. In one of these, a person conjures up images related to something he or she wants to retain. To remember the name "Peggy," you might imagine a pirate with a wooden (peg) leg. Such a tactic could be helpful as long as you do not end up calling her "Pegleggy."

A semantic approach entails tacking on words to what you wish to recall. For example, in a music appreciation class that one of us (Hal Arkowitz) took in elementary school, the teacher asked the class to associate the main musical theme of the classical piece, the *Peer Gynt Suite*, with the following rather silly sentence: "Morning is dawning and Peer Gynt is yawning and music is written by Grieg." The tie-in with the phrase was designed to help the kids remember the name of the composer.

Although Glisky and Glisky found support for these visual and semantic techniques, among others, they cautioned that memory improvements in the laboratory do not necessarily translate to enhancements in daily life, because these benefits depend on people practicing and using the tactics regularly. This gap in efficacy may be widest for strategies that take considerable time and effort to learn. Also, improvements in one area of memory often do not generalize to others.

Studies have found some support for the validity of the saying "Use it or lose it." The more we use our memory – for example, reading, doing crossword puzzles, and playing board games – the better it may be, probably because such activities involve considerable use of memory. Of course, those with better memories may also be more likely to exercise their minds in the first place, accounting for some (but probably not all) of the association between good memory and amount of cognitive stimulation.

Fit Body, Fit Mind

If Jagger is as physically fit as he looks, his mind may be following suit. Some studies have found that higher levels of aerobic exercise are associated with better memory in older adults. Although many of these studies do not prove that aerobic exercise causes the memory improvements, some do suggest a causal connection. When psychologist Stanley Colcombe of the University of Illinois at Urbana-Champaign and his colleagues reviewed 18 controlled studies addressing this association in 2003, they found evidence that aerobic exercise did indeed lead to enhancements in memory.

Sustained aerobic activity may not be the only way to keep your mind agile and your memory sharp. In a study published in 2011 neurologist

Ruth Ruscheweyh of the University of Münster in Germany and her colleagues assessed total physical activity in 62 older adults over 6 months. Their questionnaire included both formal exercise and daily routines such as walking to work, climbing stairs, and gardening. The researchers linked reported increases in overall activity, no matter its type, with improvements in episodic memory at the end of 6 months. The greater the rise in activity levels, the bigger the memory boost. Thus, keeping physically active through regular workouts along with everyday errands and tasks may be the best recipe for reinvigorating your powers of recollection. (For more on the connection between physical and mental fitness in old age, see "Fit Body, Fit Mind?" by Christopher Hertzog, Arthur F. Kramer, Robert S. Wilson, and Ulman Lindenberger, *Scientific American Mind*, July/August 2009.)

The research suggests that many memory techniques as well as a physically and mentally energetic lifestyle can improve memory in older adults. We still have a long way to go before we have highly effective methods, but given the vigor of this field, we can expect great progress in the near future.

Further Reading

Draaisma, D. (2013). *The nostalgia factory: Memory, time and ageing*. New Haven, CT: Yale University Press.

Glisky, E. L., & Glisky, M. L. (2008). Memory rehabilitation in older adults. In D. Tuss, G. Winocur, & I. Robertson (Eds.), *Cognitive neurorehabilitation: Evidence and applications* (2nd ed.) (pp. 541–562). Cambridge: Cambridge University Press.

Winningham, R. (2009). *Train your brain: How to maximize memory ability in older adults*. Amityville, NY: Baywood Publishing Company.

Section 9

Psychotherapy and Other Approaches to Change

Introduction

Many decades ago, psychotherapy was more of an art than a science. Many therapists relied on their intuitions and gut hunches, and simply did what they thought were the best ways to help clients change. There was little or no research to guide them to which approaches were most effective for different problems. Then, approximately 40 years ago, clinical psychology and psychiatry researchers turned their attention to research aimed at evaluating the effectiveness of different psychotherapies. As a result, we now have solid data on which therapies work reasonably well for a wide variety of problems. But we still have a long way to go.

Some therapists argue that their preferred approach is superior to others. Others believe that most or all therapies are equally effective due to elements they share, such as empathy, support, and feedback. Which view is correct? Does it matter what type of therapy one receives? In this section of the book, we examine this debate and find some truth to both points of view.

Facts and Fictions in Mental Health, First Edition. Hal Arkowitz and Scott O. Lilienfeld.
© 2017 John Wiley & Sons, Inc. Published 2017 by John Wiley & Sons, Inc.

Psychotherapy is often used in conjunction with other approaches, most commonly psychotropic medications. The evidence suggests that in many cases of depression, the combination may be more effective than each one singly.

Another approach sometimes employed in conjunction with psychotherapy is the use of domesticated animals. Some psychologists have argued that psychotherapy combined with interactions with animals, known as animal-assisted therapy (AAT), may be more effective than psychotherapy without AAT. Is that the case? In this section, we take a closer look at this question.

People with problems often seek help from sources other than psychotherapy, such as self-help books. Sales of these books are in the millions of dollars each year with several thousands of new ones appearing annually. Some troubled people obtain help only from these books, but many psychotherapists also use them as part of their treatment approach. Authors of self-help books frequently make unrealistic claims about how following their advice can cure people's problems. In this section, we will learn whether such books have value in helping people suffering from psychological distress.

People often turn to another source for help with personal problems: media "shrinks" such as Dr. Phil. Their shows attract huge audiences with many people undoubtedly believing that they employ valid therapeutic principles and methods that are helpful to their guests. Typically, these and other celebrities interact with an individual, couple, or family seeking help for psychological problems. Most use a highly directive approach and tell people what they need to change and how to change it – what we call the "just do it" approach. Some audience members may take this "just do it" approach to heart and use it on themselves as well as friends and family members. Are these media shrinks helpful? Are the methods they use well validated by research?

Many people form their impressions of how therapists work from the media, especially television and movies. Like the media shrinks discussed above, many portray mental health professionals as all-knowing and omnipotent, possessing the answers to complex problems that plague us. Still other depictions of psychotherapy in the media portray a therapy in which the patient lies on a couch while the therapist tries to get to the unconscious historical "roots" of the problem, saying very little in the process. How effective are approaches like this?

The myths discussed in this section have a practical impact on those who believe them. They convey misleading information about psychotherapy that may lead people to avoid needed psychotherapy or to seek psychotherapy with unrealistic expectations. In this section, we examine several questions about psychotherapy and related approaches.

- Are all therapies equally effective?
- Is the effectiveness of different psychotherapies due to elements that they share in common like empathy and support or to factors specific to the different therapies?
- Is animal-assisted psychotherapy more effective than psychotherapy alone?
- Does the addition of medication increase the effectiveness of psychotherapy?
- How helpful are self-help books?
- How helpful are media shrinks?
- How accurate are the portrayals of psychotherapy in the media?
- Why do people sometimes resist changing when they know that doing so would improve the quality of their lives?

38

Are all Psychotherapies Created Equal?

As a prospective client searches for a psychotherapist, numerous questions may spring to mind. How experienced is the therapist? Has he or she helped people with problems like mine? Is he or she someone I can relate to? Yet it may not occur to clients to ask another one: What type of therapy does the clinician deliver? People often assume that the brand of therapy offered is irrelevant to the effectiveness of treatment. Is this assumption correct?

Psychologists do not agree on whether the "school" of therapy predicts its effectiveness. In a survey in 2006 by psychologists Charles Boisvert of Rhode Island College and David Faust of the University of Rhode Island, psychotherapy researchers responded to the statement that "in general, therapies achieve similar outcomes" with an average score of 6 on a 7-point scale, indicating strong agreement. In contrast, psychologists in practice averaged a rating of 4.5, signifying that they agreed only moderately with that position.

As we will discover, both camps can justify their point of view. Although a number of commonly used psychotherapies are broadly comparable in their effects, some options are less well suited to certain conditions, and a few may even be harmful. In addition, the differences

Facts and Fictions in Mental Health, First Edition. Hal Arkowitz and Scott O. Lilienfeld.
© 2017 John Wiley & Sons, Inc. Published 2017 by John Wiley & Sons, Inc.

among therapies in their effectiveness may depend partly on the kinds of psychological problems that clients are experiencing.

Tale of the Dodo Bird

At least 500 different types of psychotherapy exist, according to one estimate by University of Scranton psychologist John Norcross. Given that researchers cannot investigate all of them, they have generally concentrated on the most frequently used approaches. These include behavior therapy (altering unhealthy behaviors), cognitive-behavior therapy (altering maladaptive ways of thinking), psychodynamic therapy (resolving unconscious conflicts and adverse childhood experiences), interpersonal therapy (remedying unhealthy ways of interacting with others), and person-centered therapy (helping clients to find their own solutions to life problems).

As early as 1936, Washington University psychologist Saul Rosenzweig concluded after perusing the literature that one therapy works about as well as any other. At the time, many of the principal treatments fell roughly into the psychodynamic and behavioral categories, which are still widely used today. Rosenzweig introduced the metaphor of the dodo bird, after the feathered creature in Lewis Carroll's *Alice in Wonderland*, who declared, following a race, that "everyone has won, and all must have prizes." The "Dodo Bird verdict" has since come to refer to the claim that all therapies are equivalent in their effects.

This verdict gained traction in 1975, when University of Pennsylvania psychologist Lester Luborsky and his colleagues published a review of relevant research suggesting that all therapies work equally well. It gathered more momentum in 1997, when University of Wisconsin–Madison psychologist Bruce E. Wampold and his coauthors published a meta-analysis (quantitative review) of more than 200 scientific studies in which "bona fide" therapies were compared with no treatment. By bona fide, they meant treatments delivered by trained therapists, based on sound psychological principles, and described in publications. Wampold's team found the differences in the treatments' effectiveness to be minimal (and they were all better than no treatment).

One explanation for the Dodo Bird effect is that virtually all types of psychotherapy share certain core features. In a classic 1961, book the late psychiatrist Jerome Frank of the Johns Hopkins University argued that all effective therapies consist of clearly prescribed roles for healer and client. They present clients with a plausible theoretical rationale and provide them with specific therapeutic rituals, he wrote. They also take place in a setting, usually a comfortable office, associated with the alleviation of distress. Later writers elaborated on Frank's thinking, contending that effective therapies require empathy on the part of the clinician, close rapport between practitioner and client, and shared therapeutic goals.

Today many authors argue that these and other common elements are even more powerful than the features that distinguish one therapy from another. To take just one example, Wampold concluded in a 2001 analysis that the therapeutic alliance – the strength of the bond between a therapist and his or her client – accounts for about 7% of therapeutic effectiveness but that the school of the therapy accounts for only about 1%. Most of the remaining 92% is presumably caused by other factors, such as the personalities of the therapist and client.

Is the Dodo Bird Extinct?

Although most researchers agree that common factors play key roles in psychotherapy, some doubt that all methods are equally effective. Even Wampold has been careful to note that his conclusion holds for only bona fide treatments; it does not extend to all 500 or so therapies. For example, few experts would contend that rebirthing therapy, premised on the dubious idea that we must "relive" the trauma of our birth to cure neurosis, works as well as cognitive-behavior therapy for most psychological conditions.

Moreover, research suggests that even among accepted therapies, the type of treatment does matter under certain circumstances. A 2001 review by University of Pennsylvania psychologist Dianne Chambless and Virginia Polytechnic Institute psychologist Thomas Ollendick revealed that behavior therapy and cognitive-behavior therapy are more effective than many, and probably most, other treatments for anxiety disorders and for childhood and adolescent depression and behavioral problems. In addition, in a 2010 meta-analysis psychologist David Tolin of the Institute of Living in Hartford, Connecticut, found that these same two therapy types produce better results than psychodynamic therapy for anxiety and mood disorders.

The Dodo Bird verdict must also be qualified by evidence indicating that several widely used therapies do not work and may actually harm. For example, in a 2003 review psychologist Richard McNally of Harvard University and his colleagues evaluated crisis debriefing. In this treatment for warding off posttraumatic stress symptoms, therapists urge those exposed to emotionally fraught events such as shootings or earthquakes to try to reexperience the feelings they had during the event soon after it. McNally's team concluded that this treatment is inert at best and possibly damaging, perhaps because it interferes with natural coping mechanisms.

In light of such findings, a search for a therapist should at least sometimes involve a consideration of the type of treatment he or she practices. It is true that ingredients, such as empathy, that cut across effective therapies are potent and that various established techniques are roughly equivalent for a broad range of difficulties. Yet under certain circumstances, the therapeutic method can matter. For example, if a clinician espouses an approach outside the scientific mainstream – one that does not fall under the broad categories we have listed here – you should not assume that this treatment will be as helpful as others. If you suffer from an anxiety disorder or one of the other conditions for which behavior and cognitive-behavior interventions work well, then someone who practices one of those two types is probably a good bet.

Of course, scientists have systematically assessed only a minority of the psychotherapies invented so far for their efficacy in treating the numerous psychological difficulties that afflict humankind. In the coming decade, we hope that further research clarifies whether the brand of therapy makes a difference in an individual's recovery from psychological distress.

Further Reading

Hunsley, J., & Di Guilio, G. (2002). Dodo bird, phoenix, or urban legend? The question of psychotherapy equivalence. *Scientific Review of Mental Health Practice*, *1*(1), 11–22.

Wampold, B. E., & Imel, Z. (2015). *The great psychotherapy debate: The evidence for what makes psychology work*. New York, NY: Routledge.

39

Do Self-Help Books Help?

Have you ever purchased a self-help book? If so, you are like most Americans. In 2003 alone, publishers put out more than 3,500 new self-help titles, ringing up more than $650 million in sales. Many of the buyers cannot or will not seek psychotherapy, but surveys by John C. Norcross of the University of Scranton and others indicate that 80% or more of psychotherapists recommend such books to their patients. How well are self-help books fulfilling their purpose?

Authors of self-help books often make grandiose promises that invite a skeptical look. Consider the title of a best-seller by Anthony Robbins: *Awaken the Giant Within: How to Take Immediate Control of Your Mental, Emotional, Physical and Financial Destiny!* (Free Press, 1992). The dust jacket describes Robbins as an "acknowledged expert in the psychology of change." Yet he lacks any formal mental health credentials. Elsewhere, Robbins has made eyebrow-raising claims, such as that he can cure any psychological problem in a session, make someone fall in love with you in 5 minutes and even revive brain-dead individuals. (If he can do this with enough people, he might sell even more books.)

Even trained psychologist authors are not immune to hyperbole. Wayne Dyer, a counseling psychologist, wrote *You'll See It When You*

Facts and Fictions in Mental Health, First Edition. Hal Arkowitz and Scott O. Lilienfeld.
© 2017 John Wiley & Sons, Inc. Published 2017 by John Wiley & Sons, Inc.

Believe It: The Way to Your Personal Transformation (Harper Paperbacks, 2001). The dust jacket promises that "through belief you can make your most impossible dreams come true, turn obstacles into opportunities, rid yourself of guilt and inner turmoil, and spend every day doing the things you love to do." That's nice work if you can get it.

In view of how much time, money, and effort buyers spend on these materials, not to mention the hopes they raise, it is remarkable how little the average person knows about their effectiveness. Moreover, as clinical psychologist Gerald M. Rosen of the University of Washington has noted, professional psychological organizations have done little to educate the public concerning the strengths and weaknesses of self-help. Still, some researchers have conducted informative studies of the effects of self-help books, or as they call it "bibliotherapy."

Typically investigators recruit participants with a specific problem (such as depression, panic attacks, or obesity). They take objective measures of the problem before and after the bibliotherapy and compare such statistics with a group that gets no book or any other treatment (the "control" group); the intervening period usually lasts 4 to 12 weeks. Some studies also compare bibliotherapy with face-to-face psychotherapy.

Results generally demonstrate that bibliotherapy leads to greater mental health improvements than no treatment, and it often equals the benefits obtained by psychotherapy. Before you log on to Amazon.com or rush to the bookstore, however, let us describe the limitations of this research.

Small sample size. Only a tiny percentage of self-help books has been evaluated; a larger sampling may show different effects.

Minor problems. Many studies have employed subjects with relatively minor problems (such as mild fears of public speaking), which may be more amenable to self-help strategies than serious problems are.

Uneven results. Improvements occur for some but not all people, and many of those who do get better are still left with significant symptoms.

Study conditions yield greater success. Study volunteers may be more motivated than casual bookstore or airport browsers who purchase the same book. Subjects may be especially encouraged to read the book because researchers often call to monitor how they are doing. (In contrast, one of us [Hal Arkowitz] has had a self-help book for more than 30 years entitled *How to Get Control of Your Time and Your Life.* He has not yet found the time to read it. Maybe he should take part in one of these studies.)

Combined treatments. One review found that bibliotherapy study participants also met with therapists for 36 minutes on average per week, making it difficult to separate how much of the positive effects are attributable to psychotherapy versus bibliotherapy.

Box 39.1   Using Self-Help Books Wisely

- Choose books based on research or on valid psychological principles of change. See if the author makes any references to published research that support his or her claims. Some books that have been used with good effect in bibliotherapy studies are *Feeling Good: The New Mood Therapy,* by David D. Burns (Avon, 1999); *Mind Over Mood: Change How You Feel by Changing the Way You Think,* by Dennis Greenberger and Christine Padesky (Guilford Press, 1995); and *Coping With Panic: A Drug-Free Approach to Coping with Anxiety Attacks,* by George Clum (Self Change Systems, 1999).
- Examine the credentials of the author. Proclaiming oneself an expert (or appearing on *Oprah*) does not an expert make.
- Be wary of books that make promises that they obviously cannot keep, such as curing a phobia in 5 minutes or fixing a failing marriage in a week. Typically these books are based on the personal biases and preferences of the author rather than on valid psychological principles.
- Beware of authors that offer "one size fits all" solutions. For example, a book that tells you to always express your anger to your spouse fails to take into account the complexity of the people involved and the specifics of the marriage.
- If the problem is a serious one, such as clinical depression, obsessive-compulsive disorder, or schizophrenia, you are better off seeking professional treatment than reading a self-help book.

False hopes. Some self-help books may be unable to deliver on their expansive promises. As a result, readers may perceive their lack of change as personal failures and even see themselves as hopeless cases ("false hope syndrome"). When unreasonable expectations for self-change go unmet, people feel frustrated and despondent and may give up trying to change.

Even when self-help works, it may not work as well as psychotherapy. A 2007 review by Marisa Menchola, along with University of Arizona colleague Arkowitz and Brian Burke of Fort Lewis College, examined this possibility. In contrast to previous reviews, it included only studies in which contact with a therapist or researcher was minimal and in which subjects suffered from serious problems, such as major depression or panic disorder. Overall, bibliotherapy was better than no treatment, although psychotherapy was still superior to bibliotherapy. Certain self-help books can be valuable resources for personal change – especially if readers follow some simple tips in Box 39.1. A famous Latin phrase, however, remains apt: *Caveat emptor!* ("Buyer beware!")

Further Reading

Menchola, M., Arkowitz, H., & Burke, B. (Eds.). (2007). Efficacy of self-administered treatments for depression and anxiety. *Professional Psychology: Research and Practice, 38,* 421–429.

Rosen, G. M., Glasgow, R. E., Moore, T. M., & Barrera, M. (2015). Self-help therapy: Recent developments in the science and business of giving psychology away. In In S. L. Lilienfeld, S. J. Lynn, & J. M. Lohr (Eds.), *Science and pseudoscience in clinical psychology* (pp. 245–274). New York, NY: Guilford Press.

Scogin, F. R. (Ed.). 2003. The status of self-administered treatments [Special section]. *Journal of Clinical Psychology, 59*(3), 247–349.

40

The "Just Do It!" Trap

Why Dr. Phil and Dr. Laura Won't
Solve Your Problems

A woman who had been married for 14 years called into Dr. Laura's radio show. The woman says she recently realized that she has never loved her husband, and she informs Dr. Laura that she has told her husband that. The couple has received marriage counseling, but Dr. Laura tells the caller that counseling is useless because of her attitude, according to a YouTube recording of the episode. The conversation continues:

> DR. LAURA: What is your question for me?
> CALLER: What type of advice can you give me to try to …?
> DR. LAURA (INTERRUPTING):   Too late, too late, you were cruel.
> CALLER: At the time …
> DR. LAURA (INTERRUPTING AGAIN):   Try to make it up to him by just being nice every day. Maybe you're just broken in the I-can-feel-compassion-for-someone department.

In an episode of Dr. Phil's television show that first aired on April 1, 2009, Dr. Phil spoke to a guest who was seeking help because she gets very angry at her children and sometimes hits them. His advice: "You can stop. You can stop because you do stop for other people … It's not that you won't, it's just that you don't …"

Facts and Fictions in Mental Health, First Edition. Hal Arkowitz and Scott O. Lilienfeld.
© 2017 John Wiley & Sons, Inc. Published 2017 by John Wiley & Sons, Inc.

Participants in the Dr. Laura (Schlessinger) and the Dr. Phil (McGraw) shows seek help for a variety of personal problems, and the advice the hosts provide reaches a lot of people. In 2010 Dr. Laura's call-in show drew more than 9 million listeners per week. At about the same time, Dr. Phil attracted roughly 4 million viewers per program. Yet neither host claims to practice psychotherapy. What is more, both Schlessinger's and McGraw's typical takes on people's troubles are at odds with much of the psychological literature, which suggests that their recommendations are unlikely to work most of the time and might even do damage.

Although Schlessinger holds a California license in marriage, child, and family counseling, her Ph.D. is in physiology, not psychology, making the use of "Dr." as a qualification for giving personal advice misleading. McGraw has a psychology Ph.D. and was licensed as a psychologist in Texas until 2006, when he let his license expire.

Blaming the Victim

McGraw and Schlessinger are right to emphasize personal responsibility and discourage blaming others for problems. Yet they often take individual accountability to an extreme, implying that people are to blame for all their difficulties when, in fact, factors such as an individual's genetic makeup, personal history, and current circumstances may contribute significantly to psychological problems. Emphasizing personal control above all else can discourage people from identifying the external issues or situations that might be contributing to their problems and that might need to be addressed.

Another drawback of the Schlessinger and McGraw styles is their lack of empathy – a willingness to understand another person's thoughts, feelings, and struggles from that person's perspective. Schlessinger typically spends only a few minutes with callers, frequently interrupting them and sometimes referring to their behaviors with derogatory terms, such as "stupid." Her strongly worded advice is usually based on her socially conservative and religious views and often neglects many of the specific problems that the caller is facing. McGraw typically spends somewhat more time listening, but he comes to relatively quick conclusions about the causes of and solutions for his guests' problems, again reflecting little appreciation for the complexities of people's lives.

Recent research suggests that a lack of empathy is a handicap when trying to help people with psychological or social problems. In a 2002 quantitative review of numerous studies psychologist Arthur Bohart, then at California State University, Dominguez Hills, and his colleagues found a correlation between high levels of empathy in therapists and successful outcomes in their patients. In a 1992 study psychiatrist David Burns, then at the University of Pennsylvania School of Medicine, and his colleagues used advanced statistical techniques for distinguishing cause and effect and found that a therapist's ability to empathize not only is correlated with a patient's progress but also contributes to it. Empathy is the cornerstone of psychotherapy, both because therapists need it to provide useful and relevant guidance and because patients benefit from feeling truly understood.

Breeding Resistance

Instead of trying to understand their guests, Schlessinger and McGraw are often confrontational and directive, authoritatively telling people what to do or not to do with relatively little input from the recipients of their instructions. For example, Dr. Phil told a 19-year-old man who was considering marrying a 30-year-old woman with two children after a very short courtship: "You absolutely, unequivocally should not do this!"

However much the viewer might agree, numerous studies reveal that a directive therapist style leads many people to dig in their heels and may even worsen a situation or psychological problem. In 1985 psychologists Gerald Patterson and Marion Forgatch of the Oregon Social Learning Center concluded that directives from therapists who were coaching mothers to deal with difficult children triggered more resistant responses from the mothers than did a supportive approach involving gentle encouragement and belief in a child's ability to change. In a 1993 study psychologist William R. Miller of the University of New Mexico and his colleagues found that therapists who used more directive and confrontational statements elicited more opposition from patients who were problem drinkers. In addition, the more directive the therapists were, the more the clients drank a year after the therapy.

Most psychotherapists know that merely telling people to stop their problem behaviors is rarely helpful, and indeed no data exist to show that anyone has benefited from Schlessinger's or McGraw's advice. After a thorough search of the research literature and the Internet, we could not find a single follow-up study of the participants, formal or informal.

Because Schlessinger's and McGraw's practices are unsubstantiated, we believe that these well-known hosts need to demonstrate that they are not causing harm. Calling what they do "entertainment" or "education" does not exclude them from this requirement. Both shows inaccurately portray how mental health professionals understand and help people. Most psychological problems do not simply reflect a lack of self-control and cannot be changed by simple directives. Believing that they can could lead millions of people to ignore important biological or social causes of their troubles and fail to seek effective treatments for themselves or others.

Further Reading

Elliot, R., Bohart, A. C., Watson, J. C., & Greenberg, L. S. (2011). Empathy. *Psychotherapy: Theory, Research, and Practice, 48*, 43–49.

Salerno, S. (2005). *SHAM: How the self-help movement made America helpless.* New York, NY: Crown Publishers.

41

Can Animals Aid Therapy?

In 1857 British novelist George Eliot wrote, "Animals are such agreeable friends. They ask no questions and they pass no criticism." So it is no surprise that scholars have long been intrigued by the possibility that animals possess largely untapped therapeutic powers. But are animals good for our psychological and physical health, either as pets or as "therapists"?

Most Americans are animal lovers; about 63% of U.S. households contain one or more pets, according to the American Pet Products Manufacturers Association. Several, but not all, studies suggest that those of us who own pets tend to be somewhat happier than those of us who do not. In addition, research by Erika Friedmann and her colleagues at the University of Maryland School of Nursing shows that pet ownership predicts 1-year survival rates among victims of heart attacks.

Though interesting and potentially important, studies such as these are difficult to interpret because pet owners may differ in unmeasured ways from people who do not own pets. For example, pet owners may be better adjusted psychologically and have fewer cardiac

Facts and Fictions in Mental Health, First Edition. Hal Arkowitz and Scott O. Lilienfeld.
© 2017 John Wiley & Sons, Inc. Published 2017 by John Wiley & Sons, Inc.

risk factors (they may eat healthier diets and experience lower levels of hostility) than nonpet owners.

Easing Stress?

To unravel the potential influences of pets on well-being, researchers must conduct experiments that randomly assign some people, but not others, to receive a pet, either in the laboratory or in their home. Studies by psychologists Karen Allen of the University at Buffalo and James Blascovich of the University of California, Santa Barbara, and their colleagues demonstrate that the presence of a favorite pet during a stressful task – such as performing difficult mental arithmetic – largely prevents spikes in participants' blood pressure. In contrast, the presence of a friend does not. In addition, Allen's work shows that stressed-out, hypertensive stockbrokers who were randomly assigned to adopt either a pet dog or cat ended up with lower blood pressure than those who were not. These studies suggest that the presence of pets may lower our blood pressure and stress levels, although they do not tell us the reasons for this effect. They also do not inform us whether we would observe similar effects with other preferred stimuli, such as a good luck charm or a favorite doll.

Few would contest the claim that pets can give us comfort, especially in times of strain or loneliness. A far more controversial question concerns the effectiveness of animal-assisted therapy (AAT), defined as the use of an animal as either a treatment by itself or an addition to an existing treatment, such as psychotherapy. The animals used in various forms of AAT are a veritable menagerie: horses, dogs, cats, rabbits, birds, fish, guinea pigs, and, perhaps best known of all, dolphins. In turn, the psychological problems for which AATs are used include schizophrenia, clinical depression, anxiety disorders, eating disorders, attention-deficit hyperactivity disorder, autism, and a host of developmental disabilities.

Popularized largely by Yeshiva University psychologist Boris Levinson in the 1960s, AATs appear to be surprisingly common: a 1973 survey by Oklahoma State University psychologist Susan S. Rice and her colleagues revealed that 21% of therapists in the psychotherapy division of the American Psychological Association incorporated animals into their treatment in some fashion. Whether this percentage has changed over the past 4 decades is unknown.

Leisure Versus Therapy

Do AATs work? To make some inroads into this question, we need to distinguish between two different uses of animals: recreation and psychotherapy. Some uses of animals are purely recreational: Their goal is to allow their human companions to have fun. There is scant dispute that interacting with friendly animals can "work" for such purposes, because such activities often make people feel happier temporarily. To show that AATs work, however, researchers must demonstrate that animals produce enduring effects on people's psychological health, not merely short-term changes in mood, such as pleasure, relaxation, or excitement.

Probably the most extensively researched AAT is dolphin-assisted therapy (DAT), which is most commonly used for children with autism or other developmental disabilities. DAT is practiced not only in the United States – primarily in Florida and Hawaii – but also in Mexico, Israel, Russia, Japan, China, and the Bahamas, among other countries. Typically during DAT sessions children interact with a captive dolphin in the water while performing rudimentary manual tasks, such as placing rings on a peg. In many cases, the dolphin presumably serves as a "reinforcer" for appropriate child behaviors. Many DAT Web sites advance strong claims regarding this treatment's effectiveness; one asserts that "this field of medicine has shown extraordinary results of the therapy [DAT] and breakthroughs in outcomes" as compared with conventional treatments, including medication and therapy. Do the data support these assertions?

Psychologist Lori Marino, then at Emory University, and one of us (Scott Lilienfeld) have examined the research findings regarding DAT in two reviews, one published in 1998 and the second in 2007. We found the evidence lacking for DAT's effectiveness. In many cases, researchers had shown only that children who received DAT displayed improvements on some psychological measures as compared with children who did not. Yet such results do not exclude the possibility that these changes would have occurred with the mere passage of time. In still other cases, researchers did not rule out the possibility that reported improvements were merely short-term mood effects rather than lasting changes in symptoms. Finally, no researcher adequately excluded the possibility that the observed effects could have been produced by any animal or, for that matter, by any highly pleasurable stimulus. The research literature for other AATs appears to be no more definitive.

Hidden Costs

Why should we care about whether AATs work? After all, if children seem to enjoy them and parents are willing to pay for them, why worry? There are at least three reasons. First, AATs can produce what economists term "opportunity costs" – the time, money and effort expended in seeking out ineffective treatments. Because of such costs, parents and children may forfeit the chance to seek out effective treatments. In the case of DAT, opportunity costs are far from trivial, because treatments frequently cost $3,000 to $5,000, not including the price of travel and lodging. Second, at least some AATs may be physically hazardous. For example, in DAT it is not legally required that dolphins be screened for infectious diseases. Moreover, there have been multiple reports of children injured by dolphins in DAT sessions. Third, some AATs result in largely unappreciated costs to the animals themselves. For example, removing dolphins from the wild for transfer to DAT facilities not only separates them from their families but also often results in the death of many dolphins within each pod.

So, to the bottom line: Are animals good for our psychological and physical health? Undoubtedly, many animals can be valued companions and provide social support; they can also make us feel better in the short term. It is possible that pets can be of particular help to people with depression or to children who have been severely neglected – for whom loneliness and lack of social support are often common problems. Still, further research will be needed to investigate this possibility. Moreover, whether animals – including dolphins – produce long-term changes in the core symptoms of other psychological conditions, such as autism, developmental disabilities, or anxiety disorders, is another matter altogether. To this question, we must reserve the verdict sometimes delivered in Scottish courts: "unproven."

Further Reading

Allen, K. (2003). Are pets a healthy pleasure? The influence of pets on blood pressure. *Current Directions in Psychological Science, 12*(6), 236–239.

Fine, A. H. (Ed.). (2006). *Handbook on animal-assisted therapy: Theoretical foundations and guidelines for practice* (2nd ed.). San Diego, CA: Academic Press.

Marino, L. & Lilienfeld, S. O. (2007). Dolphin-assisted therapy: More flawed data and more flawed conclusions. *Anthrozoös, 20*(3), 239–249.

42

Psychotherapy in the Public Eye

Imagine that you've been feeling out of sorts lately. For reasons you don't understand, you're kind of depressed, are having trouble sleeping, and more irritable about things than usual. For the first time in your life, you've decided to seek professional help. When you enter the therapist's office, what do you expect to encounter?

If you're like most people, you'll expect the therapist to ask you to recline on a couch and talk about your past, especially your painful experiences in childhood. Perhaps you'll be discussing your dreams and fantasies, as well as your relationships with your parents. You may expect to do most of the talking while the therapist listens intently and analyzes your train of thought. The therapist will help you achieve a sudden and dramatic insight, perhaps triggered by a long-repressed memory or a fresh understanding of an old problem.

As we will see, these popular views of psychotherapy are largely outmoded and inaccurate. Because they have been shaped by the entertainment media, however, it is not surprising that they are widely shared. The public's misperceptions of psychotherapy matter. If people hold unduly negative views of therapists or approach treatment with unrealistic expectations, they may be reluctant to obtain help or find themselves disappointed when they do.

Popular Misinformation

Survey data suggest that many Americans hold inaccurate views of psychotherapy. For example, in a 2012 study of psychology undergraduates by psychologists Annette Taylor and Patricia Kowalski, between 63% and 70% of participants (depending on the phrasing of the question) agreed that for psychological treatment to work, therapists must first unearth the "root causes" of clients' problems in childhood. Nevertheless, decades of research on cognitive-behavior, behavioral, and interpersonal therapies demonstrate that although tracing the presumed early causes of people's difficulties can sometimes offer a helpful perspective on current problems, it is rarely a necessary ingredient for improvement. Indeed, these effective treatments focus largely on the here and now. In another survey, published in 2013 by psychologists Rick Gardner and Dana Brown of the University of Colorado in Denver, undergraduates gave an average rating of 2.6 on a 6-point scale (where 1 = Completely False and 6 = Completely True) to the item "Most psychotherapy involves a couch and exploring one's early past," suggesting that many participants perceived at least some truth in the assertion.

Other data suggest that the general public is misinformed about psychotherapists, often confusing psychologists, psychiatrists, and other treatment providers. For example, in a 2007 population-based survey of over 1,000 Americans, psychologist Rhea Farberman of the American Psychological Association reported that "most Americans cannot tell one mental health professional from another." This "role diffusion," as it has been called, may fuel the erroneous perception that most treatment providers – and perhaps psychological treatments themselves – are largely interchangeable.

Media Misportrayals

There is no shortage of media portrayals of mental health professionals. As epidemiologist Jane Pirkis of the University of Melbourne and her coauthors observed in a 2005 report, approximately 9% of prime-time television programs feature at least one therapist. Not surprisingly, the public's perception of psychotherapy as a voyage through the past, often conducted on a couch, is mirrored – and probably influenced – by the modal images of psychotherapy on the small and large screen.

As psychologists Danny Wedding of the Missouri Institute of Mental Health and Ryan Niemiec of Saint Louis Behavioral Medicine Institute reported in a 2003 analysis, the lion's share of depictions of psychotherapy in Hollywood films present treatment as psychoanalytic (Freudian) in nature. They offer the example of Woody Allen's 2003 film *Anything Else*, in in which the therapist asks the client to lie on a couch. In addition, the therapist barely speaks at all, let alone provides advice. Psychotherapy is typically portrayed in a caricatured fashion even in cartoons. In an analysis of the depiction of therapists in cartoons from 1941 to 1990, psychiatrist Glenn Walter of Northside Clinic in Sydney, Australia, found that 86% featured a couch, with minimal change across the decades. More broadly, as Wedding and Niemiec point out, many Hollywood films depict the typical course of psychotherapy as involving "sudden cures": virtually immediate psychological transformations triggered by a dramatic insight, often regarding one's childhood.

These portrayals fly in the face of reality. As psychologists John Norcross and Jessica Rogan demonstrated in a 2013 survey of 428 psychotherapists, only 27% describe themselves as "psychodynamic," meaning influenced by the teachings of Sigmund Freud and his colleagues. In addition, the iconic couch is largely a residue of psychoanalytic treatment and is uncommonly used today. Moreover, improvement in psychotherapy is almost always fairly gradual and uneven, and rarely follows upon a single remarkable discovery.

Most movies and television programs depicting psychotherapy are replete with other inaccuracies. As Niemiec and Wedding noted, blatant boundary violations, including close friendships or sexual relations between therapist and client (both of which are unethical according to professional standards), are widespread in Hollywood therapy. For example, in the *Analyze This* and *Analyze That* films (which appeared in 1998 and 2002, respectively) starring Billy Crystal and Robert De Niro, the therapist conducts treatment with his client during meals in restaurants and weddings; in the 1997 Academy Award-winning film *Good Will Hunting*, the therapist (played by Robin Williams) attempts to choke his client (played by Matt Damon) during a confrontation. Interestingly, an analysis of 250 film reviews of *Good Will Hunting* by private practice psychologist Mary Banks Gregorson revealed that only one questioned the therapist's behavior. Furthermore, scores of films foster role diffusion by failing to distinguish psychologists from psychiatrists. In a 1999 review, psychologists Richard Bischoff of the University of Nebraska at Lincoln and Annette Reiter of Marriage and Family Counseling of Pinellas in St. Petersburg, Florida, reported that only 6% of psychotherapists in films are identified as psychologists, with most described as psychiatrists or other physicians.

Therapy Stereotypes

Therapists depicted on screen appear to fall into a small number of stereotypical categories. In a 1987 review, Maryland psychiatrist Irving Schneider classified movie practitioners into three broad groups: Dr. Dippy (named after the first film featuring a therapist, *Dr. Dippy's Sanitarium*, which premiered in 1906), Dr. Wonderful, and Dr. Evil. Dr. Dippy (embodied by Mel Brooks in the 1977 film *High Anxiety*) is the prototypical "crazed" therapist. He or she seems more disturbed than many of his or her clients, and is often goofy or buffoonish. Dr. Wonderful (embodied by Judd Hirsch in the 1980 film *Ordinary People*) is kind and empathic, and can do little or no wrong. Dr. Evil (embodied by Anders Ahlbom in the 2008 film *The Girl Who Kicked the Hornet's Nest*) is cruel, often inflicting abuse on his patients. Other authors have extended Schneider's three-part taxonomy. For example, as noted in a 1999 article by reporter Scott Sleek, psychologists within the Media Watch group of Division 46 (Society for Media Psychology and Technology of the American Psychological Association) have added two more categories, Dr. Rigid, who is an emotionless killjoy, and Dr. Line-Crosser, who neglects crucial boundaries with his or her patients.

Reason for Hope?

Despite the misleading portrayals of psychotherapists on screen, there are cautious grounds for optimism. At least some recent media depictions of therapists, such as Gabrielle Byrne as Dr. Paul Weston in the recent HBO television series *In Treatment*, may be slightly more encouraging. *In Treatment* depicts Weston as a reasonably realistic therapist struggling to help his clients. He is not flawless by any means, but neither is he inept, cruel, or grossly unethical. At the same time, as one of us (Hal Arkowitz) observed in a 2008 review of the series in *Scientific American Mind*, Weston frequently engages in highly confrontational tactics with his clients; such tactics have generally been found in controlled psychotherapy research to be linked to poor outcomes.

Other data reveal that the general public holds a more positive view of psychotherapy than in previous generations. For example, in a large survey of the German population published in 2005, psychiatrists M. C. Angermeyer and H. Matschinger of the University of Leipzig reported substantial increases over the previous decade in the proportion of people willing to recommend psychotherapy for an individual with depression or schizophrenia (we are aware of no comparable U.S. survey data). These and other findings raise the possibility that in the coming years, the public's views of psychotherapy will become more closely aligned with reality.

Further Reading

Gabbard, G., & Gabbard, K. (1999). *Psychiatry and the cinema.* Washington, DC: American Psychiatric Publishing.

Wedding, D., Boyd, M. A., & Niemiec, R. M. (2005). *Movies and mental illness: Using films to understand psychotherapy.* Cambridge, MA: Hogrefe & Huber Publishers.

43

Why Don't People Change?

How many therapists does it take to change a lightbulb? Hold that thought. We will get to the answer shortly in this chapter, which addresses how difficult it is to make a change, despite our best intentions. Consider how many people engage in self-defeating patterns of behavior despite negative consequences:

- Smoking, obesity, and problem drinking can lead to chronic illness and premature death. Nevertheless, large-scale surveys of adults by the Centers for Disease Control and Prevention have found that more than 20% of American adults continue to smoke, more than 30% are significantly overweight, and approximately 15% are binge drinkers.
- People do not always comply with medical treatments. Studies indicate that between 50% and 65% of all patients do not follow their regimens and that 10% of hospital admissions among older adults result from failure to follow doctors' directions. Pauline Vincent, then at Case Western Reserve University, surveyed glaucoma patients in a 1971 study. Some 54% of the patients who knew they would go blind unless they used the eye drops as directed still did not adequately comply.

Facts and Fictions in Mental Health, First Edition. Hal Arkowitz and Scott O. Lilienfeld.
© 2017 John Wiley & Sons, Inc. Published 2017 by John Wiley & Sons, Inc.

- People who seek psychotherapy for conditions that cause them serious distress often thwart the very help they seek by being uncooperative, frequently missing sessions or dropping out of therapy altogether. One study found that more than 70% of patients receiving therapy in a community mental health center dropped out of treatment by the third session!
- Many attempts to change our behavior are unsuccessful. For example, psychologist John Norcross of the University of Scranton found that only 19% of those who had made a New Year's resolution to change some problem behavior had maintained the change when followed up 2 years later.
- People continue to engage in patterns of behavior – jealousy, dependency, nagging, anger, violence, and withdrawal, for example – that are often destructive to their significant relationships.

Some of the more common explanations for these phenomena blame an individual's characteristics such as stubbornness, resistance, addictive personality, and self-destructiveness. This reasoning is largely circular. People infer the explanation from the behavior (e.g., "He's not changing because he's stubborn") and then use that very behavior to support the explanation ("He's stubborn because he's not changing"). Clearly, we need a better understanding of why people do not change. That is where research comes in.

Confused about Change

In *Ambivalence in Psychotherapy* (Guilford Press, 2006), David E. Engle, a Tucson psychotherapist, and one of us (Hal Arkowitz) argue that dealing with ambivalence is central. In the authors' view, people who want to change but cannot are pulled in two directions by motivations to change and motivations to maintain the status quo. Several studies have demonstrated that the balance between these opposing forces can predict who changes and who does not. What gets in the way of change? Box 43.1 summarizes some of the critical factors.

Helping people change involves helping them *want* to change – rather than cajoling them through advice, persuasion, or social pressure. Research has demonstrated that such "highly directive" approaches are

> ## Box 43.1   Forces That Block Change
>
> - *Diablos conocidos* ("the devils you know"): The status quo is familiar and predictable, even though it may be uncomfortable. In contrast, change is unpredictable and arouses anxiety.
> - People fear that if they fail in their efforts to change, they will feel even worse.
> - Faulty beliefs (e.g., "Unless I am 100% successful, I consider it a failure") can impede change. When others push us to change, we often perceive these efforts as threats to our personal freedom. To retain this sense of freedom, we may resist change. Psychologists term such behavior "reactance."
> - The undesirable behaviors may serve important functions (such as the alcoholic who finds that drinking relieves stress and depression temporarily). Changing (stopping drinking) may take away the only means the person has known of dealing with this distress.

likely to backfire, making the patient increasingly likely to resist change. For example, a study by William R. Miller, R. Gayle Benefield, and J. Scott Tonigan, all then at the University of New Mexico, demonstrated that for problem drinkers, directive-confrontational styles of therapy led to significantly more resistance and poorer outcomes 1 year later than more supportive approaches did. They found that the more therapists confronted the clients, the more the clients drank. In contrast, more supportive styles were less likely to elicit such reactions and more likely to be successful.

One such approach is motivational interviewing, developed by Miller and fellow psychologist Stephen Rollnick of the Cardiff University School of Medicine in Wales. In this method, the therapist aims to enhance the client's intrinsic motivation toward change by exploring and resolving his or her ambivalence. The goal is to help the client (rather than the therapist) become the advocate for change. In other words, a client's resistance to change is seen by the therapist as ambivalence to be understood and appreciated rather than opposed directly.

To help resolve ambivalence, the therapist provides assistance in several ways. These methods include using a supportive style of therapy and highlighting client statements that reflect conflict between the person's behavior and values ("So it's important to you to be a good mother to your son, but your crack addiction interferes with this"). Such discrepancies create discomfort about the status quo and increase motivation to change. In addition, the therapist pays more attention to the client's talk about changing versus not changing, to help resolve ambivalence and tip the scales toward change. Once those uncertainties are dealt with, behavioral change often occurs.

A considerable body of research shows that motivational interviewing and related approaches are effective in helping people change alcohol and drug addiction, health-related behaviors, and disorders of anxiety, depression, eating, problem gambling, domestic violence, and even suicidal thinking. A quantitative review by Hal Arkowitz, Brian Burke of Fort Lewis College, and Marisa Menchola of the University of Arizona found a 51% improvement rate for motivational interviewing and related procedures compared with 37% for either treatment as usual or no treatment.

Apart from its use as a therapy, the ideas inherent in motivational interviewing can be used to help ourselves or a loved one change. These ideas emphasize listening and understanding hesitation about change, not opposing it, and trying to supportively strengthen the side of the person's mind that wants change.

So how many therapists *does* it take to change a lightbulb? By now you may have figured out the answer: "Just one, but the lightbulb really has to want to change." We hope this chapter will switch on your thinking about change, help you stop short-circuiting your efforts, and shed light on what you can do.

Further Reading

Arkowitz, H., Miller, W. R., & Rollnick, S. (Eds.). (2015). *Motivational interviewing in the treatment of psychological probems* (2nd ed.). New York, NY: Guilford Press.

Engle, D. E., & Arkowitz, H. (2006). *Ambivalence in psychotherapy: Facilitating readiness to change.* New York, NY: Guilford Press.

Miller, W. R., & Rollnick, S. (2013). *Motivational interviewing: Helping people change* (3rd ed.). New York, NY: Guilford Press.

Section 10
Other Myths

Introduction

Myths do not appear only in certain areas of psychology. They can be found in almost all of psychology, as well as in other disciplines and everyday life. In this section we focus on a variety of possible myths in psychology that span many areas but hold important implications for mental illness.

- Are most disorders we see in Western and European countries the same or similar to those in other parts of the world?
- Is positive thinking always helpful?
- Does a full moon really trigger strange behavior?
- How accurate is eyewitness testimony?
- Is the insanity defense frequently used in criminal trials?
- Does the insanity defense provide an easy way out for the defendant?
- Is obesity primarily due to lack of will power or to environmental factors like food advertisements?
- Are self-harming behaviors like cutting really suicide attempts or do people engage in them for other reasons?

Facts and Fictions in Mental Health, First Edition. Hal Arkowitz and Scott O. Lilienfeld.
© 2017 John Wiley & Sons, Inc. Published 2017 by John Wiley & Sons, Inc.

44

Do Psychological Disorders Differ Across Cultures?

Let us start with a little quiz. How many of these conditions have you heard of:

- *taijin kyofusho*,
- *hikikomori*,
- *hwa-byung*,
- *qi-gong* psychotic reaction?

If your score was 0 out of 4, do not feel bad: Your culture may be to blame. The first two conditions are mental illnesses largely endemic to Japan; the second two are endemic to China. Psychological disorders, or at least our labels for them, differ across cultures. But are these and other non-Western conditions truly distinct from those in the United States and Europe? Or does every mental malady, no matter how foreign-sounding in name, vary only in minor ways from a problem that is more familiar to us, such as depression or schizophrenia?

The evidence to date strongly suggests that culture can influence the expression of mental illnesses. Whether radically different cultures can give rise to entirely new psychiatric disorders, however, is a matter of fierce debate.

Facts and Fictions in Mental Health, First Edition. Hal Arkowitz and Scott O. Lilienfeld.
© 2017 John Wiley & Sons, Inc. Published 2017 by John Wiley & Sons, Inc.

This issue is of more than academic importance. Psychotherapists often consider cultural differences in their treatment, to be sure, but they typically assume that depression, for example, looks pretty much the same everywhere with minor exceptions. If so-called culture-bound syndromes – mental illnesses that are specific to a particular society – are merely variations of Western disorders, then mental health professionals in Western countries can safely continue to draw on existing knowledge about familiar disorders to treat them. In contrast, if some psychiatric ailments are entirely distinct from those in Western countries, psychologists and psychiatrists may need to start from scratch in figuring out how best to treat them.

Similar Syndromes

In the past century the presumed role of culture in mental illness has swung from one extreme to the other. For decades many cultural anthropologists, sociologists, and psychologists assumed such enormous diversity in psychiatric disorders across the globe that they were skeptical of any attempts to classify them. But that viewpoint came under serious scrutiny in 1976, when Harvard University anthropologist Jane Murphy reported powerful evidence that some syndromes did, in fact, seem to cross cultural lines.

Murphy examined two very different societies – a group of Yorubas in Nigeria and a group of Inuit Eskimos near the Bering Strait – that had experienced essentially no contact with modern culture. Yet these populations had names for disorders that appeared strikingly similar to schizophrenia, alcoholism, and psychopathy. For example, the Inuit used the term "*kunlangeta*" to describe someone (usually a man) who lies, cheats, and steals, is unfaithful to women, and does not obey elders – a sketch very much like that of a Western psychopath. When Murphy asked one of the Inuit how the group typically dealt with such an individual, he replied that "somebody would have pushed him off the ice when no one was looking." Apparently the Inuit are no fonder of psychopaths than we are.

Later research bolstered Murphy's conclusion. But the idea that some mental illnesses are present in both Western and non-Western cultures does not preclude the possibility that some disorders might exist only in certain societies. Indeed, in 1994 the American Psychiatric Association introduced an appendix of 25 culture-bound syndromes into the fourth edition of its *Diagnostic and Statistical Manual of Mental Disorders* (*DSM-IV*).

But just as soon as this appendix appeared, many scientists contested the notion that culture-bound syndromes are unique conditions, arguing that some or perhaps even all might be variants of disorders already known in Western culture by different labels. For example, some seal hunters in Greenland experience a condition called kayak angst, characterized by feelings of panic out in the ocean, along with an intense need to seek security back on land. Although kayak angst appears on some lists of culture-bound syndromes, it strongly resembles the Western condition of panic disorder with agoraphobia, which is marked by extreme fear of situations in which escape would be difficult in the event of a sudden surge of overwhelming fear.

Another possible Western illness in disguise is *taijin kyofusho*, which appeared in our quiz and is also listed in *DSM-5*'s new Glossary of Cultural Concepts of Distress. *Taijin kyofusho* is an anxiety disorder, common in Japan, marked by a fear of offending other people, typically by appearance or body odor. *Taijin kyofusho* may be an Asian form of social phobia (also called social anxiety disorder), in which people dread behaving in a fashion that is potentially embarrassing – say, making a gaffe when speaking or performing in public. Because Japanese tend to be more concerned with group harmony and cohesiveness than are Westerners, *taijin kyofusho* may be a form of social phobia in a culture that is especially sensitive to the feelings of others.

Distinct Disorders?

Nevertheless, some culture-bound syndromes may be sufficiently different from Western disorders to merit separate diagnostic criteria (see Box 44.1). In the bizarre condition of *koro*, found primarily in Southeast Asia and Africa, people fear that their sexual organs are disappearing or shrinking. *Koro* sometimes spreads in waves of mass panic and is triggered by marked anxiety. In the Malaysian condition of *amok*, which has given rise to the expression "running amok," afflicted individuals, almost all of whom are males, often respond to a perceived slight by withdrawal and brooding, followed by frenzied and uncontrolled violence.

Box 44.1   Cultivated Madness?

Some mental illnesses, such as those listed below, have no direct counterpart in our society. Scientists debate whether such ailments are distinct from problems that plague Westerners or whether they include hidden facets that will eventually tie them to illnesses we know all too well.

Name of Condition	Principal Region(s) in Which It Has Been Reported	Clinical Features
Hikikomori	Japan	Extreme social withdrawal
Dhat	India, Pakistan	Anxiety, fatigue, worries about loss of semen
Hwa-byung	Korea	Insomnia, fatigue, indigestion, aches and pains, other physical symptoms, all attributed to suppressed anger
Latah	Malaysia, Southeast Asia	Sudden and extreme startle reactions, followed by loss of control, profanity, and mimicking of others
Windigo	Central and Northeast Canada, Native American populations	Extreme anxiety, along with fears of cannibalizing others
Qi-gong psychotic reaction	China	Sudden loss of sense of reality following certain meditative practices
Ataque de nervios	Latin America	Shouting, trembling, cursing, feelings of loss of control and fear, sometimes accompanied by violent or suicidal behavior

And in the disorder of "2-D love," recently reported in Japan and some other countries, men develop what appear to be amorous relationships with animated female characters; they may carry around pillows or other tangible reminders of these characters wherever they go. Whether these mysterious maladies bear any underlying commonalities to well-documented Western psychiatric illnesses is unknown. *Koro*, for example, could be a type of hypochondriasis (hypochondria), but this possibility has received little systematic research.

Scientific disagreements aside, experts concur that culture can shape the overt expression of mental illness in significant ways. As a consequence, psychotherapists ought to give further consideration to learning more about cultural influences on mental illness and incorporating them into their treatment plans. Meanwhile scientists should use personality and laboratory tests to investigate the causes and manifestations of culture-bound syndromes to determine which of these disorders, if any, are distinct from those in Western culture. If some of these syndromes turn out to be unique, mental health professionals may need to construct and implement psychological interventions that differ in significant ways from those we recognize.

Further Reading

Guarnaccia, P. J., & Rogler, L. H. (1999). Research on culture-bound syndromes: New directions. *American Journal of Psychiatry, 156*(9), 1322–1327.

Simons, R. C., & Hughes, C. C. (Eds.). (1985). *The culture-bound syndromes: Folk illnesses of psychiatric and anthropological interest.* Boston, MA: D. Reidel/Kluwer.

45

Can Positive Thinking
Be Negative?

"Accentuate the positive," the 1944 song by Johnny Mercer and Harold Arlen cheerfully implored us. From Benjamin Franklin's 1750 *Poor Richard's Almanack* (which advised readers that "sorrow is good for nothing but sin") to today's parade of motivational speakers, Americans have long embraced an optimistic, "can do" attitude toward life. Plug "positive thinking" into Amazon.com, and you will find a never-ending supply of products designed to help us see life through rose-colored lenses, including a "Power of Positive Thinking" wall calendar and an "Overcoming Adversity with Encouragement and Affirmation" poster series.

In fact, however, positivity is not all it is cracked up to be. Although having an upbeat attitude undoubtedly has its benefits, gains such as better health and wealth from high spirits remain largely undemonstrated. What is more, research suggests that optimism can be detrimental under certain circumstances.

Facts and Fictions in Mental Health, First Edition. Hal Arkowitz and Scott O. Lilienfeld.
© 2017 John Wiley & Sons, Inc. Published 2017 by John Wiley & Sons, Inc.

Pluses of Pessimism

Despite the popular emphasis on positive thinking, academic psychology was for many decades centered on the negative. Even today a perusal of the typical psychology textbook reveals a predominance of topics dealing with the dark side of life – mental illness, crime, addiction, prejudice, and the like – probably reflecting an aim to remediate these personal and social problems.

Then, in the late 1990s, a cadre of prominent psychologists led by University of Pennsylvania psychologist Martin E. P. Seligman established a field called positive psychology. This burgeoning discipline explores the causes and consequences of happiness, character strengths and virtues, resilience, and other important aspects of psychological adaptation and health. Not all positive psychologists push cheerfulness at any cost – in a 1990 book Seligman warned that optimism "may sometimes keep us from seeing reality with the necessary clarity." But many do advocate a perspective that implies that positive thinking is good for all of us, all of the time, noted Bowdoin College psychologist Barbara Held in a 2004 article.

In fact, much of the data supporting solid benefits from positive thinking is weak. According to a 2010 review by Cornell University psychologist Anthony Ong, although most studies show that optimistic people tend to be physically healthier than others and they may also live longer, these findings come from correlational studies, which examine statistical associations between positive thinking and life outcomes but cannot tell us about cause and effect. Thus, thinking positively might make us healthier, but being healthier may instead lead us to think positively. Another interpretation of the same results: Positive thoughts and good health are the result of a third factor – being highly energetic, say – that was not measured in most of these studies. The same ambiguity plagues most studies purporting to show that optimism can lift depressed moods or boost job performance.

Even if more optimistic results about optimism eventually surface, a rosy outlook is unlikely to benefit everyone. Defensive pessimists, for example, tend to fret a great deal about upcoming stressors such as job interviews or major exams, and they overestimate their likelihood of failure. Yet this worrying works for these individuals, because it allows them to be better prepared. Work by Wellesley College psychologist Julie

Norem and her colleagues shows that depriving defensive pessimists of their preferred coping style – for example, by forcing them to "cheer up" – leads them to perform worse on tasks. Moreover, in a 2001 study of elderly community participants, Seligman and Brandeis University psychologist Derek Isaacowitz found that pessimists were less prone to depression than were optimists after experiencing negative life events, such as the death of a friend. The pessimists had likely spent more time bracing themselves mentally for unpleasant possibilities.

Another study calls into question the healing power of positive affirmations – those ubiquitous fixtures of pop psychology parodied by former comedian Al Franken as counselor Stuart Smalley ("I'm good enough, I'm smart enough, and doggonit, people like me"). In a study published in 2009, University of Waterloo psychologist Joanne Wood and her colleagues found that for participants with high self-esteem, repeating a positive affirmation ("I am a lovable person") multiple times indeed resulted in slightly better moods right afterward. But among those with low self-esteem, the positive affirmations backfired, resulting in worse moods. Wood and her colleagues conjectured that statements like Smalley's ring hollow in the minds of individuals with low self-esteem, serving only to remind them of how often they have fallen short of their life goals.

Too Much of a Good Thing?

Another potential hitch in the positive-thinking movement is that a sanguine attitude may be unhealthy when taken to an extreme, because it can become unhinged from reality. In a 2000 article University of Michigan psychologist Christopher Peterson, a founder of the positive psychology movement, distinguished realistic optimism, which hopes for the best while remaining attuned to potential threats, from unrealistic optimism, which ignores such threats.

A 2007 study by University of Virginia psychologist Shigehiro Oishi, University of Illinois psychologist Ed Diener, and Michigan State University psychologist Richard Lucas reinforces Peterson's concerns. Using analyses from several large international samples, they found that although extremely happy people are the most successful in close interpersonal relationships and volunteer work, moderately happy people are more successful than extremely happy people financially and education-ally and are also more politically active. Admittedly, Oishi and his colleagues measured happiness rather than optimism per se, although the two tend to be fairly closely associated. Still, their findings raise the possibility that although a realistically positive attitude toward the world often helps us to achieve certain life goals, a Pollyannaish attitude may have its costs – perhaps because it fosters complacency.

Positive thinking surely comes with advantages: It may encourage us to take needed risks and expand our horizons. But it has downsides as well and may not be for everyone, especially those for whom worrying and kvetching come naturally as coping mechanisms. Moreover, positive thinking may be counterproductive if it leads us to blithely ignore life's dangers. Finally, as journalist Barbara Ehrenreich warns in a 2009 book, the pervasive assumption that positive attitudes permit us to "think our way out of" illnesses such as cancer has an unappreciated dark side: It may lead people who fail to recover from these illnesses to blame themselves for not being more chipper.

Further Reading

Ehrenreich, B. (2009). *Bright-sided: How the relentless promotion of positive thinking has undermined America*. New York, NY: Metropolitan Books.

Held, B. S. (2004). The negative side of positive psychology. *Journal of Humanistic Psychology, 44*(1), 9–46.

Seligman, M. E. P., & Csikszentmihalyi, M. (2000). Positive psychology: An introduction. *American Psychologist, 55*, 5–14.

46

Does a Full Moon Really Trigger Strange Behavior?

It is the very error of the moon. She comes more near the earth than she was wont. And makes men mad.

William Shakespeare, *Othello*

Across the centuries, many a person has uttered the phrase "There must be a full moon out there" in an attempt to explain weird happenings at night. Indeed, the Roman goddess of the moon bore a name that remains familiar to us today: *Luna*, prefix of the word "lunatic." Greek philosopher Aristotle and Roman historian Pliny the Elder suggested that the brain was the "moistest" organ in the body and thereby most susceptible to the pernicious influences of the moon, which triggers the tides. Belief in the "lunar lunacy effect," or "Transylvania effect," as it is sometimes called, persisted in Europe through the Middle Ages, when humans were widely reputed to transmogrify into werewolves or vampires during a full moon.

Even today many people think the mystical powers of the full moon induce erratic behaviors, psychiatric hospital admissions, suicides, homicides, emergency room calls, traffic accidents, fights at professional

Facts and Fictions in Mental Health, First Edition. Hal Arkowitz and Scott O. Lilienfeld.
© 2017 John Wiley & Sons, Inc. Published 2017 by John Wiley & Sons, Inc.

Figure 46.1   Source: Wikimedia/Allen Watkin

hockey games, dog bites, and all manner of strange events. One survey revealed that 45% of college students believe moonstruck humans are prone to unusual behaviors, and other surveys suggest that mental health professionals may be still more likely than laypeople to hold this conviction. In 2007 several police departments in the United Kingdom even added officers on full-moon nights in an effort to cope with presumed higher crime rates.

Water at Work?

Following Aristotle and Pliny the Elder, some contemporary authors, such as Miami psychiatrist Arnold Lieber, have conjectured that the full moon's supposed effects on behavior arise from its influence on water. The human body, after all, is about 80% water, so perhaps the moon works its mischievous magic by somehow disrupting the alignment of water molecules in the nervous system.

But there are at least three reasons why this explanation doesn't "hold water," pardon the pun. First, the gravitational effects of the moon are far too minuscule to generate any meaningful effects on brain activity, let alone behavior. As the late astronomer George Abell of the University of California, Los Angeles, noted, a mosquito sitting on our arm exerts a more powerful gravitational pull on us than the moon does. Yet to the best of our knowledge, there have been no reports of a "mosquito lunacy effect." Second, the moon's gravitational force affects only open bodies of water, such as oceans and lakes, not contained sources of water, such as the human brain. Third, the gravitational effect of the moon is just as potent during new moons – when the moon is invisible to us – as it is during full moons.

There is a more serious problem for fervent believers in the lunar lunacy effect: no evidence that it exists. Florida International University psychologist James Rotton, Colorado State University astronomer Roger Culver, and University of Saskatchewan psychologist Ivan W. Kelly have searched far and wide for any consistent behavioral effects of the full moon. In all cases, they have come up empty-handed. By combining the results of multiple studies and treating them as though they were one huge study – a statistical procedure called meta-analysis – they have found that full moons are entirely unrelated to a host of events, including crimes, suicides, psychiatric problems, and crisis center calls. In their 1985 review of 37 studies entitled "Much Ado about the Full Moon," which appeared in one of psychology's premier journals, *Psychological Bulletin*, Rotton and Kelly humorously bid adieu to the full-moon effect and concluded that further research on it was unnecessary.

Persistent critics have disagreed with this conclusion, pointing to a few positive findings that emerge in scattered studies. Still, even the handful of research claims that seem to support full-moon effects have collapsed on closer investigation. In one study published in 1982 an author team reported that traffic accidents were more frequent on full-moon nights than on other nights. Yet a fatal flaw marred these findings: In the period under consideration, full moons were more common on weekends, when more people drive. When the authors reanalyzed their data to eliminate this confounding factor, the lunar effect vanished.

Where Belief Begins

So if the lunar lunacy effect is merely an astronomical and psychological urban legend, why is it so widespread? There are several probable reasons. Media coverage almost surely plays a role. Scores of Hollywood horror flicks portray full-moon nights as peak times of spooky occurrences such as stabbings, shootings, and psychotic behaviors.

Perhaps more important, research demonstrates that many people fall prey to a phenomenon that University of Wisconsin–Madison psychologists Loren and Jean Chapman termed "illusory correlation" – the perception of an association that does not in fact exist. For example, many people who have joint pain insist that their pain increases during rainy weather, although research disconfirms this assertion. Much like the watery mirages we observe on freeways during hot summer days, illusory correlations can fool us into perceiving phenomena in their absence.

Illusory correlations result in part from our mind's propensity to attend to – and recall – most events better than nonevents. When there is a full moon and something decidedly odd happens, we usually notice it, tell others about it, and remember it. We do so because such co-occurrences fit with our preconceptions. Indeed, one study showed that psychiatric nurses who believed in the lunar effect wrote more notes about patients' peculiar behavior than did nurses who did not believe in this effect. In contrast, when there is a full moon and nothing odd happens, this nonevent quickly fades from our memory. As a result of our selective recall, we erroneously perceive an association between full moons and myriad bizarre events.

Still, the illusory correlation explanation, though probably a crucial piece of the puzzle, does not account for how the full-moon notion got started. One intriguing idea for its origins comes to us courtesy of psychiatrist Charles L. Raison, now at University of Arizona, and several of his colleagues. According to Raison, the lunar lunacy effect may possess a kernel of truth in that it may once have been genuine. Raison conjectures that before the advent of outdoor lighting in modern times, the bright light of the full moon deprived people who were living outside – including many who had severe mental disorders – of sleep. Because sleep deprivation often triggers erratic behavior in people with certain psychological conditions, such as bipolar disorder (formerly called manic depression), the full moon may have been linked to a heightened rate of bizarre behaviors in long-bygone eras. So the lunar lunacy effect is, in Raison and his colleagues' terms, a "cultural fossil."

We may never know whether this ingenious explanation is correct. But in today's world at least, the lunar lunacy effect appears to be no better supported than is the idea that the moon is made of green cheese.

Further Reading

Hines, T. (2003). *Pseudoscience and the paranormal* (2nd ed.). (2003). Amherst, NY: Prometheus Books.

Raison, C. L., Klein, H. M., & Steckler, M. (1999). The moon and madness reconsidered. *Journal of Affective Disorders*, 53(1), 99–106.

Rotton, J., & Kelly, I. W. (1985). Much ado about the full moon: A meta-analysis of lunar-lunacy research. *Psychological Bulletin*, 97(2), 286–306.

47

Do the Eyes Have It? Eyewitness Testimony Is Often Inaccurate

In 1984 Kirk Bloodsworth was convicted of the rape and murder of a 9-year-old girl and sentenced to the gas chamber – an outcome that rested largely on the testimony of five eyewitnesses. After Bloodsworth had served 9 years in prison, DNA testing proved him to be innocent. Such devastating mistakes by eyewitnesses are not rare, according to a report by the Innocence Project, an organization affiliated with the Benjamin N. Cardozo School of Law at Yeshiva University that uses DNA testing to exonerate those wrongfully convicted of crimes. Since the 1990s, when DNA testing was first introduced, Innocence Project researchers have reported that 73% of the 239 convictions overturned through DNA testing were based on eyewitness testimony. One third of these overturned cases rested on the testimony of two or more mistaken eyewitnesses. How could so many eyewitnesses be wrong?

Eyewitness identification typically involves selecting the alleged perpetrator from a police lineup, but it can also be based on police sketches and other methods. Soon after selecting a suspect, eyewitnesses are asked to make a formal statement confirming the ID and to try to recall any other details about events surrounding the crime. At the trial, which may be years later, eyewitnesses usually testify in court. Because

Facts and Fictions in Mental Health, First Edition. Hal Arkowitz and Scott O. Lilienfeld.
© 2017 John Wiley & Sons, Inc. Published 2017 by John Wiley & Sons, Inc.

individuals with certain psychological disorders, such as antisocial personality disorder and substance dependence, are at high risk for criminal involvement, they are also at heightened risk for false identifications by eyewitnesses.

Surveys show that most jurors place heavy weight on eyewitness testimony when deciding whether a suspect is guilty. But although eyewitness reports are sometimes accurate, jurors should not accept them uncritically because of the many factors that can bias such reports (see Box 47.1). For example, jurors tend to give more weight to the testimony of eyewitnesses who report that they are very sure about their identifications even though most studies indicate that highly confident eyewitnesses are generally only slightly more accurate – and sometimes no more so – than those who are less confident. In addition to educating jurors about the uncertainties surrounding eyewitness testimony, adhering to specific rules for the process of identifying suspects can make that testimony more accurate.

Box 47.1   Error-Prone IDs

A number of factors can reduce the accuracy of eyewitness identifications. Here are some of them:

- extreme witness stress at the crime scene or during the identification process;
- presence of weapons at the crime (because they can intensify stress and distract witnesses);
- use of a disguise by the perpetrator such as a mask or wig;
- racial disparity between the witness and the suspect;
- brief viewing times at the lineup or during other identification procedures;
- lack of distinctive characteristics of the suspect such as tattoos or extreme height.

Source: Adapted from "Expert Testimony Regarding Eyewitness Identification," by B. L. Cutler and G. L. Wells, in *Psychological Science in the Courtroom: Consensus and Controversy*. Edited by Jennifer L. Skeem, Kevin S. Douglas, and Scott O. Lilienfeld. Guilford Press, 2009.

Reconstructing Memories

The uncritical acceptance of eyewitness accounts may stem from a popular misconception of how memory works. Many people believe that human memory works like a video recorder: The mind records events and then, on cue, plays back an exact replica of them. On the contrary, psychologists have found that memories are reconstructed rather than played back each time we recall them. The act of remembering, says eminent memory researcher and psychologist Elizabeth F. Loftus of the University of California, Irvine, is "more akin to putting puzzle pieces together than retrieving a video recording." Even questioning by a lawyer can alter the witness's testimony because fragments of the memory may unknowingly be combined with information provided by the questioner, leading to inaccurate recall.

Many researchers have created false memories in normal individuals; what is more, many of these subjects are certain that the memories are real. In one well-known study, Loftus and her colleague Jacqueline Pickrell gave subjects written accounts of four events, three of which they had actually experienced. The fourth story was fiction; it centered on the subject being lost in a mall or another public place when he or she was between 4 and 6 years old. A relative provided realistic details for the false story, such as a description of the mall at which the subject's parents shopped. After reading each story, subjects were asked to write down what else they remembered about the incident or to indicate that they did not remember it at all. Remarkably, about one third of the subjects reported partially or fully remembering the false event. In two follow-up interviews, 25% still claimed that they remembered the untrue story, a figure consistent with the findings of similar studies.

Given the dangers of mistaken convictions based on faulty eyewitness testimony, how can we minimize such errors? The Innocence Project has proposed legislation to improve the accuracy of eyewitness IDs. These proposals include videotaping the identification procedure so that juries can determine if it was conducted properly, putting individuals in the lineup who resemble the witness's description of the perpetrator, informing the viewer of the lineup that the perpetrator may or may not be in it, and ensuring that the person administering the lineup or other identification procedure does not know who the suspect is. Although only a few cities and states have adopted laws to improve the accuracy of eyewitness identifications, there seems to be a growing interest in doing so.

Expert Testimony

In addition, allowing experts on eyewitness identification to testify in court could educate juries and perhaps lead to more measured evaluation of the testimony. Most U.S. jurisdictions disallow such experts in courtrooms on the grounds that laboratory-based eyewitness research does not apply to the courtroom and that, in any case, its conclusions are mostly common sense and therefore not very enlightening. Yet psychologist Gary Wells of Iowa State University and his colleague Lisa Hasel have amassed considerable evidence showing that the experimental findings do apply to courtroom testimony and that they are often counterintuitive.

Science can and should inform judicial processes to improve the accuracy and assessment of eyewitness accounts. We are seeing some small steps in this direction, but our courts still have a long way to go to better ensure that innocent people are not punished because of flaws in this very influential type of evidence.

Further Reading

Loftus, E. F. (2007). *Eyewitness testimony: Civil and criminal* (4th ed.). Newark, NJ: LexisNexis.

Skeem, J. L., Douglas, K. S., & Lilienfeld, S. O. (Eds.). (2009). *Psychological science in the courtroom: Consensus and controversy*. New York, NY: Guilford Press.

Wells, G. L., & Hasel, L. E. (2007). Eyewitness identification: Issues in common knowledge and generalization. In E. Borgida & S. T. Fiske (Eds.), *Beyond common sense: Psychological science in the courtroom*. Oxford, England: Wiley-Blackwell.

48

The Insanity Defense on Trial

On June 20, 2001, Andrea Yates, an ex-nurse from Houston with a history of severe postpartum depression, drowned all five of her children (aged 6 months to 7 years) in a bathtub. Following a conviction in 2002 that was overturned on appeal, Yates was acquitted in 2006 as not guilty by reason of insanity. Yates's attorneys, backed by expert testimony, contended that she thought she was being persecuted by Satan and needed to protect her children from eternal damnation by killing them.

Forty-six U.S. states have some version of the insanity defense on the books, with Utah, Montana, Idaho, and Kansas disallowing it. This defense is designed to protect people who are incapable of understanding or controlling their criminal actions and to help them get treatment. Nevertheless, the idea of offenders being deemed legally innocent is hard for the public to swallow. In the case of Yates, radio talk-show host Mike Gallagher captured the sentiments of many: "So now," Gallagher opined, "officially and formally, Andrea Yates did not drown her five children, is that it?" Similarly, after the 1982 acquittal of John W. Hinckley, Jr., for the attempted assassination of President Ronald Reagan, an ABC News poll revealed that 76% of Americans believed that Hinckley – who was deemed delusional – should have been convicted.

Facts and Fictions in Mental Health, First Edition. Hal Arkowitz and Scott O. Lilienfeld.
© 2017 John Wiley & Sons, Inc. Published 2017 by John Wiley & Sons, Inc.

Although excusing the violence of Yates and Hinckley may seem wrong, the insanity defense is actually tailored to such situations. The concept of criminal "guilt" refers to more than whether a defendant committed the crime; in almost all states, it also requires that the person be deemed of sound mind when the act was performed. And although many believe the plea dumps dangerous felons back on the streets, in fact attorneys attempt the defense only rarely and typically fail in the attempt. Even when the defense succeeds, the acquitted usually end up with sentences similar to or longer than those for convictions. The main difference between an acquittal and conviction: Those acquitted on the basis of insanity are usually sent to psychiatric hospitals rather than prisons.

Origins of a Plea

In 1843 Daniel McNaughton went to 10 Downing Street in London with a plan to kill the British prime minister, Robert Peel. Mistaking Peel's secretary for Peel, McNaughton shot the secretary, who died 5 days later. McNaughton was acquitted on the grounds that he believed the government was plotting against him, but the verdict had no clear precedent and rested on fuzzy legal grounds. Reacting to public anger to the verdict, a panel of judges fashioned a guideline for insanity, now called the McNaughton rule: To be declared insane, defendants must either not have known what they were doing at the time or not have realized their actions were wrong.

The McNaughton rule, which many U.S. states adopted, hinges on cognitive factors, excusing people from legal responsibility because they lacked understanding of the crime's meaning. Some states now employ the looser guidelines set out by the American Law Institute in 1962, which broadened the insanity defense to also include cases in which a person cannot control his or her impulse to act because of a psychiatric disorder. Proponents of the defense, in either guise, regard it as a needed exception for the rare cases in which people are unable to inhibit their destructive behaviors. Most advocates believe that it is inhumane to punish individuals who did not adequately grasp what they were doing. Instead, they say, we should try to rehabilitate or least treat them.

But critics contend that excusing individuals for a crime that they unquestionably committed makes no sense. To them, the insanity defense confuses the question of whether a person should be found guilty of a crime with that of what punishment he or she should receive. Most skeptics believe that all defendants who commit a crime should be found guilty but that those with severe mental illness should sometimes receive lessened sentences.

Catering to this view, about 20 states have introduced the verdict of "guilty but mentally ill," which holds a person legally accountable for a crime but permits mental illness to be considered as a mitigating factor in sentencing. This verdict is supposed to enable an ill individual to receive the treatment he or she needs. In reality, those deemed guilty but mentally ill sometimes fail to receive adequate therapy. What is more, the verdict has not led to a clear-cut reduction in the number of insanity acquittals.

Judicious Use?

Whether or not the insanity defense is justified, it is intended only for the rare instances in which a bona fide mental disorder has obliterated the psychological brakes most of us use to stop ourselves from acting immorally. Yet many Americans perceive the insanity defense to be widely invoked and commonly successful. In a 2007 study psychologist Angela Bloechl of the University of Wisconsin–Oshkosh and her colleagues found that college students estimate that the defense is used in 30% of criminal cases and succeeds 30% of the time.

Yet data from multiple studies show that only about 1% of cases involve the plea, and only 15%–25% of those result in acquittals. Although notorious insanity plea acquittals, such as those of Yates and Hinckley, garner outsize media attention, scores of other defendants, including Jack Ruby (who killed Lee Harvey Oswald, John F. Kennedy's assassin), David Berkowitz ("Son of Sam"), Jeffrey Dahmer (serial killer), and Lee Boyd Malvo (one of the two Beltway snipers), have been convicted after pleading insanity.

Many people also believe that those acquitted on the basis of insanity get a quick and easy pass out of prison. "A few years of treatment in a mental hospital, then presto! She's all better now, free to be released into an unsuspecting public," Gallagher speculated about Yates. But only about 1% of those who use the insanity defense successfully are released immediately, and the average length of hospital stays for people let off because of insanity is about 3 years. Indeed, as of this writing, Yates remains institutionalized in a mental hospital in Kerrville, Texas, more than 15 years after her acquittal. Moreover, data collected in 1995 by sociologist Eric Silver, then at Policy Research Associates in Delmar, New York, suggest that those deemed not guilty by reason of insanity often remain in institutions just as long as people convicted of comparable crimes do; in some states, such as New York and California, they stay longer.

Thus, the insanity defense is far from a quick passage to freedom. Citizens and policy makers must understand the plea for what it is: an extremely rare exception that proves the rule that almost all individuals should be held legally responsible for their criminal actions.

Further Reading

Caplan. L. (1984). *The insanity defense and the trial of John W. Hinckley, Jr.* Boston, MA: David R. Godine.

Daftary-Kapur, T., Groscup, J. L., O'Connor, M., Coffaro, F., & Galietta, M. (2011). Measuring knowledge of the insanity defense: Scale construction and validation. *Behavioral Sciences & the Law, 29*(1), 40–63.

Silver, E., Cirincione, C., & Steadman, H. J. (1994). Demythologizing inaccurate perceptions of the insanity defense. *Law and Human Behavior, 18*(1), 63–70.

49

How Much Does the Environment Contribute to Obesity?

Obesity is a "global epidemic," according to the World Health Organization. Two thirds of American adults and one third of school-age children are either overweight or obese (defined as extremely overweight). These proportions have been rising steeply, report the latest surveys. From 1960 to 2002 the population of overweight and obese adults increased by roughly 50%, and the corresponding increase for children was 300%. Compounding the problem, obesity rates in other countries are rapidly approaching those in the United States.

What is causing this pandemic, and what can we do about it? Researchers have provided some tentative answers that fly in the face of commonly held beliefs. They suggest that the increase in obesity may be a result of environmental changes that tempt us into unhealthy habits and tend to overwhelm our psychological defenses against consuming too much and succumbing to fattening fare. In fact, environmental cues can exacerbate any innate tendency to use food as a balm for jittery nerves or sadness. Thus, many health experts advocate legislation – for instance, a tax on junk food – that promotes healthy eating. Others are trying to help individuals change their immediate eating milieu in ways that discourage overeating.

Facts and Fictions in Mental Health, First Edition. Hal Arkowitz and Scott O. Lilienfeld.
© 2017 John Wiley & Sons, Inc. Published 2017 by John Wiley & Sons, Inc.

Obesity Myths

Many people, including health care professionals, believe that obesity can be attributed simply to a lack of self-control or willpower. It is true that obese people are often unable to adequately control their eating. But lack of self-control is merely a description, not an explanation. What remains to be explained is *why* they cannot exercise self-control.

Nevertheless, doctors routinely tell their obese patients to restrict what they eat. Diet books, articles in health magazines and on Web sites, and commercial weight-loss programs also encourage people to eat less and exercise more. Unfortunately, approaches based on self-control do not seem to work very well. As sales of weight-loss books have climbed recently – from 3.6 million copies in 2005 to 4.8 million in 2007 – so has obesity. Further, two thirds of those who slim down in weight-loss programs regain their weight within a year, and almost all have put back the pounds within 5 years.

Other explanations of the increase in obesity are based on genes and psychological factors. It is true that many people are predisposed to gain weight because of their genetic makeup. But genetic factors cannot account for the sharp *increase* in the prevalence of obesity in society. The genes within a population relevant to weight do not change appreciably in 50 years. Some psychological factors may also play a role in obesity, including impulsivity, anxiety, and a tendency among some people to eat during negative emotional states. But here, too, there is no reason to believe that these characteristics have become more prevalent in recent decades. Therefore, genetic and psychological factors cannot account for the rise in obesity.

Toxic Environment

Results of a large number of studies support the conclusion that environmental cues exert a powerful influence on our eating behaviors. And unlike biological factors, our nutritional environment *has* changed radically in the past 50 years. In various publications, Yale University psychologist Kelly D. Brownell has used the term "toxic environment" to refer to this new dietary atmosphere, which is characterized by pervasive exposure to food that is energy-dense, heavily marketed, cheap, and widely accessible, accompanied by a lack of physical activity.

A 1995 report by the Institute of Medicine set the stage for future work when it concluded that the root of the obesity problem "must lie in the powerful social and cultural forces that promote an energy-rich diet and a sedentary lifestyle." More recent studies have borne out this statement. These forces, Brownell postulates, include the explosion of fast food outlets, increasingly large restaurant portion sizes, "all you can eat" buffets, the proliferation of mini markets that sell high-calorie snacks and drinks, contracts between schools and fast food and soft drink companies to sell their products in school cafeterias, and widespread powerful food advertising.

Given the importance of the environment on obesity, many researchers, including Brownell, argue that we need new laws and social policies to combat obesity. Brownell's controversial proposals suggest, for example, regulating food advertising aimed at children, prohibiting fast foods and soft drinks in schools, and subsidizing healthy foods.

Taxation is another potentially effective means of reducing consumption of harmful products, as the tobacco tax has demonstrated. Brownell and Thomas Frieden, who now heads the Centers for Disease Control and Prevention, have argued for a tax on one of the biggest contributors to obesity: sugar-sweetened beverages. Recently the U.S. Senate Finance Committee recommended such a tax to help combat obesity. Although major soft drink corporations vehemently oppose such a tax, the proposal is now on the national agenda.

Cornell University researcher Brian Wansink and his colleagues have found that cues in our personal eating environment also exert pressure on our tendencies to overeat (see Box 49.1). Based on these findings, they have suggested various ways of altering our environment to influence us to eat less. They advise, for instance, reducing portion sizes, keeping tempting food out of sight, never eating directly out of a package, and asking waiters to remove the chips or bread from the table.

Analyzing the power of environmental influences on obesity can lead to many practical suggestions for lessening their detrimental effects and encouraging lifelong healthy eating. And because obesity is a serious problem that has managed to spread to many corners of the globe, we must explore every possible avenue to reduce its prevalence.

Box 49.1   Conspicuous Consumption

Studies show that our surroundings greatly influence how much and what we eat. In his book *Mindless Eating: Why We Eat More Than We Think* (Bantam Dell, 2007), Brian Wansink, professor of consumer behavior and nutritional science at Cornell University, describes the environmental stimuli that numerous investigations have tied to overeating. Here are some of them:

- The larger the amount of food on a plate, the more we eat.
- The bigger the food container, the more we eat.
- When the food we prepare comes in large packages, we prepare and eat more than if the food comes in smaller packages.
- We eat more when the food is visible and conveniently located.
- We eat more when the food has an appealing name (such as Succulent Italian Seafood Filet) than when the same food has an ordinary name (such as Seafood Filet).
- Schoolchildren who live close to fast food outlets have a 5% higher obesity rate than do students who attend schools farther away from such stores.
- People who move from less modernized countries to more modernized ones show increased rates of obesity as compared with individuals who stay in their less modernized country.

Further Reading

Bray, G. A., & Bouchard, C. (Eds.). (2014). *Handbook of obesity* (4th ed.). Boca Raton, FL: CRC Press.

Brownell, K. D., & Battle Horgen, K. (2003). *Food fight: The inside story of the food industry, America's obesity crisis, and what we can do about it.* New York, NY: McGraw-Hill.

Wadden, T. A., Brownell, K. D., & Foster, G. D. (2002). Obesity: Responding to the global epidemic. *Journal of Consulting and Clinical Psychology, 70*(3), 510–525.

50

When Eating Becomes an Illness

"I am forever engaged in a silent battle in my head over whether or not to lift the fork to my mouth, and when I talk myself into taking the bite, I taste only shame," writes Jena Morrow in her memoir, *Hollow: An Unpolished Tale* (Moody Publishers, 2010). In her book Morrow recounts the pain and suffering she endured as she struggled to overcome the eating disorder anorexia nervosa.

Morrow's silent battle echoes those of the 0.6% of the U.S. population who will develop anorexia at some point in their life. Another 1% will experience bulimia nervosa, according to a 2007 survey by psychiatrist James I. Hudson of Harvard Medical School and his associates. Although these figures are lower than for most other psychological conditions, eating disorders can be emotionally and physically devastating.

Sufferers of both anorexia and bulimia are preoccupied with their weight and the shape of their body, and their self-esteem is based largely on how satisfied they are with these two physical characteristics. Individuals with anorexia often refuse to eat, lose significant amounts of weight, and are consumed by a fear of becoming overweight. Sufferers also have the distorted belief that they are overweight when, in fact, they are not.

Facts and Fictions in Mental Health, First Edition. Hal Arkowitz and Scott O. Lilienfeld.
© 2017 John Wiley & Sons, Inc. Published 2017 by John Wiley & Sons, Inc.

Bulimia is characterized by frequent binges during which an unusually large amount of food is consumed. People with bulimia fear that they will gain weight from their binges, and so they try to avoid putting on pounds, usually by forcing themselves to vomit or taking large amounts of laxatives and diuretics.

Proper understanding of these disorders is critical for knowing who is at risk and getting them proper treatment. Yet many people hold serious misconceptions about anorexia and bulimia. Here are five of them:

1. **Myth #1:** Eating disorders are extremely rare in men and boys.

    Fact: Although eating disorders are more common among females than males, a significant percentage of males struggle with them. Hudson and his associates found that 0.9% of females and 0.3% of males had or currently have anorexia. The corresponding figures for bulimia were 1.5% and 0.5%.

2. **Myth #2:** Anorexia is the only life-threatening eating disorder.

    Fact: Eating disorders have the highest mortality of any mental illness because of medical complications and suicide. In a 2009 paper, psychiatrist Scott Crow of the University of Minnesota Medical School and his colleagues analyzed the death records of 1,885 people who were evaluated 8–25 years previously at an eating disorders clinic at Minnesota. The mortality rates for anorexia and bulimia in this group were about the same: approximately 4%. Other investigators have found somewhat higher mortality for anorexia than for bulimia, but bulimia can be deadly, too.

3. **Myth #3:** Purging is an effective way to lose weight.

    Fact: Most people with bulimia very likely believe in this myth, or they would not vomit or use medications in an attempt to eliminate calories. Although purging is one of the formal criteria for bulimia, many people with anorexia purge as well. Yet purging is not effective for weight loss. Laxatives and diuretics cause water loss, which is soon replaced. Laxatives get rid of only 10% of the calories eaten. Vomiting is also relatively ineffective. By the time a person has induced vomiting, typically immediately after the binge has ended, the body has absorbed 50%–75% of the ingested food. Not only is purging ineffective for weight loss, it can also cause serious dehydration, electrolyte imbalances, and other problems, all of which may lead to serious illness or death.

4.   **Myth #4:** Body weight is one clue that a person has bulimia.
     Fact: Despite bingeing, individuals with bulimia have body weights that are indistinguishable on average from those who do not have the disorder. Perhaps the most obvious sign of bulimia is puffy cheeks because of the enlargement of the salivary glands from purging. Still, friends and family are often unaware that bulimia causes this physical sign. Because the disorder can be difficult to spot, those who suffer from it often fail to get the support they need to seek treatment.

     In contrast, an excessively thin appearance may be a clue that a person has anorexia. In the later stages, when an individual is 20%–30% or more underweight, the disorder becomes even more obvious.

5.   **Myth #5:** Recovery from eating disorders is rare.
     Fact: Many studies support the efficacy of a type of cognitive-behavior therapy (CBT) for bulimia in which therapists educate patients about bulimia – for example, they explain why purging is ineffective – alter dysfunctional thoughts about weight, and teach strategies for resisting the impulse to binge and purge. In a report published in 2000, psychiatrist W. Stewart Agras of the Stanford University School of Medicine and his colleagues gave 220 individuals diagnosed with bulimia either 19 sessions of CBT or of interpersonal therapy (IPT), which focuses on the interpersonal context of the problem and resolving conflicts that may contribute to the disorder. When treatment ended, 29% of those who received CBT had recovered, compared with only 6% of those who underwent IPT. One year later, however, the success rates were more comparable; 40% of the CBT recipients and 27% of those given IPT no longer had the disorder. Although there is considerable room for improvement, these findings suggest that certain types of therapy can be very helpful for bulimia.

The picture is less encouraging for anorexia. The first goal is to restore body weight to normal or near normal, something that is often achieved in a hospital. Surprisingly, 85% of hospitalized patients gain enough weight to go home, where the challenge is to keep them at a healthy weight. Some data suggest that CBT similar to that used for bulimia can prevent relapse of anorexia. In 2003 psychologist Kathleen M. Pike of Columbia University and her colleagues assigned 33 patients with anorexia who had been released from a hospital to a year of either CBT or nutritional counseling. At the end of treatment, only 22% of the CBT group had relapsed or dropped out compared with 73% of the group that received nutritional counseling. What is more, 44% of the CBT patients showed significant improvement and 17% full recovery compared with 7% and 0%, respectively, in the nutritional-counseling group. Although the results for CBT are promising, we are not close to a cure for anorexia, especially given that other researchers who have followed patients for longer have found much higher relapse rates.

Still, some individuals with anorexia do recover. And the more people who know the facts about eating disorders such as anorexia and bulimia, the sooner these serious illnesses will be recognized and treated.

Further Reading

Agras, W. S. (Ed.). (2010). *The Oxford handbook of eating disorders*. Oxford, England: Oxford University Press.

Pike, K. M., Walsh, B. T., Vitousek, K., Wilson, G. T., & Bauer, J. (2003). Cognitive behavior therapy in the posthospitalization treatment of anorexia nervosa. *American Journal of Psychiatry, 160*(11), 2046–2049.

Walsh, B. T. Attia, E., Glasofer, D. R., & Sysko, R. (Eds.). (2014). *Handbook of assessment and treatment of eating disorders*. Arlington, VA: American Psychiatric Association Publishing.

51

Self-Harm

The Cutting Edge

"You don't feel like you're hurting yourself when you're cutting. You feel like this is the only way to take care of yourself," a young woman we will call Alice told journalist Marilee Strong for her 1998 book, *A Bright Red Scream: Self-Mutilation and the Language of Pain*. As with many adolescents and young adults, Alice habitually harmed herself by cutting her arms and wrists.

Such behavior has long puzzled lay-people and scientists alike. Many have assumed that it is the same as a suicide attempt or a ploy to manipulate others. In reality, a person who deliberately engages in self-harm may be at risk of suicide, but the act is, by definition, not an attempt to mortally wound. In addition, there are numerous reasons for the behavior, attention seeking being only one of the more rare ones. Indeed, as Alice's comment suggests, people drawn to these behaviors often report that their actions bring positive psychological effects. Recent work suggests that self-injury might in some cases provide a form of pain relief, an insight that might lead to new treatments for the condition.

Facts and Fictions in Mental Health, First Edition. Hal Arkowitz and Scott O. Lilienfeld.
© 2017 John Wiley & Sons, Inc. Published 2017 by John Wiley & Sons, Inc.

Figure 51.1 Source: Anna Goodson Management/DANIEL STOLLÉ

Deliberate Destruction

In a 2009 book psychologist Matthew K. Nock of Harvard University defined nonsuicidal self-injury as "the direct and deliberate destruction of one's own body tissue in the absence of suicidal intent." By far the most common method of self-harm is cutting and scratching the skin. Other means of hurting oneself include head banging, hitting, burning, and picking at wounds, thereby interfering with their healing. In rare cases, people go to grotesque extremes, such as self-castration or plucking out their eyes.

Self-harming is neither uncommon nor new. During the late 19th century European women were known to puncture themselves with needles. More recently, the list of public figures who have self-injured includes Princess Diana, actors Johnny Depp and Angelina Jolie, singers Amy Winehouse, Courtney Love, and Marilyn Manson, and an early pioneer in sex research, Alfred Kinsey.

In 2011 psychologist E. David Klonsky of the University of British Columbia surveyed by telephone 439 randomly selected adults between the ages of 19 and 92 about whether they currently or had ever engaged in self-injury and, if so, when such behavior occurred and the types of injury inflicted. His data revealed that a staggering 6% of his sample displayed some kind of self-injurious behavior during their lifetime. Klonsky found that self-injury usually begins between the ages of 13 and 15 and is most frequent among adolescents. Only 35% of the subjects started hurting themselves at or after age 18. Half of those who harmed their own body used more than one method to do so. Results of studies on gender differences are mixed, but most find the habit to be more common among women.

Worse than the wounds themselves – although these sometimes require medical treatment – is the heightened risk of attempted and actual suicide among chronic self-injurers. Numerous researchers have found a strong association between self-harm and suicidal behaviors, such as thoughts of, plans for, and attempts at suicide, as well as completed suicide. In a 2002 review article psychiatrist David Owens of the University of Leeds in England reported that more than 5% of patients hospitalized for self-harm died by suicide within 9 years of their discharge.

Self-injury was once thought to be limited to borderline personality disorder, a serious illness marked by instability in mood, identity, impulse control, and relationships. We now know that people who physically abuse themselves very likely are afflicted with any of various mental illnesses. These ailments include major depression, bipolar disorder, anxiety disorders, eating disorders, schizophrenia, and some personality disorders, including the borderline type (see Chapter 30, this volume).

To highlight its pathological significance, nonsuicidal self-injury was for the first time categorized as a distinct condition in the 2013 edition of the American Psychiatric Association's diagnostic manual, *DSM-5*. Rather than being an official diagnosis, however, the problem appears in a section of the publication entitled "Conditions for Further Study," which lists behaviors or issues that merit further research. The new entry emphasizes that self-injury is not associated with one particular mental illness and may constitute a stand-alone problem. For example, some people might be diagnosed with major depressive disorder and nonsuicidal self-injury to distinguish that person from someone who is depressed but does not harm himself or herself.

Coping and Changing

Despite numerous attempts to determine why people deliberately hurt themselves, no one is certain of the answer. When asked why they do it, individuals most commonly say their actions help them suppress or release negative emotions, such as anxiety, anger, or depression. Psychiatrist Leo Sher, then at Columbia University, and Columbia psychologist Barbara Stanley concluded in 2009 from their review of biological research that self-injury releases opiate-like chemical messengers in the brain known as endorphins. The release leads to a euphoric state that reduces pain and offers reprieve from emotional distress, supporting the reason most self-injurers give for their behavior. This state may also explain why people such as Alice say they feel as if they are being good to themselves. A smaller percentage of afflicted individuals report that the pain helps to snap them out of an emotional numbness, that they want to punish themselves for wrongdoing, or that they are using their injuries to get attention from others.

Based on the endorphins hypothesis, some researchers have examined whether naltrexone – a drug used to treat alcohol dependence that blocks the release of these hormones in the brain – might limit this self-destructive behavior by reducing its palliative properties. So far, however, the results of studies of the effectiveness of this and other medications for the condition have been unconvincing.

For now, an approach called dialectical-behavior therapy, developed by psychologist Marsha M. Linehan of the University of Washington, offers the best hope for patients. In this therapy – which was initially designed for people with borderline personality disorder, 80% of whom self-injure – clients learn how to better tolerate stress and reduce negative feelings, among other coping strategies. The approach combines emotion-regulation techniques used in cognitive-behavior therapy with mindfulness training, which emphasizes acceptance and living in the moment. At least five well-designed studies show that dialectical-behavior therapy reduces rates of self-injury in individuals and lowers the number of suicide attempts and episodes of substance abuse in people with personality disorders.

Although its effectiveness in people with other psychological problems remains unsubstantiated, the treatment is an excellent starting point for the Alices of the world who need less harmful ways to take care of themselves.

Further Reading

Koerner, K. (2012). *Doing dialectical behavior therapy: A practical guide.* New York, NY: Guilford Press.

Nock, M. K. (Ed.). (2009). *Understanding nonsuicidal self-injury: Origins, assessment, and treatment.* Washington, DC: American Psychological Association.

Nock, M. K. (2014). *Oxford handbook of suicide and self-injury.* New York, NY: Oxford University Press.

Postscript
A Reader's Guide to Baloney Detection

As the saying goes, all good things must come to an end. For more than 8 years, we authored a column in *Scientific American Mind* on facts and fictions in mental health, an opportunity for which we are profoundly grateful. These articles have formed the basis for the chapters in this book.

We wrote these articles for a simple reason: We live in a world in which mental health literacy is more important than ever. According to survey data published in 2010 by psychiatrist Mark Olfson of Columbia University and psychologist Steven Marcus of the University of Pennsylvania, about 3% of Americans are in psychotherapy, with most of them also receiving medication. Moreover, as psychiatrist Thomas Insel, former director of the National Institute of Mental Health, observed in a 2014 strategic plan, the incidence of a number of mental health conditions, including autism spectrum disorder and major depression, has soared in recent years, although the significance of these rising rates remains a matter of controversy.

Despite its pervasiveness, many people are woefully misinformed about mental illness. This fact is worrisome because inaccurate notions about mental illness can be harmful. For example, the erroneous belief

Facts and Fictions in Mental Health, First Edition. Hal Arkowitz and Scott O. Lilienfeld.
© 2017 John Wiley & Sons, Inc. Published 2017 by John Wiley & Sons, Inc.

that people with schizophrenia are prone to violence can lead to unjusti-fied stigma (see Chapter 33, this volume). And the unsupported assump-tion that antidepressants are more effective than cognitive-behavior therapy for the long-term treatment of depression can dissuade individ-uals from seeking the most beneficial interventions for their illness (see Chapter 12, this volume).

In this concluding chapter, we will extract some of the more important lessons we can learn from this book.

A Misunderstanding Mind

Several common errors of reasoning make all of us susceptible to certain misconceptions about psychological health. For instance, the availability heuristic is a mental shortcut by which we gauge the frequency of an event by the extent to which it is fresh in our mind. For example, the mis-taken belief that most children of divorced parents display poor psychological adjustment probably stems from the fact that when a child experiences serious problems after a divorce, we often hear about it. Conversely, when a child adapts well to a divorce – as most do – his or her resilience is almost never discussed. As a result, we may think of divorce as more closely tied to psychological problems than it actually is (see Chapter 20, this volume).

Another common logical error is post hoc, ergo propter hoc, meaning "after this, therefore because of this." Our minds are continually on the lookout for connections between incidents, which may lead us to con-clude that an event preceding the emergence of a psychological condition caused the condition. For instance, many people continue to believe that childhood vaccines (especially those containing the preservative thimer-osal) cause autism because the usual time for vaccinating children – soon after they turn 1 – comes just before the first signs of autism typically become evident. This connection in time is apparently more persuasive to many than the multiple, large epidemiological studies that have debunked the link (see Chapter 16, this volume).

In addition, many misconceptions about mental illness contain a kernel of truth that can lead us to false conclusions. For example, just because dogs, horses, and some other domesticated animals provide emotional warmth that can temporarily relieve anguish does not mean that animal-assisted therapy alleviates the main symptoms of major mental disorders such as autism, schizophrenia, and anorexia nervosa (see Chapter 41, this volume).

Misled by the Messenger

As information becomes increasingly abundant and accessible, the ability to evaluate articles, books, and Web sites grows more crucial. About 3,500 self-help books appear every year, but few are based on research or are subjected to scientific scrutiny (see Chapter 39, this volume). Likewise, many psychology Web sites are replete with misinformation. In a 2012 survey of the sites of eight national autism associations, special education professor Jennifer Stephenson and her coauthors at Macquarie University in Australia found that most of them provided misleading information about the effectiveness of interventions. For example, of 33 autism treatments suggested on these sites, solid empirical support exists for only three. (Those three are grounded in the principles of behavior modification, a technique that reinforces adaptive activities.)

The mainstream media can also spread distortions, whether because of mistakes rising from deadline pressure, misunderstanding of source material, or an overzealous desire to appeal to the public. As psychologist Thomas Gilovich of Cornell University observed in his 1991 book, *How We Know What Isn't So*, reporters almost always sharpen the central point of an article and leave out peripheral details. They also routinely exaggerate claims in the service of a good story. On October 7, 2013, the front page of *The Sun*, a popular British tabloid, trumpeted: "1,200 killed by mental patients." The headline implied that psychiatric patients had murdered 1,200 people in the United Kingdom. Yet that figure included not only patients in the mental health system but also individuals who were judged retrospectively by researchers to be experiencing symptoms of mental illness, a judgment that is highly subjective.

Even when a story is more nuanced, the headline may still hold sway in people's minds. In 2014 psychologist Ullrich Ecker of the University of Western Australia and his colleagues collected data showing that deceptive headlines, such as "Fears of Fluoride in Drinking Water" (which topped an article emphasizing the safety of fluoride in water), can provoke biased inferences about the story, leading to misconceptions. Thus, readers must not only continue past the headline but must also carefully encode any details in a story that contradict or add nuance to its title. We should beware, too, of misguided attempts to create balance in stories. Journalists sometimes feel obligated to present both sides of an issue even when the scientific consensus is clearly on one side.

We hope that this book has helped educate readers about psychological health in ways that matter for both individuals and society. The tips and analyses we have offered over the years are hardly panaceas, but they can serve as a guide through the increasingly complicated maze of claims about mental health.

Further Reading

Gilovich, T. (1991). *How we know what isn't so: The fallibility of human reason in everyday life*. New York, NY: Free Press.

Jorm, A. F. (2012). Mental health literacy: Empowering the community to take action for better mental health. *American Psychologist*, 67(3), 231–243.

Index